Family Catecnism

Westminster Edition

PSALM ONE PUBLISHING

JACKSONVILLE, FL

Family Catechism – Westminster Edition

Edited by – Kevin C. Easterday

First Printing: 2016

ISBN 978-0692282175

Psalm One Publishing
P.O. Box 24084
Jacksonville, FL 32257
www.psalm1publishing.com

Introduction, Dedicatory, and Acknowledgements

"Hear, O Israel: The LORD our God, the LORD is one. 5 You shall love the LORD your God with all your heart and with all your soul and with all your might. 6 And these words that I command you today shall be on your heart. 7 You shall teach them diligently to your children, and shall talk of them when you sit in your house, and when you walk by the way, and when you lie down, and when you rise. 8 You shall bind them as a sign on your hand, and they shall be as frontlets between your eyes. 9 You shall write them on the doorposts of your house and on your gates." Deuteronomy 6:4-9.

"And Jesus came and said to them, 'All authority in heaven and on earth has been given to me. 19 Go therefore and make disciples of all nations, baptizing them in the name of the Father and of the Son and of the Holy Spirit, 20 teaching them to observe all that I have commanded you. And behold, I am with you always, to the end of the age.'" Matthew 28:18-20.

These verses serve as the premise of discipleship in the old covenant and in the new. The first is like a preamble and educational charter of the nation of Israel. Verse 4 is the well-known *shema* of Israel (possibly an Hebraic catechism question), and as our Lord Jesus later made clear, verse 5 is the first and greatest commandment (which was the answer to a catechism-like question asked of Him).[1] The second passage from Matthew's Gospel is commonly known as the "Great Commission," which is surely a charter for the Christian education of every tribe, nation, people, and tongue. Yet even these previous verses from Deuteronomy not only speak to the old covenant people of Israel, but to the Church in our day. When these two passages are combined, they form a full revelation of God's design for a godly education. However, neither of these commands are the foundation. The foundation upon which they rest is the Creator, and by connection to Him, His creation and special revelation.

Man was created to know God,[2] and to be known by God.[3] Therefore, all learning, instruction, knowledge, and wisdom has its foundation in God Himself as Creator.[4] He created all things;[5] nothing exists that does not find its existence in the One True God, in whom we live, and move, and have our being.[6] Therefore, anything we know about God or about His creation must come from Him. More specifically, Paul in Colossians 1:16, tells us that Christ is the center of everything God created; everything was created through Him and for Him.

But Christ must be revealed to any and all who would know Him.[7] And He has been revealed through God's special revelation; His Holy, inspired, infallible Word. And this Word comes to us in the preaching, reading, and meditating of it.[8] Thus, the Bible is indispensable if we are to know anything of God, or of His Son, the Lord Jesus, or of His Holy Spirit, the one who illumines our minds in the knowledge of God.[9]

Christ, Himself, claimed to be central to our knowledge of, and relationship to God. Jesus said, *"...I am the way, and the truth, and the life. No one comes to the Father except through Me,"* John 14:6. Thus, our "knowing

---

[1] Mark 12:28-30.

[2] Psalm 46:10; Romans 1:18-21.

[3] Psalm 139:1-4,15-18.

[4] Proverbs 1:1-7, 15:33; 1 Corinthians 1:19-24; Ephesians 1:17; 1 Corinthians 2:10-16.

[5] Ephesians 3:9; Colossians 1:16; Hebrews 1:2; Revelation 4:11.

[6] Acts 17:28.

[7] Matthew 11:25,27; Luke 10:21-22.

[8] Ephesians 3:5; Romans 10:14-17.

[9] 1 Corinthians 2:10.

God" only comes by knowing Christ and being in Him, which is all owing to the grace of God, and the work of the Holy Spirit in each and every believer.

Now, if we are in Him, then we love Him. If we love Him, then we keep His commandments.[10]

We are commanded, therefore, to bring up our children in the fear and discipline of the LORD.[11] God is not simply suggesting we raise them this way, or even requesting it; we are commanded to do it. We are to teach them to love God, as their God; to understand and obey the Gospel as the power of God; to know Christ, the wisdom and power of God; and to know the power of His resurrection.

Thus, putting all these ideas together, it is imperative for disciples of the Lord Jesus Christ not only to ground their own learning in Him, but also to ground everything they teach their children in Him. Every moment of every day is to be a teaching moment with an opportunity to preach the Gospel to ourselves and to our children, and to glorify and extol Christ.

However, this biblical mandate is more than simply a method of education, or a way to gain knowledge. It is a way of life, or a worldview. The Word of God is to be spoken of, and meditated on, in every part of life.[12] It is to be in front of the people of God, even as they live before the face of God. In today's world, we face the daunting challenge on a daily basis to fit the Bible into our lives. But the Bible is not supposed to fit somewhere in our lives. Rather, our lives are supposed to be fitted around it. Therefore, this *Family Catechism* is not supposed to replace the centrality of the scriptures, but to be a tool to help us better to know, understand, and apply them. If this catechism is used with a closed Bible, it will not bear nearly the fruit it would if the Bible were opened and searched, to see if these things are true.

It goes without saying that we cannot teach what we do not know. Thus, *Family Catechism* is designed for the entire church; for adults as well as children; for single people, as well as those who have a growing family. The format of this catechism is designed so that members of Christ's body will learn and grow in concert with one another. There is a suggested schedule for systematically working through the Confession and Catechisms. If used in this manner, and with the Holy Spirit's leading, the church will grow in grace together, being strengthened in the corporate body of Christ.

Thanks to the Rev. Mark S. Melton, and the session of Christ Covenant Orthodox Presbyterian Church, in Sheridan, Indiana, who contributed to this work and allowed it first to be used and distributed to the members of CCOPC. Thanks also to Mrs. Cornelia Wall for helpful tips on memorization. And finally, thanks to the Rev. Dr. Stephen C. Jennings, and ruling elders at Westminster Presbyterian Church (PCA), Jacksonville, Florida: Mr. Art Fox, Mr. Gary Furlong, and Mr. Robert Moore; for approving, proofreading, and permitting the publication of this catechism.

May our loving Father use this "tool" in the church more and more; to conform her to the likeness and image of His dear Son, and our Savior, the Lord Jesus Christ!

To God alone be glory!

Kevin C. Easterday

December 2016

Jacksonville, Florida

---

[10] John 14:15.
[11] Ephesians 6:4.
[12] Psalm 1:2; 2 Timothy 3:16.

How to Use This Catechism

The items included in *Family Catechism*, when used as intended, have been designed to accomplish four goals. The first goal is to provide each church member with a good working knowledge of the doctrinal standards of churches who have adopted the Westminster Confession of Faith and Catechisms, as a good summary of what the Bible teaches. The second goal is to provide a resource to aid private worship in the home. The third goal is to help each member and family to grow in their faith, and in the knowledge of the Lord Jesus Christ. And the fourth goal, is to help each member to be able to share his or her own faith in whatever place or calling he or she is divinely appointed.

In order to reach the first goal, we have included the Westminster Confession of Faith and Catechisms, along with the Children's Catechism. We have also included: the Apostle's Creed, and the Nicene Creed; explanation of the five "*Solas*" of the Reformation; and a summary of the "five points" of Calvinism. For the second goal, we have included portions of the Westminster Directory for Family Worship (in modern English), as well as some forms of prayer to be used in family worship from *The Valley of Vision* (also modernized). Though the Directory for Family Worship is not binding on any Church denomination today, it is a good resource for families to be reminded, challenged, and helped in their practice of private worship. For the third goal, we have included a modern English version of *The Sum of Saving Knowledge*. This resource was originally published along with the Westminster Confession of Faith and Catechisms for many years, and is a very good summary of what it means to have faith and believe in Jesus Christ. The fourth goal is not so much tied to any one resource, but is tied to the effort expended by each one of us as we learn together what it means to be a disciple of Jesus Christ, and to fulfill His "Great Commission."

What is catechism? Our English word is similar to the Greek word which means, "To sound from above." Catechism is sometimes called the Socratic Method, because it was employed by the Greek Philosopher, Socrates. Therefore, it is a very tried and true method of teaching. Moreover, Donald Van Dyken provides a helpful analogy for what it means to "catechize." If one wanted to find a submarine submerged, one would use sonar by pointing the signal downward in order to "see" what bounces back. Catechism, then, is a way to ask a particular question in order to "see" what bounces back. Because we adhere to doctrinal standards, we seek a common answer to a common question concerning the doctrines of the Church. Some churches today believe "rote" answers are not beneficial, but that each one should put the answer in his or her own words. However, this goes contrary to what we believe about biblical interpretation. If each Bible verse has only one true meaning, but several applications, then our meaning must be the same, even though we could spend a lifetime considering how we should apply it. Therefore, the Confession and Catechisms provide a standard, meaningful answer for what the Bible teaches.

Another analogy we may make concerning confessions and catechisms is that they are like the glossary of a book. The glossary is like a dictionary, only it does not provide an exact definition of a word, but the way the word is used in the book. The Confessions and Catechisms are a glossary of biblical truths, systematically formatted into summary statements.

Why not just use the Bible? Some churches state, "No creed but Christ; no book but the Bible," but in this, they are really saying that each person in the church has a right to interpret the Bible for himself. But if there are 100 members of a particular church, there could be 100 different interpretations of the same Bible verse. Our foundation is the Bible alone, yet we use the standards in order to have a singular interpretation of it. As you look at the Confession and Catechisms, you will see that there are summary statements along with footnotes of the Scripture reference. These summary statements are based upon the Scripture that is referenced. For instance, in the Shorter Catechism, question 1: "What is the chief end of man?" there are several Bible verses listed for the two short summary statements given in the answer: "Man's chief end of is to glorify God, and to enjoy Him forever." Therefore, every statement and question in our standards is based on what the Bible says in answer to a particular question.

If you are looking at the amount of information included in this catechism, you may be wondering where to begin. You may even be a bit intimidated. That is okay. Perhaps the best suggestion for you to remember is this rule: set reasonable goals. If a child, or even an adult is determined to memorize the Shorter Catechism in a few months' time, that may be too aggressive. For this reason, we have included a suggested schedule for memorization of the catechisms over the course of a year. You may want to come up with your own schedule over a longer period of time. The point is to make a goal, and stick with it.

That brings us to the second rule: track your progress. Tracking your child's progress helps to encourage him or her to continue, but you should also track yours so that your child can see that it is important to you, as well. If you are married, but have no children yet, track your progress together as a couple. If you are single, you might consider being accountable to someone else in tracking your progress. This will give you incentive to stick with it. We have included tracking sheets you can fill out in the back of the catechism.

The third rule? Keep at it. Even if you go several days without looking at the material, pick up where you left off. If you have children, they will probably remind you after a few days. You might look at this work as filling up a jar with change from your pocket. If you add in little by little, you will eventually have a pretty good sum of money. It is the same with biblical truth. Psalm 119:11 says, *"Your word I have hidden in my heart, that I might not sin against You."* If we all take in these truths little by little, it will help us greatly in our struggle against sin.

Mrs. Wall's Memorization Tips

PRAY first. Ask God to help you concentrate and not be distracted from learning.

SAY the words out loud, slowly repeating them several times.

WRITE the words out several times. Or, perhaps make some memory flash cards.

BREAK the verse into parts and memorize one section at a time.

COVER the verse and see if you can say it to yourself. If not, repeat the steps above.

ASK someone to listen to your memory work.

REVIEW, REVIEW, REVIEW! To keep what you have memorized fresh in your mind, you must refer to it often.

FIND ways to make your memorization fun and challenging.

BE ASSURED! Our heavenly Father is pleased that we have obeyed His command to hide His word in our hearts with the purpose of not sinning against Him.

Suggestions and Schedule for Memorizing the Catechism

Ideally, the order of memorization of the catechisms could flow from a yearly reading of the Confession of Faith. The table below has been organized so that your family may read the Confession through 52 weeks of the year. The catechisms are placed in the week according to the chapter of the Confession to be read. This means memorizing the catechism will not be done sequentially. If you do not want to memorize the catechism this way, but choose to do it in order of the questions, there is nothing wrong with that. However, it would be beneficial for the whole church if it is done each year together. Essentially, each family would all be studying the same thing at the same time. But, you and your church may use whatever order you want; this is merely a suggestion.

Secondly, as has already been stated in the Introduction, keep your Bible open. When you read the Confession and Catechisms, look up the Scripture references. Learning the Catechisms without an open Bible is like baking a cake with no ingredients. You can follow the cake recipe to the letter, pretending to mix everything in the bowl, but without the ingredients you will not have the delicious results of your labors. We cannot taste and see that the Lord is good without eating His Word (Jeremiah 15:16).

Week	WCF	Children's	WSC	WLC
1	Chapter 1, sections 1-4	Q14-15	Q1-2	Q1-3
2	Chapter 1, sections 5-10	None	None	Q4
3	Chapter 2, sections 1-3	Q1-5, 9-11	Q3-5	Q5-8
4	Chapter 3, sections 1-3	Q6-8, 12-13	Q6-7	Q9-12
5	Chapter 3, sections 4-8	None	Q8	Q13-14
6	Chapter 4; Chap. 5, sec. 1	Q16-21	Q9-11	Q15-18
7	Chap. 5, sec. 2-7; Chap. 6, sec. 1	None	None	Q19
8	Chapter 6, sections 2-4	Q28-33, 35	Q13-16	Q21-22, 24
9	Chapter 6, sections 5-6	Q34, 36-38	Q17-19	Q23, 25, 27
10	Chapter 7, sections 1-3	Q22-27, 41-44	Q12, 20	Q20, 28-30
11	Chap. 7, sec. 4-6; Chap. VIII, sec. 1	None	None	Q31-34
12	Chapter 8, section 2	Q45-51, 137-139	Q21-22	Q26, 35-39
13	Chapter 8, sections 3-5	Q61-72	Q23-24	Q40-43
14	None	None	Q25-27	Q44-50
15	Chapter 8, sections 6-8	None	Q28	Q51-56
16	Chapter 9	Q59-60	None	Q57
17	Chapter 10, sections 1-3	Q39-40	Q29-31	Q58-59, 67-68
18	Chap. 10 sec. 4; Chap. 11, sec. 1-3	Q52-53	Q32-33	Q60, 70
19	Chap. 11, sec. 4-6; Chap. 12; Chap. 13, sec. 1	Q54	None	Q71
20	Chap. 13, sec. 2-3; Chap. 14, sec. 1	None	Q34-36	Q74-75, 77-78
21	Chap. 14, sec. 2-3; Chap. 15, sec. 1-2	Q55-58	Q85-86	Q72-73, 153
22	Chap. 15, sec. 3-6; Chap. 16, sec. 1	None	Q87	Q76
23	Chap. 16, sec. 2-7; Chap. 17, sec. 1	None	None	None
24	Chap. 17, sec. 2-3; Chap. 18, sec. 1-3	None	None	Q79-80
25	Chap. 18, sec. 4; Chap. 19, sec. 1-2	None	Q39-40	Q81, 91-93

Week	WCF	Children's	WSC	WLC
26	Chapter 19, sections 3-5	Q73	Q41	Q94-96, 98
27	Chapter 19, sections 6-7	None	Q43	Q97, 99-101
28	None	Q74-81	Q42, 44-48	Q102-107
29	None	Q82-85	Q49-56	Q108-114
30	None	Q86-90	Q57-62	Q115-120
31	None	Q91-92	Q63-66	Q121-127
32	None	Q93-94	Q67-69	Q128-134
33	None	Q95-98	Q70-75	Q135-141
34	None	Q99-102	Q76-81	Q142-148
35	Chapter 20, sections 1-3	Q103-104	Q82-84	Q149-152
36	Chap. 20, sec. 4; Chap. 21, sec. 1-3	Q105-106	Q98	Q178-180, 185
37	Chapter 21, sections 4-6	None	None	Q181-184
38	Chapter 21, sections 7-8	Q107-108	Q99	186-188
39	None	Q109-121	Q100-106	Q189-195
40	Chapter 22, sections 1-6	None	Q107	Q196
41	Chap. 22, sec. 7; Chap. 23; Chap. 24, sec. 1-2	None	None	None
42	Chap. 24, sec. 3-6; Chap 25, sec. 1-2	None	None	Q62, 64-65
43	Chap. 25, sec. 3-6; Chap 26	None	None	Q61, 63, 66
44	None	None	Q88	Q69, 82-83, 86, 154
45	Chapter 27, section 1	None	Q89-90	Q155-160
46	Chapter 27, sections 2-5	Q122-125	Q91-93	Q161-164
47	Chapter 28, sections 1-5	Q126-132	Q94-95	Q165-166
48	Chap. 28, sec. 6-7; Chap. 29, sec. 1-3	Q133-135	Q96	Q167-169
49	Chapter 29, sections 4-8	Q136	Q97	Q170-172
50	Chapter 30, sections 1-2	None	None	Q173-177
51	Chap. 30, sec. 3-4; Chap. 31	None	None	Q84
52	Chapters 32-33	Q140-145	Q37-38	Q85, 87-90

Notes

The Historic Creeds of Christianity

The Apostle's Creed

I BELIEVE IN GOD the Father Almighty, Maker of Heaven and earth.

I BELIEVE IN JESUS CHRIST, His only Son, our Lord, who was conceived by the Holy Spirit and born of the Virgin Mary. He suffered under Pontius Pilate, was crucified, died, and was buried; He descended into hell. The third day He rose again from the dead. He ascended into heaven and is seated at the right hand of God the Father Almighty. From there He will come to judge the living and the dead.

I BELIEVE IN THE HOLY SPIRIT, the holy catholic church,[13] the communion of saints, the forgiveness of sins, the resurrection of the body, and the life everlasting. Amen

The Nicene Creed

WE BELIEVE IN ONE GOD, the Father Almighty, Maker of heaven and earth, of all things visible and invisible.

AND IN ONE LORD JESUS CHRIST, the only-begotten Son of God, begotten of His Father before all worlds, God of God, Light of Light, very God of very God, begotten, not made, being of one substance with the Father; by whom all things were made; who for us and for our salvation came down from heaven, and was incarnate by the Holy Spirit of the virgin Mary, and was made man; and was crucified also for us under Pontius Pilate; He suffered and was buried; and the third day He rose again according to the Scriptures, and ascended into heaven, and is seated at the right hand of the Father; and He shall come again, with glory, to judge both the living and the dead; whose kingdom shall have no end.

AND WE BELIEVE IN THE HOLY SPIRIT, the Lord and giver of life, who proceeds from the Father and the Son; who with the Father and the Son together is worshipped and glorified; who spoke by the prophets; and we believe in one holy catholic and apostolic church; we acknowledge one baptism for the remission of sins; and we look for the resurrection of the dead, and the life of the world to come. Amen.

---

[13] The word "catholic" is a word used to describe the worldwide unity of the Church of Jesus Christ. As it is used in the creed, it does not refer to the Roman Catholic Church.

The Five Sola's of the Reformation

The Protestant Reformation of the 16th Century emphasized five important statements regarding salvation. Each of these Latin statements begins with the word *sola*. Because the Roman Catholic Church had perverted the gospel of Jesus Christ, and obscured the clear teaching of Scripture regarding how men, women, boys, and girls are saved, the Reformers thought it necessary to clearly and distinctly summarize what the Bible teaches. They did so through the five terms listed below.

1. *Sola Scriptura* – The Bible Alone

The Bible alone is authoritative and teaches all that is necessary for salvation and how to live as a Christian.

2. *Soli Christo* – Christ Alone

Salvation is only through Jesus Christ made possible by His perfect obedience and sacrifice of Himself.

3. *Sola Gratia* – Grace Alone

Salvation is only by God's grace, and not because of anything else.

4. *Sola Fide* – Faith Alone

Salvation is accomplished only through faith in Jesus Christ, and that faith is a gift only given according to the will of God, and by the operation of the Holy Spirit.

5. *Soli Deo Gloria* – To the Glory of God Alone

Salvation from beginning to end is to God's Glory alone.

The SOLAS Summary:

Salvation is known to us because of the Bible alone; that it is by grace alone, through faith alone, in Christ alone, to the Glory of God alone.

Sola's Memory Song (See page 165 for the music)

We know from Sola Scriptura,

We are saved by Sola Gratia,

Through Sola Fide,

In Soli Christo,

To Soli Deo Gloria.

The Five Points of Calvinism – "TULIP"

This content is attributed to the Catechism Manual of Christ Covenant OPC in Sheridan, Indiana.

The acrostic **TULIP** is the most familiar way of delineating the doctrines of Grace. While this acrostic is well known, there are more helpful means of defining and articulating what it is we mean by the "doctrines of grace." A brief summary statement of each of these five doctrines follows.

<u>T</u>otal depravity

By "total depravity" what we are to understand is that man is utterly lacking in his ability to (in and of himself) respond to the good news of salvation through Christ alone. That is why some describe this first doctrine as "total inability." It does not mean that human beings are as wicked or evil as they could possibly be; it simply says to us that every faculty of man's being has been horribly affected and "deadened" by sin in the fall of Adam. The whole man - his mind, his heart, and especially, his will - has been so affected by the fall that he is in a state of utter and complete inability to comply with God's commandments. cf. Romans 1:18-32; 3:10-18; 5:12-19; Ephesians 2:1-3; Colossians 2:13.

<u>U</u>nconditional election

"Unconditional election" (a doctrine often misunderstood and misrepresented) teaches us that a gracious and loving God has "out of mere grace, according to the sovereign good pleasure of His own will, chosen from the whole human race...a certain number of persons to redemption in Christ... Those chosen were neither better nor more deserving than the others..." (Canons of Dortrecht, first main point of doctrine, article 7). God's election unto salvation is unconditional in that it is not predicated on anything we do (not even our "choosing") or anything we are. It finds its basis in our sovereign God's mere good pleasure. When properly understood, this glorious doctrine strikes a death blow to all human pride as well as the pervasive sense of self-sufficiency, characteristic of mankind. cf. John 15:16; Acts 13:48; Romans 8:29-30; 9:10-13, 16; Ephesians 1:4-5, 11; 2 Thessalonians 2:13; 2 Timothy 1:9.

<u>L</u>imited atonement

The third doctrine of grace, "Limited Atonement," while fitting nicely into the *TULIP* acrostic, is less than helpful because of its 'limitations.' If not properly explained, it can easily lead one to conclude that God is limited, that He can only save some. Thus, terms like "particular redemption" or "efficacious atonement" are better descriptions of what this doctrine actually entails. Very simply, limited atonement or particular redemption teaches us that Christ's atonement, the redemptive nature of His death on the cross, was for a particular people. It was for the elect of God and only for the elect. It was "limited" in that sense and in no other. cf. Isaiah 53:11; Matthew 20:28; John 6:37-39; Hebrews 9:28.

<u>I</u>rresistible grace

"Irresistible Grace" has been referred to by some as "effectual call" or "efficacious grace," that is, it effects or accomplishes God's desired end. It is the doctrine that teaches us that God, through the agency of regeneration, replaces our heart of stone with a heart of flesh, thus causing the elect of God to be perfectly willing and desirous of receiving Christ unto salvation. Irresistible grace does not suggest either raw determinism or God forcing us to believe in Him against our will. Rather, this doctrine teaches us that salvation is all of grace, the grace of God applied to unregenerate men and women resulting in a change of their "want to." As God gives this grace to sinners, they willingly choose to believe and receive (John 1:12). However, without the application of this grace, none would choose to believe. cf. John 1:12-13; 5:25; 6:45; Acts 16:14; Romans 3:21-26.

Perseverance of the saints

The final doctrine of grace (Perseverance of the Saints) is one of the most precious and freeing truths in all of Scripture. It gives assurance to the child of God that God is indeed able to save from first to last, from beginning to end. C. H. Spurgeon, in refuting those who argued that one can never be absolutely sure of his or her final destination, once said, "I grant that my atonement, or bridge to heaven is more narrow than yours. However, yours only goes half way across the chasm and mine goes all the way. In our scheme, the sinner must furnish the other half." Perseverance of the Saints (sometimes called "preservation" of the saints) teaches us that the child of God will persevere, he will be preserved in his faith because it is God who has begun that good work and He will bring it to completion (Philippians 1:6). Once again, salvation is seen to be entirely of God, from first to last. cf. Psalm 37:28; Isaiah 45:17; Matthew 10:22; John 6:37-40; 10:27-30; 17:9-18; Hebrews 7:25; 1 John 2:19, 25.

The Sum of Saving Knowledge

This work, jointly published in 1650 by two Scottish theologians David Dickson and James Durham, was printed for many years along with the Westminster Confession of Faith and Catechisms, even though it was developed independently of the Assembly. Although it was never adopted by the Church, it is helpful as a summary of the doctrines contained in Standards. It has been edited to make it easier to read in modern English.

Heading I.

Man's Woeful Condition by Nature, Through Breaking the Covenant of Works.
"He destroys you, O Israel, for you are against me, against your helper." Hosea 13:9.

I. The almighty and eternal God, the Father, the Son, and the Holy Ghost, three distinct persons in the one and the same undivided Godhead, equally infinite in all perfections, did, before time, most wisely decree, for His own glory, whatsoever comes to pass in time: and does in a most holy and infallible manner execute all His decrees, without being partaker of the sin of any creature.

II. This God, in six days, made all things of nothing, very good in their own kind: in particular, He made all the holy angels; and He made Adam and Eve, the first man and woman and root of all mankind, both upright and able to keep the law written in their hearts. They were naturally bound to obey this law under penalty of death. But God was not bound to reward their service until He entered into a covenant or contract with them, which also included their children after them; to give them eternal life, upon condition of perfect and personal obedience; threatening them with death in case they should fail. This is the covenant of works.

III. Both angels and men were subject to the change of their own free will, as history has unfolded, (God having reserved to himself the incommunicable property of being naturally unchangeable), for many angels of their own free will fell into sin from their first estate, and became devils. Adam and Eve, being enticed by Satan, one of these devils speaking as a serpent, broke the covenant of works in eating the forbidden fruit. Once they sinned, they, and their children after them as branches of the root and included in the same covenant with them, not only became liable to eternal death, but also lost all ability to please God. They truly did become, by nature, enemies of God, and of all spiritual good, by which their whole being was corrupted and inclined only to evil continually. This is called original sin, the bitter root of all the sins which are committed daily, in thought, word, and deed.

Heading II.

The Remedy Provided in Jesus Christ for the Elect by the Covenant of Grace.
"He destroys you, O Israel, for you are against me, against your helper." Hosea 13:9.

I. Although mankind was brought into this miserable condition by his own actions, he is not able to help himself out of it, nor is he willing to be helped out of it by God. Rather, it is his natural inclination, because of sin, to remain ignorant of his condition until he dies. Yet God, according to the richness of His glorious grace, has revealed in His word a way for sinners to be saved from their condition by faith in Jesus Christ, God's Eternal and only Begotten Son. This salvation in Christ is made sure because of the covenant of redemption, made and agreed upon between God the Father and God the Son, in the council of the Trinity, before the world began.

II. The covenant of redemption may be summed up in this: God, of His own free grace and for His own glory, before the world began, chose a people for Himself from all of mankind, in order to give to them His only Son to be their Redeemer. Christ, as that one and only Redeemer, who is fully God in His divine nature, was willingly to take upon Himself the conditions of the covenant of redemption in that, He was to humble Himself by coming into this world as a man, and to take to Himself a true soul and a body, thus having a fully human nature. These two natures were joined inseparably together in the one Man, Jesus Christ. He was also willingly to submit Himself to the law, so that by His perfect obedience, He would make salvation sure, by giving His own righteousness to be accounted to sinful men. Christ also was to satisfy divine justice on behalf of His people by suffering the cursed death of the cross, in order to ransom and redeem His people from sin and death, so they might have the reward of life in His name. Along with these benefits His people would receive all the saving graces by which His atoning work was to be applied effectually to each of them in due time by means of the Holy Spirit's appointment. These conditions Christ, the Son of God, accepted before the world began.

III. And in the fullness of time Christ came into the world, to accomplish what is commonly called the covenant of grace. He was born of the Virgin Mary; subjected Himself to the law, and completely paid the debt of His people's sin on the cross, thus accomplishing all the work His Father gave Him to do. However, even though this covenant of redemption was made before the world began, and Christ actually accomplished all of His redeeming work in time in the covenant of grace, He has always been working, even since the fall of Adam, in applying all these benefits to His chosen people by His Spirit working faith in them and uniting them to Himself, and is ever living to intercede for them before the throne of God.

IV. For the accomplishment of these two covenants, of which they could rightly be said to be one in the same – the covenant of redemption having an eternal aspect, and the covenant of grace being the outworking of that covenant in time – Christ was given the offices of Prophet, Priest, and King in order that God's chosen people might partake of His grace. He was given the office of Prophet, to reveal all saving knowledge to His people, and to persuade them to believe and obey. He was given the office of Priest, to offer up Himself as a sacrifice once for all, and to intercede on their behalf continually before the Father, making their worship and service to God acceptable. And He was given the office of King, to subdue them to Himself, to feed and rule them by His means of grace, and to defend them and conquer all their enemies and His.

Heading III.

The Outward Means Appointed to Make the Elect Partakers of This Covenant, Along with the Inexcusable Condition of the Rest of Mankind.
"For many are called, but few are chosen." (Matthew 22:14).

I. The outward and ordinary means for making His chosen ones to be partakers of the covenant of grace are given with such wisdom, that His people will most assuredly and without failure be converted and saved by them. Additionally, these means also serve to condemn those who stumble because of their unbelief. Among the means of grace to be mentioned are these four in particular: 1) the word of God, 2) the sacraments, 3) prayer, and 4) the Church. By the preaching of the Word of God, the Lord makes a genuine offer of grace through the gospel to all sinners; who are to receive it by faith in Jesus Christ; who are also to confess their sins; and who are to accept Christ and His rule over them. To these and to their children, Christ offers the benefits and privileges of the covenant of grace. In the sacraments, God signifies and seals to those who receive them by faith, the benefits of the covenant of grace. By prayer, God's people are daily reminded to receive His mercy and grace in Christ in order to give them strength and confidence in His promises. And in the Church, He will provide His people with those who will shepherd their souls and encourage them towards godliness. All of these means must be received and acted upon by faith. Therefore, only true believers will gain peace and comfort by the effectual use of them.

II. The covenant of grace was known to the people of God in the Old Testament in His unfolding revelation of the gospel, in the giving of the law and ordinances, and in the prophecies of the Messiah to come. The covenant was known to the people of God in the New Testament with the revelation of the Lord Jesus Christ. Yet, these two different eras of God's people do not signify two separate covenants of grace. There is one covenant of grace with a difference in the outward administration from the Old to the New. The Old Testament administration of the covenant included sacrifices, circumcision, and the paschal lamb. These sacraments pointed forward to Christ, in whom was the fulfillment of them all. Once His work of fulfillment was accomplished, He established the covenant in simpler ordinances of baptism and the Lord's Supper. Although the new administration of the covenant is less ceremonial, yet the reality of Christ's victory over sin, death, and hell is made more meaningful, even in these simpler ordinances.

Heading IV.

The Blessings which are Effectually Conveyed by the Means of Grace to the Lord's Elect, or Chosen People.
"For many are called, but few are chosen." (Matthew 22:14).

I. These outward ordinances are not beneficial to those without faith. But to those who are given faith to believe in the Lord Jesus, by the power of His Spirit, He effectually applies all these saving graces He purchased for them in the covenant of redemption, making a lasting change in them. In particular, He does four things: 1) He converts or regenerates them by giving spiritual life to them. They are given new life so that they may understand the gospel, may be renewed in their wills, and may have their sinful desires changed into godly ones. He also helps them to put away their sin nature, and gives them a spiritual desire for obedience to His commands; 2) He gives them saving faith, by which they truly embrace Him and believe the gospel; 3) He gives them repentance by making them hate their sins and be truly sorry for them so that they turn from them and desire to serve God in righteousness; and, 4) He sanctifies them by giving them increasing grace and strength so that they persevere in the faith and in their spiritual obedience to the law of God, bearing much fruit in their good works as God gives them opportunities to serve.

II. Along with this inward change of their disposition towards God, He also changes their status from being alienated from Him, into a covenant relationship with Him by faith. This change of status includes the following four things: 1) He justifies them by imputing to them Christ's perfect obedience in exchange for their disobedience, along with the pardoning of their sins, which the Lord Jesus paid for with His life upon the cross, 2) He reconciles and purchases their peace with God so that they are no longer His enemies, 3) He adopts them into His family so that they no longer are children of wrath, but true sons of God who are blessed with all the spiritual privileges rightly belonging to His sons, and 4) after their warfare in this life is ended, He perfects them in holiness and blessedness, taking first their souls to be with Him at death; and then, at the last day, both their souls and bodies will be joyfully joined together again in the resurrection. In the Day of Judgment, all the wicked shall be sent away to hell, along with Satan who they followed. But Christ's own chosen and redeemed ones, the true believers who followed Him, will remain forever with Him in the state of His eternal glory.

The Practical Use of Saving Knowledge

The following is contained in the Holy Scriptures and summarized in the Westminster Confession of Faith and Catechisms:

The primary use of Christian doctrine is to convince us of our sin, of God's righteousness and our own unrighteousness, and of just the penalty of all the sins we have committed against a holy God, (John 16:8). This doctrine shows us that, along with Adam, we have broken the covenant of works, and so must humble ourselves and repent. But it also shows us that if we truly believe in Christ, we will be included in the covenant of grace and be saved, we will have assurance that our faith is well founded and strengthened by Christ, and that Christ is working in us to bear much fruit.

The condition of the covenant of works, or of the law, is summed up in this statement: "If you perfectly obey all that God has commanded, and do not fail at any point, you shall be saved. But if you fail, you shall surely die," (Romans 10:5; Galatians 3:10, 12).

The covenant of grace in the gospel of Jesus Christ may be summed up by this statement: "If you flee from the wrath you deserve for your disobedience, and come to the only, true Redeemer, Jesus Christ, (who is able to save to the uttermost all who come to God through Him), you shall not die, but have eternal life," (Romans 10:8-9, 11).

In order to convince us of our sins, of our unrighteousness and of deserving the just penalty for sins committed under the law, or covenant of works; these scriptures, among many more, may be useful.

I. For Convincing Ourselves We are Sinners According to the Law, consider Jeremiah 17:9-10.

> *"The heart is deceitful above all things, and desperately sick; who can understand it? 10 'I the LORD search the heart and test the mind, to give every man according to his ways, according to the fruit of his deeds.'"*

This teaches us at least these two things:

1. The fountain of all our disobedience and sin against God is in our hearts, which also definitely includes the mind, the will, all desires and affections, and all the powers of the soul. Every part of our, heart, mind, and soul is corrupted and defiled with original sin. Not only does this corruption make our minds not able to understand and grasp saving truth, but it also leads us to carry out rebellion against God. Instead of being obedient to God's commands, we obey our own evil lusts and desires: "*The heart is deceitful above all things, and desperately sick.*" Moreover, the heart is unsearchably wicked, so that no one, not even ourselves, can know our own hearts. This is the result of the fall of man into sin as Genesis 6:5 says, "*...Every intention of the thoughts of his heart was only evil continually.*" It is the Lord who saw this, whose testimony must be

trusted in this and all other matters concerning man He created. This is what the Bible tells us is the truth about ourselves. However, experience also teaches us that this is true. Until God humbles us and makes us to deny ourselves, we will never look to God's goodness in what He has commanded, but will solely follow our own, fleshly self-interest. This corruption of the heart rules over us and is the source of our disobedience, as well as the means by which we fall headlong into sin.

2. We will be judged before God's judgment seat for all our sins; not only for the original sin of Adam, but also for the sins we have committed ourselves, as verse 10 says, "*I the LORD search the heart and test the mind, to give every man according to his ways, according to the fruit of his deeds.*"

Thus, we must say to our own soul, "What God and my guilty conscience bears witness to is that my heart is deceitful above all things, and desperately sick; and that every intention of my heart, in my sinful nature, is only evil continually: Therefore, I am convinced that this is true."

This is how we are convinced of our sins by use of the law.

II. For Convincing Ourselves of Righteousness by the Law, consider Galatians 3:10.

> "*For all who rely on works of the law are under a curse; for it is written, 'Cursed be everyone who does not abide by all things written in the Book of the Law, and do them.'*"

In this verse, the apostle Paul teaches us at least these three things:

1. Because we are naturally sinful, the Bible tells us that we are not able to be justified before a holy God by our own obedience to the law. By trying to justify ourselves in our obedience, we put ourselves under the curse of the law, as the verse says, "*For all who rely on works of the law are under a curse.*"

2. Furthermore, since we are sinners by nature, we cannot perfectly perform all the duties of the law. At our best, we may be obedient to particular points of the law. But even in this, we stumble at other points, or waver in our obedience even to the points to which we have been obedient. The law requires perfect and perpetual obedience to all points, thus Paul quotes Deuteronomy 27:26, "*Cursed be everyone who does not abide by all things written in the Book of the Law, and do them.*"

3. Taking these two together; that we are under the curse of the law to obey it perfectly and perpetually, it is this that condemns us, and so we cannot be justified, "*Cursed be everyone who does not abide by all things written in the Book of the Law, and do them.*"

If we remain under the curse of the law and cannot be justified by our obedience to it, then none of the displeasure and wrath of God is taken away from us. We also face the danger of God's wrath being all the more hot against us, making us more miserable in soul and body in this life, in our death, and in the punishment that awaits us, unless God shows us mercy and grace.

Therefore we, as sinners, must say to our own soul, "Since I have broken the covenant of works, and have been placed under the curse of the law, and since I cannot justify myself in perfect and perpetual obedience to God's law, then I am under the wrath of God for my sinning against Him times without number. Because this is true, I am worthy of His punishment and wrath, both in this life, and that which is to come. Therefore, I believe I cannot justify myself before God even in my best obedience to His commands."

This is how we are convinced that only true righteousness according to the law is what justifies us before a holy God.

III. For Convincing Ourselves of Judgment by the Law, consider 2 Thessalonians 1:7-10.

"…when the Lord Jesus is revealed from heaven with his mighty angels [8] in flaming fire, inflicting vengeance on those who do not know God and on those who do not obey the gospel of our Lord Jesus. [9] They will suffer the punishment of eternal destruction, away from the presence of the Lord and from the glory of his might, [10] when he comes on that day to be glorified in his saints, and to be marveled at among all who have believed, because our testimony to you was believed.

In this passage, the apostle Paul teaches us that our Lord Jesus, who is Mediator for all who believe on His name, shall, at the last day, come armed with flaming fire in order to judge, condemn, and destroy all those who have not believed in God; who have not received the grace offered in the gospel of Jesus Christ; and who have not obeyed His word. These have chosen to remain in their natural state of sin under the bondage of the law, or covenant of works.

Therefore, we must say to our own soul: "What I have been warned of, and will be done with me at the last day, by the righteous Judge of the world, is justice towards my own sinfulness. I am further warned that if I do not believe in God while in this life, and do not receive and obey the teachings of the gospel of Christ, I will be separated from God and His eternal glory, and will be tormented in soul and body forever in hell. Therefore, I am convinced that God is just in His judgment, and have reason to thank God profoundly, because He has warned me to flee from the wrath to come."

This is how we may be convinced of the just judgment of God, for remaining under the covenant of works, if we do not obey the gospel of our Lord Jesus, and placed under the covenant of grace.

IV. For Convincing Us of Our Unrighteousness, and the Judgment We Shall Incur Should We Shun the Gospel of Grace.

In order to convince us that we will incur greater judgment by shunning the gospel, or covenant of grace, we must understand at least these three things: 1) we must understand that not believing in Jesus Christ, or refusing the covenant of grace offered by the gospel, is an even greater and more dangerous sin than all other sins we might commit. The reason it is a greater sin is because not believing in Christ is equal to rejecting God's mercy in Him, as He is the only way to be freed from sin and wrath, and be reconciled to God; 2) we must understand that the only way we will be accounted as righteous before a holy God is if we possess faith in Christ, because God requires no other condition but faith in Him, and further testifies from heaven, that He is well pleased to justify sinners upon their having faith in Him; and 3) we must understand that unless we believe on Christ, and unless we are accounted as righteous because we have received faith as God's gift in Christ Jesus, judgment shall follow. This judgment comes to us in two ways: if we do not truly believe on Christ for salvation in this life, we will not be pardoned of our sins, the works of the devil will not be destroyed in us, and we will not be empowered and perfected by the work of sanctification, thus, we will be constantly under God's wrath. In the second judgment, which is the life of the world to come, God's wrath will not be turned away, we will be condemned for our unrighteousness, and will be cast, along with all of Satan's followers, into hell forever.

In order to bolster this argument, the following passages of Scripture, among many others that could be cited, serve as a contrast between the great sin of not believing in Christ and shunning the covenant of grace, and the magnificence of God's grace by which He offers His only Son in the covenant of grace. For instance, look at the fair offer of grace as it is made, Isaiah 55:3. *"Incline your ear, and come to me; hear, that your soul may live; and I will make with you an everlasting covenant, my steadfast, sure love for David."* This means that if we believe in Christ and are reconciled to God, God will give to us His only Son along with all other graces in Him. This is repeated by Paul in Acts 13:34.

This offer is not to a particular people only, like the Jews of the Old Testament, but to all who hear the free offer of the gospel. Paul's proclamation in Acts 16:31 says, "…*Believe in the Lord Jesus, and you will be saved, you and your household.*" This statement is for any and all who would believe in Christ for salvation. What is the reason this offer should be made to all men? John 3:16 says, "*For God so loved the world, that he gave his only Son, that whoever believes in him should not perish but have eternal life.*" If this great salvation is offered in the Lord Jesus to all who hear it, and we do not believe in Him, but look for our happiness in some other way, what else could be said of us? Do we not vainly fool ourselves, and forsake the mercy we might obtain in Christ Jesus? Jonah 2:8-9 says, "*Those who pay regard to vain idols forsake their hope of steadfast love.* ⁹ *But I with the voice of thanksgiving will sacrifice to you; what I have vowed I will pay. Salvation belongs to the* LORD!" Moreover, 1 John 5:10-11 says, "*Whoever believes in the Son of God has the testimony in himself. Whoever does not believe God has made him a liar, because he has not believed in the testimony that God has borne concerning his Son.* ¹¹ *And this is the testimony, that God gave us eternal life, and this life is in his Son.*" And finally, Jesus Himself testifies that there is no sin like the sin of unbelief as He says in John 15:22, "*If I had not come and spoken to them, they would not have been guilty of sin, but now they have no excuse for their sin.*" These all serve to convince us of the greatness of our sin of not believing in Christ.

For convincing us that righteousness only comes by faith in Jesus Christ, consider Romans 10:3-4, which says, "*For, being ignorant of the righteousness of God, and seeking to establish their own, they did not submit to God's righteousness.* ⁴ *For Christ is the end of the law for righteousness to everyone who believes.*" And also Acts 13:39, "*and by him everyone who believes is freed from everything from which you could not be freed by the Law of Moses.*" And also 1 John 1:7, "*But if we walk in the light, as he is in the light, we have fellowship with one another, and the blood of Jesus his Son cleanses us from all sin.*"

For convincing us we are to be judged unless we embrace this righteousness, consider 1 John 3:8, "*Whoever makes a practice of sinning is of the devil, for the devil has been sinning from the beginning. The reason the Son of God appeared was to destroy the works of the devil.*" And Hebrews 9:14, "*how much more will the blood of Christ, who through the eternal Spirit offered himself without blemish to God, purify our conscience from dead works to serve the living God.*"

But if we do not embrace this righteousness, our doom is already pronounced, as Jesus says in John 3:18-19, "*Whoever believes in him is not condemned, but whoever does not believe is condemned already, because he has not believed in the name of the only Son of God.* ¹⁹ *And this is the judgment: the light has come into the world, and people loved the darkness rather than the light because their works were evil.*"

For these reasons, we who desire to believe must say to our own souls:

"What has been said here is sufficient to convince all God's chosen people of the greatness of the sin of unbelief, or of refusing to seek Christ for the forgiveness of their sins, and to flee from the wrath to come. What has been said here is sufficient to convince them that faith in Christ is the only way to obtain righteousness and peace with God, and life eternal with Him as offered in the covenant of grace. And what has been said here is sufficient to convince them of the wisdom of Christ, in His destroying the works of the devil in His beloved ones, and sanctifying and saving all those who believe in Him. May all these things be sufficient to convince me also! Therefore, if what the Spirit has said in these or other like scriptures is sufficient to convince the people of God throughout the world, of the grace of God in Christ, of the forgiveness of sins, of the justification that comes by faith in Christ, and of the sanctification His Spirit performs in them, then I should also be convinced of these truths as they pertain to me."

If these things are understood by us, we should repent of our sins, believe on Christ, and say sincerely to the Lord words like Psalm 27:8, "*You have said, 'Seek my face.' My heart says to you, 'Your face,* LORD, *do I seek.'*" "Lord, I have heard your gospel of the everlasting covenant of grace, and of all the saving mercies that I may receive in Christ to the salvation of my soul. I sincerely embrace Jesus Christ freely offered to me. I believe in Him; I beg You to help me in the places I still have doubt. I give myself completely to You, and desire to serve You as long as I live. My hope of salvation is only in Your great power to save me. I trust You to perfect me, and to work by Your Holy Spirit in, and through me. I hope in Your mercy because it endures forever. Please do unto me as You will, and do not forsake the work of Your hands. Amen."

If we pray this prayer in sincerity of heart, we may be assured of our forgiveness through Christ.

For Strengthening Our Faith Who Have Been Included in the Covenant of Grace.

Many true believers are at times weak in their faith and have doubts about their justification before God, and wonder if they really are saved. Some who profess faith deceive themselves and have a false sense of security. Therefore, it is important for us to know how we may be strengthened in our faith and have a firm sense of security regarding our salvation. In order to foster a good hope towards salvation, the following, among many other scriptures, may be brought to bear against fear and doubt.

1. Consider 2 Peter 1:1-10 as a solid ground for faith:

> *Simeon Peter, a servant and apostle of Jesus Christ, To those who have obtained a faith of equal standing with ours by the righteousness of our God and Savior Jesus Christ: ² May grace and peace be multiplied to you in the knowledge of God and of Jesus our Lord. ³ His divine power has granted to us all things that pertain to life and godliness, through the knowledge of him who called us to his own glory and excellence, ⁴ by which he has granted to us his precious and very great promises, so that through them you may become partakers of the divine nature, having escaped from the corruption that is in the world because of sinful desire. ⁵ For this very reason, make every effort to supplement your faith with virtue, and virtue with knowledge, ⁶ and knowledge with self-control, and self-control with steadfastness, and steadfastness with godliness, ⁷ and godliness with brotherly affection, and brotherly affection with love. ⁸ For if these qualities are yours and are increasing, they keep you from being ineffective or unfruitful in the knowledge of our Lord Jesus Christ. ⁹ For whoever lacks these qualities is so nearsighted that he is blind, having forgotten that he was cleansed from his former sins. ¹⁰ Therefore, brothers, be all the more diligent to confirm your calling and election, for if you practice these qualities you will never fall.*

Here Peter teaches us at least these four things, so that we may be helped in knowing how to be made strong in our faith.

1. Believers in Christ Jesus, who have fled to him for forgiveness of sins and from the wrath to come, no matter how weak they are in the faith, are called brothers. They are addressed as children of their heavenly Father, just as all the saints who have come before have been.

2. Even though we may have doubts about our calling and election, Peter says to the children of God that if we are diligent, our calling and election will be confirmed, "…*be all the more diligent to confirm your calling and election.*"

3. Along with diligence, which even false brothers may seem to have, we need to take heed that we do not become discouraged in confirming our faith, "*Therefore, brothers, be all the more diligent.*"

4. In order to be sure of both our calling and election, we must allow the Spirit to work in us by faith, which makes it firm within us and helps us bear fruit in our new obedience. In this, we must be constant: "*for if you practice these qualities you will never fall;*" understanding that these qualities in verses one through eight confirm both the soundness of our faith and the fruits that come because of it.

2. Paul encourages us further in Romans 8:1-4.

> *"There is therefore now no condemnation for those who are in Christ Jesus. ² For the law of the Spirit of life has set you free in Christ Jesus from the law of sin and death. ³ For God has done what the law, weakened by the flesh, could not do. By sending his own Son in the likeness of sinful flesh and for sin, he condemned sin in the flesh, ⁴ in order that the righteous requirement of the law might be fulfilled in us, who walk not according to the flesh but according to the Spirit."*

Here the apostle Paul teaches us at least these four things about having a solid foundation in the faith:

1. If we have sense of our sins, and fear of God's wrath for them, and flee for forgiveness to Jesus Christ alone, as He is the only Mediator and all-sufficient Redeemer of God's people; and, having fled to Christ, strive against our own flesh and the corruptness of our whole nature, and are diligent to follow the teachings of the Spirit in God's Word: then Paul says we are true believers in Christ Jesus, *"who walk not according to the flesh but according to the Spirit."*

2. Even though we flee to Christ, and strive against sin, and are fearful of God's wrath and condemnation, Paul says we are no longer in any danger of condemnation, *"There is therefore now no condemnation for those who are in Christ Jesus."*

3. By nature, all of us are bound under the law of sin and death, or the covenant of works. Yet, when we believe in Christ, we are set free. This is why Paul says of true believers, *"The law of the Spirit of life,"* or the covenant of grace, *"has set you free in Christ Jesus from the law of sin and death,"* or covenant of works.

4. The fountain from which this freedom flows is the covenant of redemption. In this covenant, which is the agreement between God the Father, God the Son, and God the Spirit, the Son agreed to take upon Himself the curse of the law, so that we, who are under that curse, who do not have the power to cast off our chains, could be delivered from its prison house. Moreover, Paul teaches us this doctrine in these four branches: 1) the law was weak, in that it was impossible for the law to make us alive in Christ and righteous before a holy God; 2) this weakness and inability of the law is not the fault of the law, but the fault of our sinful flesh, which is not able to pay the penalty of sin, nor is it able to render perfect obedience, *"the law, weakened by the flesh;"* 3) our righteousness and salvation, which was impossible to be obtained by the law of the flesh, is accomplished by God sending His own Son, Jesus Christ, in His perfect flesh, Who is alone able to obey it perfectly, and by Whose perfect flesh, which was condemned and punished on our behalf, is the perfect sacrifice acceptable to God so that we might be set free; and 4) because He is the perfection of the law and is the perfect sacrifice for sins, the penalty required by the law is perfectly satisfied. Justice is done, the law is upheld, and the righteousness of God is fulfilled. Christ fulfilled all the work of the covenant of redemption by His perfect obedience on our behalf, by His paying the full debt of all our sins, and by His working in us through our sanctification so that we may render new obedience to Him. Therefore, we are to, *"...walk not according to the flesh but according to the Spirit."*

Good Reasons to Believe

In order to build up our confidence upon the solid ground of Christ's work, we are given at least these four good reasons and special motivations to believe in Jesus Christ.

The first good reason is because of God's sincere invitation to believe in Him as is written Isaiah 55:1.

"Come, everyone who thirsts, come to the waters; and he who has no money, come, buy and eat! Come, buy wine and milk without money and without price. ² Why do you spend your money for that which is not bread, and your labor for that which does not satisfy? Listen diligently to me, and eat what is good, and delight yourselves in rich food. ³ Incline your ear, and come to me; hear, that your soul may live; and I will make with you an everlasting covenant, my steadfast, sure love for David. ⁴ Behold, I made him a witness to the peoples, a leader and commander for the peoples."

Since we have already seen, in the preceding paragraphs, the precious ransom Christ paid for our redemption, and the rich blessings He purchased for us, we see further here:

1. God's free and gracious offer of Christ and His grace to every soul, without exception, who truly desire to be saved from sin and wrath: *"Come, everyone who thirsts."*

2. He invites all sinners who stand at a distance from God to come and take from Him the riches of His grace, which run in Christ like a river: to wash away sin, and to assuage His wrath: *"...come to the waters."*

3. If we should stand back from approaching Him because of our own sense of sinfulness or unworthiness, and the inability we have to do any good, the Lord specially calls upon us, saying, *"...and he who has no money, come, buy and eat!"*

4. He shows us that we will be satisfied fully with the food He has to offer, which is grace, and even more grace, so that we will embrace His offer with a full heart. Not only this, but He invites us to make use of His grace and the blessings we have in Christ Jesus, freely, without the thought of what we should pay, *"Come, buy wine and milk without money and without price."*

5. He addresses our own inclination to seek righteousness and life by other means; to try to earn His favor by our own performance to satisfy the law's demands. He knows how reluctant we are to embrace Christ Jesus, and to accept the terms of free grace through Him. Therefore, the Lord lovingly reminds us that our way will not lead to life: *"Why do you spend your money for that which is not bread, and your labor for that which does not satisfy?"*

6. The Lord promises us complete satisfaction in embracing the grace of Christ, and even true contentment, and the fullness of spiritual pleasure, saying, *"Listen diligently to me, and eat what is good, and delight yourselves in rich food."*

7. Faith comes by hearing. This is why He calls for us to come near and hear the explanation of grace in Christ, and calls upon us to believe and trust in God: *"Incline your ear, and come to me."* When we hear this word preached, the Lord promises that if this offer of His grace is truly received by faith, then we shall pass from death to life; from being enemies of God, to being members of His household, being at peace with Him. In other words, we shall be included in His gracious and unbreakable covenant: *"...hear, that your soul may live; and I will make with you an everlasting covenant."* God declares in this everlasting covenant, the same promise of everlasting love He showed to David (cf. Acts 13:34), and the promise of salvation through David's greater Son, Jesus Christ. He declares, *"...and I will make with you an everlasting covenant, my steadfast, sure love for David."* By saying *"sure love,"* He means all the saving graces, such as righteousness, peace, joy in the Holy Spirit, adoption, sanctification, and glorification, and all the eternal riches of God in Christ Jesus.

8. To confirm this *"sure love,"* and to persuade us of the reality of this covenant He makes with us, the following four gifts are given to us in the Lord Jesus:

1) Christ is given to us as the seed of David and true heir to his kingdom. Acts 13:34 mentioned above, gives to Christ, "*the holy and sure blessings of David*," and Jesus is then given to us, who along with Him have these blessings (cf. John 4:10).

2) He has given Christ as witness to us, both of the sure and saving mercies granted to us in the covenant of redemption, and also of the Father's willingness and purpose to give them to us who embrace the offer: "*Behold, I made him a witness to the peoples.*" Moreover, Christ is the perfect witness, in that, He is party to the covenant of redemption in eternity; He is by office, Mediator (1 Timothy 2:5), the Messenger of the covenant (Malachi 3:1), Who has been given the authority to reveal it; He is declared to be the Seed of the woman who would bruise the serpent's head (Genesis 3:15); He is the only, suffering servant Who set forth the great benefits of redemption in the promises, types, and sacrifices of the Old Testament; Who is fully revealed in the New Testament; He revealed Himself at first, dimly, speaking by His Spirit, through the prophets, and He came Himself, in the fullness of time, and bore witness to all things belonging to this covenant, and of God's willingness to make His people partakers of it. He did this by taking on Himself our flesh to be united to His divine nature, by preaching the good news of the gospel with His own mouth, by paying the price of our redemption on the cross, and by drawing close to God, all His people, which He is still doing to this day, and will continue to do until the Last Day.

3) God has given us a gift of Christ by making Him a leader over us. "*Behold, I made him…a leader…for the peoples.*" First, He leads us into covenant with God and thus begins our journey of salvation in Him. But He also brings us through all the difficulties of this life and through all our afflictions and temptations, until the day He comes to bring us into life eternal with Him. All of this is accomplished by the Holy Spirit's working in us through the Word; showing us Christ's example of His trust in God and faithful obedience, enabling us to do the same; and in giving us great comfort, even in the valley of the shadow of death, that we may rest in His arms, as sheep to a gentle Shepherd.

4) God has given us a gift of Christ by making Him a commander: "*Behold, I made him…commander for the peoples.*" Christ faithfully exercises His rule by giving to His Church: laws and ordinances, elders and deacons, higher courts and assemblies among them, so that there is order in His Church. He exercises His rule over us by subduing all His people by His Word and Spirit, so that we are all under His discipline in order that He might rid us of our corruption. And lastly, He rules over us by his wisdom and power, so that we be preserved and protected from our enemies.

Therefore, we are strengthened in our faith by saying to our own souls: "If I receive the offer of free grace, which is made to me, a sinner, with my whole heart, as it thirsts for righteousness and salvation; then I may truly lay hold to that everlasting covenant, with all the sure and saving mercies belonging to Christ, the true Son and King, Who sits forever on the throne of David."

If we pray this prayer with sincerity of heart, then all that is Christ's belongs to us in Him.

The second good reason and special motivation to embrace Christ and believe in Him, is the earnest offer God makes to us to be reconciled to Him in Christ Jesus. The basis of this is put forth in 2 Corinthians 5:19-21:

> "*That is, in Christ God was reconciling the world to himself, not counting their trespasses against them, and entrusting to us the message of reconciliation. [20] Therefore, we are ambassadors for Christ, God making his appeal through us. We implore you on behalf of Christ, be reconciled to God. [21] For our sake he made him to be sin who knew no sin, so that in him we might become the righteousness of God.*

In these verses, Paul is putting forth at least these nine doctrines:

1. Even if we now have a redeemed soul, we were born into a natural state of being an enemy of God. The word reconciliation presupposes this. We cannot now be reconciled unless we were once enemies. Thus, reconciliation makes us friends with God, instead of enemies with Him.

2. Since the fall of Adam, Christ Jesus, the eternal Son of God, as Mediator between God and man, has been about making friendship, by His Word and Spirit, between God and the people He chose in Christ: "...*in Christ God was reconciling the world to himself.*"

3. This way or means of reconciliation has always been the same since the fall of man, that is, by the acknowledgement of the sins we have committed, and of our being enemies of God, and of our need for our sins to be taken away, which has always been through Christ's substitutionary sacrifice (in the Old Testament peoples through the types and shadows of the sacrificial system). Because of faith in Christ, and our true repentance for sin, God does not count our sins against us, which is why Paul says, "...*in Christ God was reconciling the world to himself, not counting their trespasses against them.*"

4. Thus, the preaching of the gospel is throughout the whole Bible, and it serves to do the following three things: 1) It serves to make people sensible of their sins, and of their being enemies of God and in danger of His wrath against them; 2) The Word of God serves to teach people the way God has prepared for them once again to be His friends, that is through Christ and the covenant of grace, and; 3) The Word of God serves to teach men how they are to behave towards God as friends, after they are reconciled to Him; that is, to take care not to sin against Him, and to strive with all their hearts to obey His commandments. This is why Paul calls the Word of God the "*message of reconciliation,*" because it teaches us of our need of reconciliation, how to obtain it, and how to keep it, all being made with God through Christ.

5. Although the hearing, believing, and obeying of this "*message of reconciliation*" belongs to all those to whom this gospel is preached, yet the authority to preach it belongs only to those who are called to the gospel ministry and are ordained for the work. Paul makes this clear in verse 19, "...*entrusting to us the message of reconciliation.*"

6. Because this "*message of reconciliation*" is only to be preached by ministers of the gospel, these ministers must behave themselves as Christ's messengers, and should closely follow their commission Jesus spoke in Matthew 28:19-20, "The Great Commission." These faithful ministers are to be received by the people as ambassadors sent from God, as Paul says, "*Therefore, we are ambassadors for Christ, God making his appeal through us.*"

7. Paul also put forward (both in this text and by his own example) that faithful and earnest ministers should always be calling upon everyone who hears them, to acknowledge their sins and of their being a natural enemy of God, and to do so with serious and solemn warnings. The ministers should also call upon their hearers to embrace Christ and the covenant of grace, and encourage them, because of the abundant grace God gives to His people, to increase in love towards God, living holy lives before Him. This is what he means when he says, "*We implore you on behalf of Christ, be reconciled to God.*"

8. There is also a responsibility Paul places on the hearers of this "*message of reconciliation.*" The minister says, "*We implore you on behalf of Christ, be reconciled to God.*" What must the hearer do? Is it possible that any offer of friendship could be greater, than the offer of friendship to an enemy, especially to one who had done so much to wrong the other who now offers His friendship? O wonder of wonders! If this offer of friendship is rejected, how fearful is the wrath this rejection will incur? The right responsibility of the hearer, then, is to accept the offer of friendship.

9. Lastly, we are shown the richness of God's grace in this offer of reconciliation. Our Lord Jesus, as party to the covenant of redemption, and in His office of Mediator, took the sins of His people and forfeited His innocence. He was condemned and put to death in order that His innocence could be given to us. This is our righteousness before a holy God, Christ. Thus Paul says, "*For our sake he made him to be sin who knew no sin, so that in him we might become the righteousness of God.*"

Therefore, may we, as weak believers who constantly need our faith strengthened, say to our own soul:

"If God shows me the great love He has for me in Christ, as offered by His duly appointed ministers of the gospel, and has offered me friendship in this "*message of reconciliation,*" then I shall, through the empowering Holy Spirit, embrace His offer through Christ, with the full purpose of striving against sin, and serving God with all my heart, soul, mind, and strength; as constantly as I can and as He gives me grace to do so. May God give me this comfort and strength: that as surely as my sins condemned the Lord Jesus and put Him to death, so too, has His righteousness and life been imputed to me. To God alone be glory!"

If we pray this prayer with sincerity of heart, then we may be assured of our reconciliation with God.

The third good reason and special motivation to believe in Christ, is because God has not only commanded that we believe in Christ, but that we also live in loving obedience to His commands, in that order. This is shown to us in 1 John 3:23.

> "*And this is his commandment, that we believe in the name of his Son Jesus Christ and love one another, just as he has commanded us.*"

These five doctrines are being put forward by John the Apostle:

1. To be reconciled to God and believe in Christ is not simply a request, but a command. Those who do not accept the sweet invitation of God, shall find that they must stand before the sovereign authority of the highest Majesty to explain the reason for their disobedience. Thus, John says, "*this is his commandment, that we believe in the name of his Son Jesus Christ.*"

2. This commandment is a commandment of the gospel. This means that it is the highest command given, and there is no other command anyone could follow that will bring about the remedy for sins committed. If we do not obey this command, there is another command that follows, "Depart from me, you cursed, into the eternal fire prepared for the devil and his angels," (Matthew 25:41). That commandment will not remedy sins, but justly punish them. However, this commandment, to believe in Christ, also pleases God when it is obeyed by faith (1 John 3:22), without which it is impossible to please God (Hebrews 11:6).

3. This verse also teaches us that, we who hear the gospel must have faith to believe in Christ no matter how weak or strong our consciences are towards our own sinfulness. In other words, those whose consciences are weak may believe that their sins are so wicked that God could not possibly forgive them all. Those who have stronger consciences may believe that their sins were not so bad, and thus, not considering their great need of Christ. Both of these situations require caution. We, as sinners, are condemned and are lost without Christ. And we must acknowledge our sinfulness, no matter how great or small we think our sins are (everyone should believe their sins are great before a holy God). Once we acknowledge our sins, we must have faith in Christ that He is able to save us from them. Everyone who comes to Him for salvation, must have faith. Therefore, the command, "*believe in the name of his Son Jesus Christ,*" is given to all, because all need to acknowledge their sinfulness and need of Christ and believe He is able to save them. No one can acknowledge their sins, yet not believe in Christ, and be saved. Likewise,

no one can believe in Christ, yet not acknowledge their sins, and be saved. True faith in Christ will always make us acknowledge our sins, and it will also give us confidence that Christ will save us from them.

4. If we obey this commandment, to believe in Christ, our salvation is on solid ground for a few particular reasons. First, Jesus is the promised Messiah, upon Whom our faith rests. He is the only Perfect One, Who is completely equipped to carry out His three-fold office of Prophet, Priest, and King. Secondly, we have embraced a savior, Who is able to save to the uttermost all who come to the Father through Him. He is called Jesus because He saves His people from their sins (Matthew 1:21). Thirdly, our salvation rests on the Rock Who is Christ, Who is the very and Only Son of God, Who is worthy to be the object of saving faith and worship.

5. If we believe in Christ, though we are freed from the curse of the law, we are not freed from the commandments and obedience of the law, but are bound to a new and even greater obligation. "...*believe in the name of his Son Jesus Christ and love one another, just as he has commanded us.*" To believe in Christ implies that we love God. If we believe in Christ and love God, then we must love each other. The two tables of the law are inseparably joined in this commandment. We are to love God in believing in Christ, and love one another (especially to those in the household of faith, Galatians 6:10). Therefore, we are not freed from our obligation to the moral law, but because of love, we are more obligated to it.

Therefore, may we, as weak believers, see the firm ground of our faith and say to our own soul:

"If I have a true sense of my own sinfulness, and fear of God's wrath; and, at the command of God, I flee to Jesus Christ, as the only remedy of my sin and misery; and I have engaged my heart to obedience to the law of love, then my faith is not a false presumption or dead, but is true, saving faith. May I live to obey the law of love in Christ!"

If we pray this prayer with sincerity of heart, then we may be assured that our faith is genuine.

The fourth good reason and special motivation to believe in Christ, is to obtain good assurance of life if we believe and obey; and proper, godly fear of all doubting as put forward in John 3:35-36.

> "*The Father loves the Son and has given all things into his hand.* [36] *Whoever believes in the Son has eternal life; whoever does not obey the Son shall not see life, but the wrath of God remains on him.*"

These verses put forward at least these five doctrines:

1. The Father is well pleased and satisfied with all the duties Christ performed as our Redeemer and the surety of our salvation, even in our being made perfect in holiness by Him. This is the meaning of, "*The Father loves the Son and has given all things into his hand.*" Because God is pleased, satisfied, and has accepted all Christ has done, He is likewise pleased with all those who are included in His work. Moreover, God has made all these things to abound toward us, as Paul says in Ephesians 1:8.

2. By saying, "*The Father...has given all things into his hand,*" God means to tell us that all He has required to fulfill the covenant of redemption, He has given to the Son. The Father has given to the Son all authority in heaven and earth; all the riches of His grace, of the Spirit and of life; and all the power and ability to accomplish His will. God did not give all these things to a mere man, but to Christ, Who has two distinct natures in one person. In the person of Christ there is the union of Christ's divine nature with His fully human nature. Because of this, Christ is able to fulfill all things as the fullness of the Godhead dwelling in human form. He is fully God and fully man, yet one Lord.

3. To those who believe in Christ with their whole heart, there is great assurance of life in the covenant of grace, and reconciliation with God through Him, as the first part of verse 36 says, "*Whoever believes in the Son has eternal life.*" Notice that the believer has eternal life, not just the possibility of eternal life; it is a certainty. How is it so certain? First, God has purposefully and irrevocably elected His chosen ones to eternal life (Ephesians 1:3-14; Romans 11:29). Secondly, it is He who has called His people, and He is faithful and will do it (Romans 8:30; Hebrews 10:23). Thirdly, this promise and everlasting covenant is made by God who does not change (Isaiah 55:3; James 1:17). Fourthly, God gives signs and seals, such as the sacrament of the Lord's Supper, as a pledge or earnest of the eternal blessings of the covenant (1 Corinthians 11:23-26-26). Fifthly, He appointed Christ, the fountain and head of life, to be our advocate and intercede for us, who has gone to prepare a place that will never decay nor be destroyed (Romans 8:34; John 14:1-3). And lastly, He has made His Spirit to dwell in us so that we may know His righteousness, peace, and joy within ourselves as a pledge of everlasting life in His kingdom which cannot be shaken (Romans 14:7; 1 Corinthians 2:12; Hebrews 12:28).

4. A warning is given, "*…whoever does not obey the Son shall not see life.*" Because of the preceding statement, "*Whoever believes in the Son has eternal life,*" we should understand that it is not just disobedience to Christ that prohibits eternal life, but also disbelief in Him. This tells us that we must know, both what it means to believe in Christ, and what it means to be obedient to Him.

5. Furthermore, we are warned that if we do not receive both Christ and His teachings, we will once again bear the wrath of God. As sinners, we are already under God's wrath (Ephesians 2:3), and, as we have seen above, sinners who remain in their sin are still subjected to the conditions of the covenant of works. But we shall endure even greater condemnation, if we, having seen the Light of the World and been freely offered His grace, reject it, and we love darkness rather than light, then this double wrath shall remain and be firmly fixed upon us, which is why our verse says, "*…but the wrath of God remains on him.*"

Therefore, may we, as weak believers, see the firm ground of our faith and say to our own soul:

"If I believe in Christ and His teachings, it may be because I am drawn towards the promise of eternal life, or because I fear God's wrath. Both of these are spiritually healthy reasons to come to Christ. However, I need to ensure that I truly believe in Him, and that I know what it means to be obedient to Him. This is the way I may be assured of life in His name. May I constantly heed the commandment to believe and obey!"

If we pray this prayer with sincerity of heart, then we may be assured that we have eternal life.

The Evidences of True Faith

Thus far we have laid the foundations of faith, and given good reasons to believe. Now, in order for us to know if we have a true and lively faith in Christ, we must consider these four things: 1) we have an obligation to keep the moral law all of our days. Although we have been freed from the law of sin and death, we have not been freed from obedience to the gospel and to Christ. Our love of Him should increase our obligation, not lessen it. We do not keep the moral law as a covenant of works to obtain salvation from God, but out of our love for God and our neighbor; 2) we must endeavor to grow in the daily practice of godliness and righteousness; 3) we must ensure our "new" obedience comes from our faith in Christ and from proper motives, so that we obey from a good conscience; and 4) we must acknowledge that our obedience flows from Christ Jesus, as He is fountain of all good works, and that only by His Spirit can we produce good fruit.

In order to convince us that we are bound to keep the moral law, we first look at Matthew 5:16-20:

> *"In the same way, let your light shine before others, so that they may see your good works and give glory to your Father who is in heaven.* [17] *Do not think that I have come to abolish the Law or the Prophets; I have not come to abolish them but to fulfill them.* [18] *For truly, I say to you, until heaven and earth pass away, not an iota, not a dot, will pass from the Law until all is accomplished.* [19] *Therefore whoever relaxes one of the least of these commandments and teaches others to do the same will be called least in the kingdom of heaven, but whoever does them and teaches them will be called great in the kingdom of heaven.* [20] *For I tell you, unless your righteousness exceeds that of the scribes and Pharisees, you will never enter the kingdom of heaven."*

In this passage, Our Lord is teaching us:

1. As we are justified by faith, we are also to give evidence of God's grace by doing good works, which is why He says, *"…let your light shine before others, so that they may see your good works and give glory to your Father who is in heaven."*

2. Our good works do not justify us, but they do point to God. Those who see us, whether they are Christians or not, converted or unconverted, may see these things and be edified or drawn to God so to give Him glory, as Jesus says, *"…so that they may see your good works and give glory to your Father who is in heaven."*

3. Lest we are to believe that the moral law is not binding on us, Christ firmly states that He did not come to destroy the law: *"Do not think that I have come to abolish the Law or the Prophets."*

4. Jesus did not want us to misunderstand Him regarding the law. We are prone to believe that freedom from the curse of the law makes us free from the law itself; that the doctrine of grace loosens the obligation to obedience to the law. But if that were the case, the law would be destroyed and the prophets would have been mistaken. Christ not only came to save us from our sins, but to make us holy. Thus He says, *"Do not think that I have come to abolish the Law or the Prophets."*

5. On the contrary, Christ says He has come in the covenant of grace, so that His people will be obedient, and thus fulfill the law and the prophets, *"I have not come to abolish them but to fulfill them."*

6. The obligation of the moral law, in all its points, regarding all its holy duties, is perpetual, and shall not cease until the end of the world, that is, *"until heaven and earth pass away."*

7. God has preserved His holy Word from the beginning, and it shall be carefully preserved even to the end of the world. There is not one small word or ink stroke that will fall away from the scriptures. This is what Jesus is saying in verse 18.

8. Those who break the moral law of God and teach others to follow their example will be in danger of being cast out of the fellowship of the true Church. They neither will find favor with God, nor with men. But those who are obedient to the law and teach others to do the same by their example, and their counsel to follow the true teaching of Scripture, as far as they are able in this life to do; these will be highly esteemed by both God and men.

9. When Jesus says, *"…unless your righteousness exceeds that of the scribes and Pharisees, you will never enter the kingdom of heaven,"* He means personal righteousness and holiness of every true Christian must be founded by faith in His righteousness, not dependent upon one's own righteousness. Jesus also means that a Christian must not be hypocritical like the Pharisees of Jesus' day. The Pharisees took pride in all their

duties of righteousness and holiness, but it was only outward observance. They neglected the inward, spiritual parts of their obedience, not caring about mercy and love they should have shown to both God and others, but only caring about what their service looked like to others. They were really trying to commend themselves to God by their own good works, and rejected the righteousness they could have had by faith in Jesus. A Christian's obedience must be more than all this; we must learn to grasp the full extent of the spiritual meaning of the law, and have a respect to all the commandments. We must labor to cleanse ourselves from all filthiness of flesh and spirit, which is part of our sin nature, and not think of our service as more than what it is. Our righteousness is not what justifies us, we must therefore be clothed with the imputed righteousness of Christ, or else we cannot be saved.

The second evidence to true faith is that the believer endeavors to put godliness and righteousness into practice, and to grow in the exercise of these graces daily. 2 Peter 1:5-8 says,

> *For this very reason, make every effort to supplement your faith with virtue, and virtue with knowledge, 6 and knowledge with self-control, and self-control with steadfastness, and steadfastness with godliness, 7 and godliness with brotherly affection, and brotherly affection with love. 8 For if these qualities are yours and are increasing, they keep you from being ineffective or unfruitful in the knowledge of our Lord Jesus Christ. 9 For whoever lacks these qualities is so nearsighted that he is blind, having forgotten that he was cleansed from his former sins.*

1. The apostle Peter teaches here that believers, in order to find evidence of precious faith in themselves, should endeavor to add to their faith seven other "sister" graces. The first is virtue. Virtue may be defined as the active exercise and practice of all moral duties. Adding this practice of moral duties to faith is so that faith may not be idle, but may be working in our lives. The second is knowledge. Knowledge serves to furnish our faith with God's truths that we must believe. Additionally knowledge informs our faith so that we may know how to practice these moral duties of virtue, and also may know how they are to be done appropriately. The third is self-control, which serves to help us use all things pertaining to our own pleasure in moderation so that we may not be unfit for the duties of virtue. The fourth is steadfastness, which serves to govern our perseverance. Steadfastness will help us to persevere when we meet with difficulties or hard circumstances; it will help us not to grow tired of doing good works, nor to grow weary or to grumble when the Lord disciplines us. The fifth is godliness. Godliness helps us by making our worship and devotion beneficial both to the inward spirit, and the outward and physical capabilities, so that we may perform properly all the duties God has called us to do. The sixth is brotherly affection, which makes us hold in high esteem and love all those who have faith in Christ, and in whom God's image is seen by us. The final grace is love, which keeps our hearts ready to do good to all men, whether they are a brother in Christ or not, upon all occasions appointed to us by God's providence.

2. Though it is true that there is still corruption and weakness in we who are godly; yet Peter exhorts us to endeavor to do our best, using all our abilities to join these graces to our faith, building them upon each other and growing in using them effectively. This is the meaning of, "…*make every effort to supplement your faith.*"

3. In verse 9, Peter assures us as we endeavor to render this diligent obedience unto the Lord, so shall we prove the soundness of our own faith. And, if we do not possess these graces, we may likewise deceive ourselves.

The third evidence of true faith is obedience to the law, which must be done through faith in Christ, as Paul teaches us in 1 Timothy 1:5, "*Now the purpose of the commandment is love from a pure heart, from a good conscience and from sincere faith (NKJV).*"

Here, Paul teaches us at least these seven doctrines:

1. Obedience to the law must flow from love, and love from a pure heart, and a pure heart from a good conscience, and a good conscience from a true faith. This is the only way obedience to the law is considered by God to be a good work.

2. The whole purpose of the law is not so that we may be justified by our obedience to it, as the Pharisees falsely taught. For it is impossible that we can be justified by the law, because every sin we commit against the law condemns us. The whole purpose of the law is so that we may express love from a pure heart.

3. If this is the true purpose of the law, this should make us flee to Christ with love in our hearts made pure by true faith in Him. We understand that we are condemned before Him for our disobedience, but because of faith, we are justified.

4. Faith teaches us that we can never obey the law out of our own love, unless our hearts and our consciences have been made pure by Jesus Christ, or because we are now seeking Him to do so.

5. False faith goes to Christ without having obtained His righteousness through justification, and merely wants to obey the law for its own merit. But true and sincere faith understands in order to be justified, it must flee to Christ for His righteousness. False faith does not see itself as guilty of breaking the law. Sincere faith knows it is guilty, and rests upon Christ. This is why Paul says in Romans 10:4, "*For Christ is the end of the law for righteousness to everyone who believes.*"

6. In order for love to act as it is supposed to in us, it is necessary that our hearts learn to hate all sin and uncleanness, and be steadfast in all holiness, "*Now the purpose of the commandment is love from a pure heart (NKJV).*"

7. Sincere faith is able to make our consciences good and our hearts pure. Moreover, we become lovingly obedient to the law, because when Christ's blood is seen by our faith to quiet the law's justice against us, then our consciences become quiet also; our hearts do not entertain the love of sin, but rather compel us to fear and obey the Lord, because of His great mercy. Further, we obey all His commandments out of love for Him and for His free gift of justification, which by grace He has bestowed on us. The purpose of the law is love, in that it obtains more obedience to God through faith in Christ than any other way.

The fourth evidence of true faith is the keeping of our communion with Christ, the fountain of all graces, and of all good works, as shown in Jesus' words in John 15:5, "*I am the vine; you are the branches. Whoever abides in me and I in him, he it is that bears much fruit, for apart from me you can do nothing.*"

Jesus uses the example of a vine to teach us,

1. We are, by nature, wild, thorny branches until we are changed by Him when we embrace Him in the gospel. Moreover, He is that noble vine, having all life and sap of grace in Himself, and is able to change our very nature when we come to Him, and to communicate His Spirit and life to as many as shall believe in Him. This is the meaning of, "*I am the vine; you are the branches.*"

2. Christ loves to have us so united to Him so that we will not be separated at any time by unbelief. He promises this mutual habitation of us in Him, and He in us, by joining faith and love in us with His Word and Spirit. All these things He is working in us and are inseparable.

3. The only way we may do even the least good work is if we are engrafted by faith into the true vine, which is Christ. Any work we do that does not rely upon Christ's Spirit and life is fruitless and void, and is no good work at all. This is what He means when He says, "*...for apart from me you can do nothing.*"

4. This mutual habitation is the fountain and infallible cause of our perseverance in good works, and our bearing much fruit. *"Whoever abides in me and I in him, he it is that bears much fruit."* Our abiding in Christ presupposes at least these three things: 1) That we have heard the joyful sound of the gospel, which makes the offer of Christ to us, who are lost sinners according to the law; 2) That we have embraced the gracious offer of Christ with our whole hearts, and; 3) That by receiving Him we have become the sons of God (John 1:12), and are incorporated into His mystical body; that He may dwell in us, as His temple, and we dwell in Him, as if residing in His dwelling of righteousness and life. Moreover, our abiding in Christ means that we call upon His name in all our prayers to God, and rely upon His strength in all our service to Him. Our abiding in Christ means that we have true contentment with His sufficiency, not seeking righteousness in ourselves or any other thing. Our abiding in Christ means that we will be steadfast in our belief of Him, in our reliance upon Him and asking for His help. It also means that we will be steadfast in our contentment of all He gives us, not seeking the pleasures of the flesh, or of the world, or of Satan. And finally, our abiding in Christ means we will be steadfast in upholding the truth of God's word, and defend His person.

Therefore, may we, as watchful believers, strengthen our faith and obedience and say to our own soul:

"If I daily seek Christ Jesus for cleansing my conscience and affections from the guilt and filth of sins I have committed against the law, and if I seek His help in order for Him to give me the ability to obey the law in love, then I have evidence of true faith in myself."

Moreover, if we are sleepy and sluggish in our belief, in order for us to be diligent and stir ourselves up to good works, we should say to ourselves:

"If these things are necessary for the evidence of true faith, and I do not see them in my life, I have deceived myself. If I am deceived, I will perish. I must, therefore, daily seek Christ for the cleansing of my conscience and affections from the guilt and filth of my own sins against the law, and I must daily seek His help in order for Him to give me the ability to obey the law in love."

And, finally, we are comforted by Jesus' words in John 6:37, *"All that the Father gives me will come to me, and whoever comes to me I will never cast out."* In this, we see that those who are elected by God for life and salvation by Jesus Christ will come to Him, be joined in covenant with Him, keep communion with Him, and will never be cast out.

Therefore, let those, who do not earnestly seek Christ for remission of sin, and new life in Him; from all the reasons that have been put forth here; say to his or her own soul, that he or she may be awakened:

"If I am not convinced, either by the law or the gospel, that I am a sinner, convicted, condemned, and worthy of judgment; and if I do not seek Christ daily for remission of my sins, and new life in Him, then I cannot expect any evidence of saving faith or of being in covenant and communion with God. But if I seek Him now for the remission of my sins, and I seek from Him new life in His name, then I will be forgiven of my sins, and given new life. If I pray this prayer in faith, John 1:9 promises me, 'If we confess our sins, he is faithful and just to forgive us ours sins and to cleanse us from all unrighteousness.' May God do unto me as He has promised!"

<u>Notes</u>

The Westminster Confession of Faith
Chapter I – Of the Holy Scripture.

I. Although the light of nature and the works of creation and providence do so far manifest the goodness, wisdom, and power of God, as to leave men unexcusable;[1] yet are they not sufficient to give that knowledge of God and of His will, which is necessary unto salvation.[2] Therefore it pleased the Lord, at sundry times, and in divers manners, to reveal Himself, and to declare that His will unto His Church;[3] and afterwards, for the better preserving and propagating of the truth, and for the more sure establishment and comfort of the Church against the corruption of the flesh, and the malice of Satan and of the world, to commit the same wholly unto writing:[4] which maketh the Holy Scripture to be most necessary;[5] those former ways of God's revealing His will unto His people being now ceased.[6]

II.   Under the name of Holy Scripture, or the Word of God written, are now contained all the books of the Old and New Testament, which are these:

Of the Old Testament:

Genesis	II Chronicles	Daniel
Exodus	Ezra	Hosea
Leviticus	Nehemiah	Joel
Numbers	Esther	Amos
Deuteronomy	Job	Obadiah
Joshua	Psalms	Jonah
Judges	Proverbs	Micah
Ruth	Ecclesiastes	Nahum
I Samuel	The Song of Songs	Habakkuk
II Samuel	Isaiah	Zephaniah
I Kings	Jeremiah	Haggai
II Kings	Lamentations	Zechariah
I Chronicles	Ezekiel	Malachi

---

[1] Psalm 19:1-3; Romans 1:19-20, 1:32, 2:1, 2:14-15.
[2] 1 Corinthians 1:21, 2:13-14.
[3] Hebrews 1:1.
[4] Proverbs 22:19-21; Isaiah 8:19-20; Matthew 4:4,7,10; Luke 1:3-4; Romans 15:4.
[5] 2 Timothy 3:15; 2 Peter 1:19.
[6] Hebrews 1:1-2.

Of the New Testament:

The Gospels according to

Matthew	Corinthians II	To Titus
Mark	Galatians	To Philemon
Luke	Ephesians	The Epistle to the Hebrews
John	Philippians	The Epistle of James
The Acts of the Apostles	Thessalonians I	The first and second Epistles of Peter
Paul's Epistles to the	Thessalonians II	The first, second, and third Epistles of John
Romans	To Timothy I	The Epistle of Jude
Corinthians I	To Timothy II	The Revelation of John

All which are given by inspiration of God to be the rule of faith and life.[7]

III. The books commonly called Apocrypha, not being of divine inspiration, are no part of the canon of the Scripture; and therefore are of no authority in the Church of God, nor to be any otherwise approved, or made use of, than other human writings.[8]

IV. The authority of the Holy Scripture, for which it ought to be believed and obeyed, dependeth not upon the testimony of any man, or Church; but wholly upon God (who is truth itself) the author thereof: and therefore it is to be received because it is the Word of God.[9]

V. We may be moved and induced by the testimony of the Church to a high and reverent esteem of the Holy Scripture.[10] And the heavenliness of the matter, the efficacy of the doctrine, the majesty of the style, the consent of all the parts, the scope of the whole (which is, to give all glory to God), the full discovery it makes of the only way of man's salvation, the many other incomparable excellencies, and the entire perfection thereof, are arguments whereby it doth abundantly evidence itself to be the Word of God: yet notwithstanding, our full persuasion and assurance of the infallible truth and divine authority thereof, is from the inward work of the Holy Spirit bearing witness by and with the Word in our hearts.[11]

VI. The whole counsel of God concerning all things necessary for His own glory, man's salvation, faith, and life, is either expressly set down in Scripture, or by good and necessary consequence may be deduced from Scripture: unto which nothing at any time is to be added, whether by new revelations of the Spirit, or traditions of men.[12] Nevertheless we acknowledge the inward illumination of the Spirit of God to be necessary for the saving understanding of such things as are revealed in the Word:[13] and that there are some circumstances concerning the worship of God, and government of the Church, common to human actions and societies, which are to be ordered by the light of nature and Christian prudence, according to the general rules of the Word, which are always to be observed.[14]

---

[7] Luke 16:29,31; Ephesians 2:20; 2 Timothy 3:16; Revelation 22:18-19.
[8] Luke 24:27,44; Romans 3:2; 2 Peter 1:21.
[9] 1 Thessalonians 2:13; 2 Timothy 3:16; 2 Peter 1:19, 21; 1 John 5:9.
[10] 1 Timothy 3:15.
[11] Isaiah 59:21; John 16:13-14; 1 Corinthians 2:10-12; 1 John 2:20,27.
[12] Galatians 1:8-9; 2 Thessalonians 2:2; 2 Timothy 3:15-17.
[13] John 6:45, 1 Corinthians 2:9-12.
[14] 1 Corinthians 11:13-14, 14:26,40.

VII. All things in Scripture are not alike plain in themselves, nor alike clear unto all:[15] yet those things which are necessary to be known, believed, and observed for salvation, are so clearly propounded and opened in some place of Scripture or other, that not only the learned, but the unlearned, in a due use of the ordinary means, may attain unto a sufficient understanding of them.[16]

VIII. The Old Testament in Hebrew (which was the native language of the people of God of old), and the New Testament in Greek (which, at the time of the writing of it was most generally known to the nations), being immediately inspired by God, and, by His singular care and providence kept pure in all ages, are therefore authentical;[17] so as, in all controversies of religion, the Church is finally to appeal unto them.[18] But, because these original tongues are not known to all the people of God, who have right unto, and interest in the Scriptures, and are commanded, in the fear of God, to read and search them,[19] therefore they are to be translated into the vulgar language of every nation unto which they come,[20] that the Word of God dwelling plentifully in all, they may worship Him in an acceptable manner;[21] and, through patience and comfort of the Scriptures, may have hope.[22]

IX. The infallible rule of interpretation of Scripture is the Scripture itself: and therefore, when there is a question about the true and full sense of any Scripture (which is not manifold, but one), it must be searched and known by other places that speak more clearly.[23]

X. The supreme judge by which all controversies of religion are to be determined, and all decrees of councils, opinions of ancient writers, doctrines of men, and private spirits, are to be examined; and in whose sentence we are to rest; can be no other but the Holy Spirit speaking in the Scripture.[24]

Chapter II – Of God, and of the Holy Trinity.

I. There is but one only,[25] living, and true God:[26] who is infinite in being and perfection,[27] a most pure spirit,[28] invisible,[29] without body, parts,[30] or passions,[31] immutable,[32] immense,[33] eternal,[34]

---

[15] 2 Peter 3:16.
[16] Psalm 119:105,130.
[17] Matthew 5:18.
[18] Isaiah 8:20; John 5:39,46; Acts 15:15.
[19] John 5:39.
[20] 1 Corinthians 14:6,9,11-12,24,27-28.
[21] Colossians 3:16.
[22] Romans 15:4.
[23] Acts 15:15-16; 2 Peter 1:20-21.
[24] Matthew 22:29,31; Acts 28:25; Ephesians 2:20.
[25] Deuteronomy 6:4; 1 Corinthians 8:4,6.
[26] Jeremiah 10:10; 1 Thessalonians 1:9.
[27] Job 11:7-9, 26:14.
[28] John 4:24.
[29] 1 Timothy 1:17.
[30] Deuteronomy 4:15-16; Luke 24:39; John 4:24.
[31] Acts 14:11,15.
[32] Malachi 3:6; James 1:17.
[33] 1 Kings 8:27; Jeremiah 23:23-24.
[34] Psalm 90:2; 1 Timothy 1:17.

incomprehensible,[35] almighty,[36] most wise,[37] most holy,[38] most free,[39] most absolute,[40] working all things according to the counsel of His own immutable and most righteous will,[41] for His own glory;[42] most loving,[43] gracious, merciful, long-suffering, abundant in goodness and truth, forgiving iniquity, transgression, and sin;[44] the rewarder of them that diligently seek Him;[45] and withal, most just and terrible in His judgments,[46] hating all sin,[47] and who will by no means clear the guilty.[48]

II. God hath all life,[49] glory,[50] goodness,[51] blessedness,[52] in and of Himself; and is alone in and unto Himself all-sufficient, not standing in need of any creatures which He hath made,[53] nor deriving any glory from them,[54] but only manifesting His own glory in, by, unto, and upon them: He is the alone fountain of all being, of whom, through whom, and to whom are all things;[55] and hath most sovereign dominion over them, to do by them, for them, or upon them whatsoever Himself pleaseth.[56] In His sight all things are open and manifest;[57] His knowledge is infinite, infallible, and independent upon the creature,[58] so as nothing is to Him contingent, or uncertain.[59] He is most holy in all His counsels, in all His works, and in all His commands.[60] To Him is due from angels and men, and every other creature, whatsoever worship, service, or obedience He is pleased to require of them.[61]

III. In the unity of the Godhead there be three persons, of one substance, power, and eternity; God the Father, God the Son, and God the Holy Ghost.[62] The Father is of none, neither begotten, nor proceeding: the Son is eternally begotten of the Father:[63] the Holy Ghost eternally proceeding from the Father and the Son.[64]

---

[35] Psalm 145:3.
[36] Genesis 17:1; Revelation 4:8.
[37] Romans 16:27.
[38] Isaiah 6:3; Revelation 4:8.
[39] Psalm 115:3.
[40] Exodus 3:14.
[41] Ephesians 1:11.
[42] Proverbs 16:4; Romans 11:36.
[43] 1 John 4:8,16.
[44] Exodus 34:6-7.
[45] Hebrews 11:6.
[46] Nehemiah 9:32-33.
[47] Psalm 5:5-6.
[48] Exodus 34:7; Nahum 1:2-3.
[49] John 5:26.
[50] Acts 7:2.
[51] Psalm 119:68.
[52] Romans 9:5; 1 Timothy 6:15.
[53] Acts 17:24-25.
[54] Job 22:2-3.
[55] Romans 11:36.
[56] Daniel 4:25,35; 1 Timothy 6:15; Revelation 4:11.
[57] Hebrews 4:13.
[58] Psalm 147:5; Romans 11:33-34.
[59] Ezekiel 11:5; Acts 15:18.
[60] Psalm 145:17; Romans 7:12.
[61] Revelation 5:12-14.
[62] Matthew 3:16-17, 28:19; 2 Corinthians 13:14; 1 John 5:7.
[63] John 1:14,18.
[64] John 15:26; Galatians 4:6.

Chapter III – Of God's Eternal Decree.

I. God from all eternity did, by the most wise and holy counsel of His own will, freely, and unchangeably ordain whatsoever comes to pass:[65] yet so, as thereby neither is God the author of sin,[66] nor is violence offered to the will of the creatures, nor is the liberty or contingency of second causes taken away, but rather established.[67]

II. Although God knows whatsoever may or can come to pass upon all supposed conditions,[68] yet hath He not decreed anything because He foresaw it as future, or as that which would come to pass upon such conditions.[69]

III. By the decree of God, for the manifestation of His glory, some men and angels[70] are predestinated unto everlasting life, and others fore-ordained to everlasting death.[71]

IV. These angels and men, thus predestinated, and fore-ordained, are particularly and unchangeably designed, and their number so certain and definite, that it cannot be either increased or diminished.[72]

V. Those of mankind that are predestinated unto life, God, before the foundation of the world was laid, according to His eternal and immutable purpose, and the secret counsel and good pleasure of His will, hath chosen, in Christ, unto everlasting glory,[73] out of His mere free grace and love, without any foresight of faith or good works, or perseverance in either of them, or any other thing in the creature, as conditions, or causes moving Him thereunto:[74] and all to the praise of His glorious grace.[75]

VI. As God hath appointed the elect unto glory, so hath He, by the eternal and most free purpose of His will, fore-ordained all the means thereunto.[76] Wherefore they who are elected, being fallen in Adam, are redeemed by Christ,[77] are effectually called unto faith in Christ by His Spirit working in due season, are justified, adopted, sanctified,[78] and kept by His power through faith, unto salvation.[79] Neither are any other redeemed by Christ, effectually called, justified, adopted, sanctified, and saved, but the elect only.[80]

VII. The rest of mankind God was pleased, according to the unsearchable counsel of His own will, whereby He extendeth or withholdeth mercy, as He pleaseth, for the glory of His sovereign power over His creatures, to pass by; and to ordain them to dishonour and wrath, for their sin, to the praise of His glorious justice.[81]

---

[65] Romans 9:15,18, 11:33; Ephesians 1:11; Hebrews 6:17.
[66] James 1:13,17; 1 John 1:5.
[67] Proverbs 16:33; Matthew 17:12; John 19:11; Acts 2:23, 4:27-28.
[68] 1 Samuel 23:11-12; Matthew 11:21,23; Acts 15:18.
[69] Romans 9:11,13,16,18.
[70] Matthew 25:41; 1 Timothy 5:21.
[71] Proverbs 16:4; Romans 9:22-23; Ephesians 1:5-6.
[72] John 13:18; 2 Timothy 2:19.
[73] Romans 8:30; Ephesians 1:4,9,11; 1 Thessalonians 5:9; 2 Timothy 1:9.
[74] Romans 9:11,13,16; Ephesians 1:4,9.
[75] Ephesians 1:6,12.
[76] Ephesians 1:4-5, 2:10; 2 Thessalonians 2:13; 1 Peter 1:2.
[77] 1 Thessalonians 5:9-10; Titus 2:14.
[78] Romans 8:30; Ephesians 1:5; 2 Thessalonians 2:13.
[79] 1 Peter 1:5.
[80] John 6:64-65, John 8:47, 10:26, 17:9; Romans 8:28-39; 1 John 2:19.
[81] Matthew 11:25-26; Romans 9:17-18,21-22; 2 Timothy 2:19-20; 1 Peter 2:8; Jude 4.

VIII. The doctrine of this high mystery of predestination is to be handled with special prudence and care,[82] that men attending the will of God revealed in His Word, and yielding obedience thereunto, may, from the certainty of their effectual vocation, be assured of their eternal election.[83] So shall this doctrine afford matter of praise, reverence, and admiration of God,[84] and of humility, diligence, and abundant consolation to all that sincerely obey the Gospel.[85]

Chapter IV – Of Creation.

I. It pleased God the Father, Son, and Holy Ghost,[86] for the manifestation of the glory of His eternal power, wisdom, and goodness,[87] in the beginning, to create, or make of nothing, the world, and all things therein whether visible or invisible, in the space of six days; and all very good.[88]

II. After God had made all other creatures, He created man, male and female,[89] with reasonable and immortal souls,[90] endued with knowledge, righteousness, and true holiness, after His own image;[91] having the law of God written in their hearts,[92] and power to fulfil it:[93] and yet under a possibility of transgressing, being left to the liberty of their own will, which was subject unto change.[94] Beside this law written in their hearts, they received a command, not to eat of the tree of the knowledge of good and evil, which while they kept, they were happy in their communion with God,[95] and had dominion over the creatures.[96]

Chapter V – Of Providence.

I. God the great Creator of all things doth uphold,[97] direct, dispose, and govern all creatures, actions, and things,[98] from the greatest even to the least,[99] by His most wise and holy providence,[100] according to His

---

[82] Deuteronomy 29:29; Romans 9:20, 11:33.
[83] 2 Peter 1:10.
[84] Romans 11:33; Ephesians 1:6.
[85] Luke 10:20; Romans 8:33, 11:5-6,20; 2 Peter 1:10.
[86] Genesis 1:2; Job 26:13, 33:4; John 1:2-3; Hebrews 1:2.
[87] Psalm 33:5-6, 104:24; Jeremiah 10:12; Romans 1:20.
[88] Genesis 1:1-31; Acts 17:24; Colossians 1:16; Hebrews 11:3.
[89] Genesis 1:27.
[90] Genesis 2:7; Ecclesiastes 12:7; Matthew 10:28; Luke 23:43.
[91] Genesis 1:26; Ephesians 4:24; Colossians 3:10.
[92] Romans 2:14-15.
[93] Ecclesiastes 7:29.
[94] Genesis 3:6; Ecclesiastes 7:29.
[95] Genesis 2:17, 3:8-11,23.
[96] Genesis 1:26,28.
[97] Hebrews 1:3.
[98] Job 38-41; Psalm 135:6; Daniel 4:34-35; Acts 17:25-26,28.
[99] Matthew 10:29-31.
[100] Psalm 104:24, 145:17; Proverbs 15:3.

infallible fore-knowledge,[101] and the free and immutable counsel of His own will,[102] to the praise of the glory of His wisdom, power, justice, goodness, and mercy.[103]

II. Although, in relation to the fore-knowledge and decree of God, the first Cause, all things come to pass immutably, and infallibly:[104] yet, by the same providence, He ordereth them to fall out, according to the nature of second causes, either necessarily, freely, or contingently.[105]

III. God in His ordinary providence maketh use of means,[106] yet is free to work without,[107] above,[108] and against them at His pleasure.[109]

IV. The almighty power, unsearchable wisdom, and infinite goodness of God so far manifest themselves in His providence, that it extendeth itself even to the first fall, and all other sins of angels and men;[110] and that not by a bare permission,[111] but such as hath joined with it a most wise and powerful bounding,[112] and otherwise ordering and governing of them, in a manifold dispensation, to His own holy ends;[113] yet so, as the sinfulness thereof proceedeth only from the creature, and not from God, who, being most holy and righteous, neither is, nor can be, the author or approver of sin.[114]

V. The most wise, righteous, and gracious God doth oftentimes leave for a season His own children to manifold temptations, and the corruption of their own hearts, to chastise them for their former sins, or to discover unto them the hidden strength of corruption, and deceitfulness of their hearts, that they may be humbled;[115] and, to raise them to a more close and constant dependence for their support upon Himself, and to make them more watchful against all future occasions of sin, and for sundry other just and holy ends.[116]

VI. As for those wicked and ungodly men whom God, as a righteous Judge, for former sins, doth blind and harden,[117] from them He not only withholdeth His grace, whereby they might have been enlightened in their understandings, and wrought upon in their hearts;[118] but sometimes also withdraweth the gifts which they had,[119] and exposeth them to such objects as their corruption makes occasions of sin;[120] and, withal, gives them over to their own lusts, the temptations of the world, and the power of Satan:[121] whereby it

---

[101] Psalm 94:8-11; Acts 15:18.
[102] Psalm 33:10-11; Ephesians 1:11.
[103] Genesis 45:7; Psalm 145:7; Isaiah 63:14; Romans 9:17; Ephesians 3:10.
[104] Acts 2:23.
[105] Genesis 8:22; Exodus 21:13; Deuteronomy 19:5; 1 Kings 22:28,34; Isaiah 10:6-7; Jeremiah 31:35.
[106] Isaiah 55:10-11; Hosea 2:21-22; Acts 27:31,44.
[107] Job 34:20; Hosea 1:7; Matthew 4:4.
[108] Romans 4:19-21.
[109] 2 Kings 6:6.
[110] 2 Samuel 16:10, 24:1; 1 Kings 22:22-23; 1 Chronicles 10:4,13-14, 21:1; Acts 2:23, 4:27-28; Romans 11:32-34.
[111] Acts 14:16.
[112] 2 Kings 19:28; Psalm 76:10.
[113] Genesis 50:20; Isaiah 10:6-7,12.
[114] Psalm 50:21; James 1:13-14,17; 1 John 2:16.
[115] 2 Samuel 24:1; 2 Chronicles 32:25-26,31.
[116] Psalm 73, 77:1-12; Mark 14:66-72; John 21:15-17; 2 Corinthians 12:7-9.
[117] Romans 1:24,26,28, 11:7-8.
[118] Deuteronomy 29:4.
[119] Matthew 13:12, 25:29.
[120] Deuteronomy 2:30; 2 Kings 8:12-13.
[121] Psalm 81:11-12; 2 Thessalonians 2:10-12.

comes to pass that they harden themselves, even under those means which God useth for the softening of others.[122]

VII. As the providence of God doth in general reach to all creatures, so after a most special manner, it taketh care of His Church, and disposeth all things to the good thereof.[123]

Chapter VI – Of the Fall of Man, of Sin, and of the Punishment thereof.

I. Our first parents, being seduced by the subtlety and temptation of Satan, sinned, in eating the forbidden fruit.[124] This their sin God was pleased, according to His wise and holy counsel, to permit, having purposed to order it to His own glory.[125]

II. By this sin they fell from their original righteousness and communion, with God,[126] and so became dead in sin,[127] and wholly defiled in all the parts and faculties of soul and body.[128]

III. They being the root of all mankind, the guilt of this sin was imputed,[129] and the same death in sin and corrupted nature conveyed, to all their posterity descending from them by ordinary generation.[130]

IV. From this original corruption, whereby we are utterly indisposed, disabled, and made opposite to all good,[131] and wholly inclined to all evil,[132] do proceed all actual transgressions.[133]

V. This corruption of nature, during this life, doth remain in those that are regenerated;[134] and although it be, through Christ, pardoned and mortified, yet both itself and all the motions thereof are truly and properly sin.[135]

VI. Every sin, both original and actual, being a transgression of the righteous law of God, and contrary thereunto,[136] doth, in its own nature, bring guilt upon the sinner;[137] whereby he is bound over to the wrath

---

[122] Exodus 7:3, 8:15,32; Isaiah 8:14, 6:9-10; Acts 28:26-27; 2 Corinthians 2:15-16; 1 Peter 2:7-8.
[123] Isaiah 43:3-5,14; Amos 9:8-9; Romans 8:28; 1 Timothy 4:10.
[124] Genesis 3:13; 2 Corinthians 11:3.
[125] Romans 11:32.
[126] Genesis 3:6-8; Ecclesiastes 7:29; Romans 3:23.
[127] Genesis 2:17; Ephesians 2:1.
[128] Genesis 6:5; Jeremiah 17:9; Romans 3:10-19; Titus 1:15.
[129] Genesis 1:27-28, 2:16-17; Acts 17:26; Romans 5:12,15-19; 1 Corinthians 15:21-22,49.
[130] Genesis 5:3; Job 14:4, 15:14; Psalm 51:5;.
[131] Romans 5:6, 7:18, 8:7; Colossians 1:21.
[132] Genesis 6:5, 8:21; Romans 3:10-12.
[133] Matthew 15:19; Ephesians 2:2-3; James 1:14-15.
[134] Proverbs 20:9; Ecclesiastes 7:20; Romans 7:14,17-18,23; James 3:2; 1 John 1:8,10.
[135] Romans 7:5,7-8,25; Galatians 5:17.
[136] 1 John 3:4.
[137] Romans 2:15, 3:9,19.

of God,[138] and curse of the law,[139] and so made subject to death,[140] with all miseries spiritual,[141] temporal,[142] and eternal.[143]

Chapter VII – Of God's Covenant with Man.

I. The distance between God and the creature is go great, that although reasonable creatures do owe obedience unto Him as their Creator, yet they could never have any fruition of Him as their blessedness and reward, but by some voluntary condescension on God's part, which He hath been pleased to express by way of covenant.[144]

II. The first covenant made with man was a covenant of works,[145] wherein life was promised to Adam, and in him to his posterity,[146] upon condition of perfect and personal obedience.[147]

III. Man by his fall having made himself incapable of life by that covenant, the Lord was pleased to make a second,[148] commonly called the covenant of grace; wherein He freely offereth unto sinners life and salvation by Jesus Christ, requiring of them faith in Him, that they may be saved,[149] and promising to give unto all those that are ordained unto life His Holy Spirit, to make them willing and able to believe.[150]

IV. This covenant of grace is frequently set forth in Scripture by the name of a Testament, in reference to the death of Jesus Christ the Testator, and to the everlasting inheritance, with all things belonging to it, therein bequeathed.[151]

V. This covenant was differently administered in the time of the law, and in the time of the gospel:[152] under the law, it was administered by promises, prophecies, sacrifices, circumcision, the paschal lamb, and other types and ordinances delivered to the people of the Jews, all fore-signifying Christ to come:[153] which were, for that time, sufficient and efficacious, through the operation of the Spirit, to instruct and build up the elect in faith in the promised Messiah,[154] by whom they had full remission of sins, and eternal salvation; and is called, the Old Testament.[155]

VI. Under the gospel, when Christ, the substance,[156] was exhibited, the ordinances in which this covenant is dispensed are the preaching of the Word, and the administration of the sacraments of Baptism and the

---

[138] Ephesians 2:3.
[139] Galatians 3:10.
[140] Romans 6:23.
[141] Ephesians 4:18.
[142] Lamentations 3:39; Romans 8:20.
[143] Matthew 25:41; 2 Thessalonians 1:9.
[144] 1 Samuel 2:25; Job 9:32-33; Job 22:2-3, 35:7-8; Psalm 100:2-3, 113:5-6; Isaiah 40:13-17; Luke 17:10; Acts 17:24-25.
[145] Galatians 3:12.
[146] Romans 10:5, 5:12-20.
[147] Genesis 2:17; Galatians 3:10.
[148] Genesis 3:15; Isaiah 42:6; Romans 8:3, 3:20-21; Galatians 3:21.
[149] Mark 16:15-16; John 3:16; Romans 10:6,9; Galatians 3:11.
[150] Ezekiel 36:26-27; John 6:44-45.
[151] Luke 22:20; 1 Corinthians 11:25; Hebrews 7:22, 9:15-17.
[152] 2 Corinthians 3:6-9.
[153] Romans 4:11; 1 Corinthians 5:7; Colossians 2:11-12; Hebrews 8,9,10.
[154] John 8:56; 1 Corinthians 10:1-4; Hebrews 11:13.
[155] Galatians 3:7-9,14.
[156] Colossians 2:17.

Lord's Supper:[157] which, though fewer in number, and administered with more simplicity, and less outward glory; yet, in them, it is held forth in more fullness, evidence, and spiritual efficacy,[158] to all nations, both Jews and Gentiles;[159] and is called the New Testament.[160] There are not therefore two covenants of grace, differing in substance, but one and the same, under various dispensations.[161]

Chapter VIII – Of Christ the Mediator.

I. It pleased God, in His eternal purpose, to choose and ordain the Lord Jesus, His only begotten Son, to be the Mediator between God and man;[162] the Prophet,[163] Priest,[164] and King,[165] the Head and Saviour of His Church,[166] the Heir of all things,[167] and Judge of the world:[168] unto whom He did from all eternity give a people, to be His seed,[169] and to be by Him in time redeemed, called, justified, sanctified, and glorified.[170]

II. The Son of God, the second person in the Trinity, being very and eternal God, of one substance and equal with the Father, did, when the fullness of time was come, take upon Him man's nature,[171] with all the essential properties and common infirmities thereof, yet without sin:[172] being conceived by the power of the Holy Ghost, in the womb of the virgin Mary, of her substance.[173] So that two whole, perfect, and distinct natures, the Godhead and the manhood, were inseparably joined together in one person, without conversion, composition, or confusion.[174] Which person is very God, and very man, yet one Christ, the only Mediator between God and man.[175]

III. The Lord Jesus, in His human nature thus united to the divine, was sanctified and anointed with the Holy Spirit, above measure,[176] having in Him all the treasures of wisdom and knowledge;[177] in whom it pleased the Father that all fullness should dwell;[178] to the end that, being holy, harmless, undefiled, and full of grace and truth,[179] He might be thoroughly furnished to execute the office of a mediator and surety.[180]

---

[157] Matthew 28:19-20; 1 Corinthians 11:23-25.
[158] Jeremiah 31:33-34; Hebrews 12:22-28.
[159] Matthew 28:19; Ephesians 2:15-19.
[160] Luke 22:20.
[161] Psalm 32:1; Acts 15:11; Romans 3:21-23,30, 4:3,6,16-17,23-24; Galatians 3:14,16; Hebrews 13:8.
[162] Isaiah 42:1; John 3:16; 1 Timothy 2:5; 1 Peter 1:19-20.
[163] Acts 3:22.
[164] Hebrews 5:5-6.
[165] Psalm 2:6; Luke 1:33.
[166] Ephesians 5:23.
[167] Hebrews 1:2.
[168] Acts 17:31.
[169] Psalm 22:30, Isaiah 53:10; John 17:6.
[170] Isaiah 55:4-5; 1 Corinthians 1:30; 1 Timothy 2:6.
[171] John 1:1,14; Galatians 4:4; Philippians 2:6; 1 John 5:20.
[172] Hebrews 2:14,16-17, 4:15.
[173] Luke 1:27,31,35; Galatians 4:4.
[174] Luke 1:35; Romans 9:5; Colossians 2:9; 1 Timothy 3:16; 1 Peter 3:18.
[175] Romans 1:3-4; 1 Timothy 2:5.
[176] Psalm 45:7; John 3:34.
[177] Colossians 2:3.
[178] Colossians 1:19.
[179] John 1:14; Hebrews 7:26.
[180] Acts 10:38; Hebrews 7:22, 12:24.

Which office He took not unto Himself, but was thereunto called by His Father,[181] who put all power and judgment into His hand, and gave Him commandment to execute the same.[182]

IV. This office the Lord Jesus did most willingly undertake;[183] which that He might discharge, He was made under the law,[184] and did perfectly fulfil it,[185] endured most grievous torments immediately in His soul,[186] and most painful sufferings in His body;[187] was crucified, and died;[188] was buried, and remained under the power of death; yet saw no corruption.[189] On the third day He arose from the dead,[190] with the same body in which He suffered,[191] with which also he ascended into heaven, and there sitteth at the right hand of His Father,[192] making intercession,[193] and shall return to judge men and angels at the end of the world.[194]

V. The Lord Jesus, by His perfect obedience, and sacrifice of Himself, which He, through the eternal Spirit, once offered up unto God, hath fully satisfied the justice of His Father;[195] and purchased, not only reconciliation, but an everlasting inheritance in the kingdom of heaven, for all those whom the Father hath given unto Him.[196]

VI. Although the work of redemption was not actually wrought by Christ till after His incarnation, yet the virtue, efficacy, and benefits thereof were communicated unto the elect in all ages successively from the beginning of the world, in and by those promises, types, and sacrifices, wherein He was revealed, and signified to be the seed of the woman which should bruise the serpent's head; and the Lamb slain from the beginning of the world: being yesterday and to-day the same, and forever.[197]

VII. Christ, in the work of mediation, acteth according to both natures, by each nature doing that which is proper to itself:[198] yet, by reason of the unity of the person, that which is proper to one nature, is sometimes in Scripture attributed to the person denominated by the other nature.[199]

VIII. To all those for whom Christ hath purchased redemption, He doth certainly and effectually apply and communicate the same,[200] making intercession for them,[201] and revealing unto them, in and by the Word, the mysteries of salvation,[202] effectually persuading them by His Spirit to believe and obey, and governing

---

[181] Hebrews 5:4-5.
[182] Matthew 28:18; John 5:22,27; Acts 2:36.
[183] Psalm 40:7-8; John 10:18; Philippians 2:8 Hebrews 10:5-10.
[184] Galatians 4:4.
[185] Matthew 3:15, 5:17.
[186] Matthew 26:37-38; Matthew 27:46; Luke 22:44.
[187] Matthew 26-27.
[188] Philippians 2:8.
[189] Acts 2:23-24,27, 13:37; Romans 6:9.
[190] 1 Corinthians 15:3-4.
[191] John 20:25,27.
[192] Mark 16:19.
[193] Romans 8:34; Hebrews 7:25, 9:24.
[194] Matthew 13:40-42; Acts 1:11, 10:42; Romans 14:9-10; 2 Peter 2:4; Jude 6.
[195] Romans 3:25-26, 5:19; Ephesians 5:2; Hebrews 9:14,16, 10:14.
[196] Daniel 9:24,26; John 17:2; Ephesians 1:11,14; Colossians 1:19-20; Hebrews 9:12,15.
[197] Genesis 3:15; Galatians 4:4-5; Hebrews 13:8; Revelation 13:8.
[198] Hebrews 9:14; 1 Peter 3:18.
[199] John 3:13; Acts 20:28; 1 John 3:16.
[200] John 6:37,39, 10:15-16.
[201] Romans 8:34; 1 John 2:1-2.
[202] John 15:13,15, 17:6; Ephesians 1:7-9.

their hearts by His Word and Spirit;[203] overcoming all their enemies by His almighty power and wisdom, in such manner, and ways, as are most consonant to His wonderful and unsearchable dispensation.[204]

Chapter IX – Of Free Will.

I. God hath endued the will of man with that natural liberty, that is neither forced, nor by any absolute necessity of nature determined to good or evil.[205]

II. Man, in his state of innocency, had freedom and power to will and to do that which was good, and well pleasing to God;[206] but yet, mutably, so that he might fall from it.[207]

III. Man, by his fall into a state of sin, hath wholly lost all ability of will to any spiritual good accompanying salvation:[208] so as, a natural man, being altogether averse from that good,[209] and dead in sin,[210] is not able, by his own strength, to convert himself, or to prepare himself thereunto.[211]

IV. When God converts a sinner, and translates him into the state of grace, He freeth him from his natural bondage under sin;[212] and, by His grace alone, enables him freely to will and to do that which is spiritually good;[213] yet so, as that by reason of his remaining corruption, he doth not perfectly, nor only, will that which is good, but doth also will that which is evil.[214]

V. The will of man is made perfectly and immutably free to do good alone, in the state of glory only.[215]

Chapter X – Of Effectual Calling.

I. All those whom God hath predestinated unto life, and those only, He is pleased in His appointed and accepted time effectually to call,[216] by His Word and Spirit,[217] out of that state of sin and death, in which they are by nature, to grace and salvation by Jesus Christ;[218] enlightening their minds spiritually and savingly to understand the things of God,[219] taking away their heart of stone, and giving unto them a heart

---

[203] John 14:26, 17:17; Romans 8:9,14, 15:18-19; 2 Corinthians 4:13; Hebrews 12:2.
[204] Psalm 110:1; Malachi 4:2-3; 1 Corinthians 15:25-26; Colossians 2:15.
[205] Deuteronomy 30:19; Matthew 17:12; James 1:14.
[206] Genesis 1:26; Ecclesiastes 7:29.
[207] Genesis 2:16-17, 3:6.
[208] John 15:5; Romans 5:6, 8:7.
[209] Romans 3:10,12.
[210] Ephesians 2:1,5; Colossians 2:13.
[211] John 6:44,65; 1 Corinthians 2:14; Ephesians 2:2-5; Titus 3:3-5.
[212] John 8:34,36; Colossians 1:13.
[213] Romans 6:18,22; Philippians 2:13.
[214] Romans 7:15,18-19,21,23; Galatians 5:17.
[215] Ephesians 4:13; Hebrews 12:23; 1 John 3:2; Jude 24.
[216] Romans 8:30, 11:7; Ephesians 1:10-11.
[217] 2 Corinthians 3:3,6; 2 Thessalonians 2:13-14.
[218] Romans 8:2; Ephesians 2:1-5; 2 Timothy 1:9-10.
[219] Acts 26:18; 1 Corinthians 2:10,12; Ephesians 1:17-18.

of flesh;[220] renewing their wills, and, by His almighty power determining them to that which is good,[221] and effectually drawing them to Jesus Christ:[222] yet so, as they come most freely, being made willing by His grace.[223]

II. This effectual call is of God's free and special grace alone, not from anything at all foreseen in man,[224] who is altogether passive therein, until being quickened and renewed by the Holy Spirit,[225] he is thereby enabled to answer this call, and to embrace the grace offered and conveyed in it.[226]

III. Elect infants, dying in infancy, are regenerated, and saved by Christ through the Spirit,[227] who worketh when, and where, and how He pleaseth:[228] so also, are all other elect persons who are uncapable of being outwardly called by the ministry of the Word.[229]

IV. Others, not elected, although they may be called by the ministry of the Word,[230] and may have some common operations of the Spirit,[231] yet they never truly come unto Christ, and therefore cannot be saved:[232] much less can men, not professing the Christian religion, be saved in any other way whatsoever, be they never so diligent to frame their lives according to the light of nature, and the law of that religion they do profess.[233] And to assert and maintain that they may, is very pernicious, and to be detested.[234]

Chapter XI – Of Justification.

I. Those whom God effectually calleth, He also freely justifieth;[235] not by infusing righteousness into them, but by pardoning their sins, and by accounting and accepting their persons as righteous, not for anything wrought in them, or done by them, but for Christ's sake alone; nor by imputing faith itself, the act of believing, or any other evangelical obedience to them, as their righteousness, but by imputing the obedience and satisfaction of Christ unto them,[236] they receiving and resting on Him and His righteousness by faith; which faith they have not of themselves, it is the gift of God.[237]

---

[220] Ezekiel 36:26.
[221] Deuteronomy 30:6; Ezekiel 11:19, 36:27; Philippians 2:13.
[222] John 6:44-45; Ephesians 1:19.
[223] Psalm 110:3; Song of Solomon 1:4; John 6:37; Romans 6:16-18.
[224] Romans 9:11; Ephesians 2:4-5,8-9; 2 Timothy 1:9; Titus 3:4-5.
[225] Romans 8:7; 1 Corinthians 2:14; Ephesians 2:5.
[226] Ezekiel 36:27; John 5:25, 6:37.
[227] Luke 18:15-16; John 3:3,5; Acts 2:38-39; Romans 8:9; 1 John 5:12.
[228] John 3:8.
[229] Acts 4:12; 1 John 5:12.
[230] Matthew 22:14.
[231] Matthew 7:22, 13:20-21; Hebrews 6:4-5.
[232] John 6:64-66, 8:24.
[233] John 4:22, 14:6, 17:3; Acts 4:12; Ephesians 2:12.
[234] 1 Corinthians 16:22; Galatians 1:6-8; 2 John 9-11.
[235] Romans 8:30, 3:24.
[236] Jeremiah 23:6; Romans 3:22,24-25,27-28, 4:5-8, 5:17-19; 1 Corinthians 1:30-31; 2 Corinthians 5:19,21; Ephesians 1:7; Titus 3:5,7.
[237] Acts 10:43, 13:38-39; Galatians 2:16; Ephesians 2:7-8; Philippians 3:19.

II. Faith, thus receiving and resting on Christ and His righteousness, is the alone instrument of justification;[238] yet is it not alone in the person justified, but is ever accompanied with all other saving graces, and is no dead faith, but worketh by love.[239]

III. Christ, by His obedience and death, did fully discharge the debt of all those that are thus justified, and did make a proper, real, and full satisfaction to His Father's justice in their behalf.[240] Yet, inasmuch as He was given by the Father for them;[241] and His obedience and satisfaction accepted in their stead;[242] and both freely, not for anything in them; their justification is only of free grace;[243] that both the exact justice, and rich grace of God, might be glorified in the justification of sinners.[244]

IV. God did, from all eternity, decree to justify all the elect,[245] and Christ did, in the fullness of time, die for their sins, and rise again for their justification:[246] nevertheless, they are not justified, until the Holy Spirit doth, in due time, actually apply Christ unto them.[247]

V. God doth continue to forgive the sins of those that are justified:[248] and although they can never fall from the state of justification;[249] yet they may, by their sins, fall under God's fatherly displeasure, and not have the light of His countenance restored unto them, until they humble themselves, confess their sins, beg pardon, and renew their faith and repentance.[250]

VI. The justification of believers under the old testament was, in all these respects, one and the same with the justification of believers under the new testament.[251]

Chapter XII – Of Adoption.

All those that are justified, God vouchsafeth, in and for His only Son Jesus Christ, to make partakers of the grace of adoption:[252] by which they are taken into the number, and enjoy the liberties and privileges of the children of God,[253] have His name put upon them,[254] receive the spirit of adoption,[255] have access to the throne of grace with boldness,[256] are enabled to cry, Abba, Father,[257] are pitied,[258] protected,[259] provided

---

[238] John 1:12; Romans 3:28, 5:1.
[239] Galatians 5:6; James 2:17,22,26.
[240] Isaiah 53:4-6,10-12; Daniel 9:24,26; Romans 5:8-10,19; 1 Timothy 2:5-6; Hebrews 10:10,14.
[241] Romans 8:32.
[242] Matthew 3:17; 2 Corinthians 5:21; Ephesians 5:2.
[243] Romans 3:24; Ephesians 1:7.
[244] Romans 3:26; Ephesians 2:7.
[245] Romans 8:30; Galatians 3:8; 1 Peter 1:2,19-20.
[246] Romans 4:25; Galatians 4:4; 1 Timothy 2:6.
[247] Galatians 2:16; Colossians 1:21-22; Titus 3:3-7.
[248] Matthew 6:12; 1 John 1:7,9, 2:1-2.
[249] Luke 22:32; John 10:28; Hebrews 10:14.
[250] Psalm 32:5, 51:7-12, 89:31-33; Matthew 26:75; Luke 1:20; 1 Corinthians 11:30,32.
[251] Romans 4:22-24; Galatians 3:9,13-14; Hebrews 13:8.
[252] Ephesians 1:5.
[253] John 1:12; Romans 8:17; Galatians 4:4-5.
[254] Jeremiah 14:9; 2 Corinthians 6:18; Revelation 3:12.
[255] Romans 8:15.
[256] Romans 5:2; Ephesians 3:12.
[257] Galatians 4:6.
[258] Psalm 103:13.
[259] Proverbs 14:26.

for,[260] and chastened by Him as by a Father;[261] yet never cast off,[262] but sealed to the day of redemption,[263] and inherit the promises,[264] as heirs of everlasting salvation.[265]

Chapter XIII – Of Sanctification.

I. They who are once effectually called and regenerated, having a new heart and a new spirit created in them, are further sanctified, really and personally, through the virtue of Christ's death and resurrection,[266] by His Word and Spirit dwelling in them:[267] the dominion of the whole body of sin is destroyed,[268] and the several lusts thereof are more and more weakened and mortified;[269] and they more and more quickened and strengthened in all saving graces,[270] to the practice of true holiness, without which no man shall see the Lord.[271]

II. This sanctification is throughout, in the whole man;[272] yet imperfect in this life, there abiding still some remnants of corruption in every part:[273] whence ariseth a continual and irreconcilable war; the flesh lusting against the Spirit, and the Spirit against the flesh.[274]

III. In which war, although the remaining corruption, for a time, may much prevail;[275] yet through the continual supply of strength from the sanctifying Spirit of Christ, the regenerate part doth overcome;[276] and so, the saints grow in grace,[277] perfecting holiness in the fear of God.[278]

---

[260] Matthew 6:30,32; 1 Peter 5:7.
[261] Hebrews 12:6.
[262] Lamentations 3:31.
[263] Ephesians 4:30.
[264] Hebrews 6:12.
[265] Hebrews 1:14; 1 Peter 1:3-4.
[266] Acts 20:32; Romans 6:5-6; 1 Corinthians 6:11; Philippians 3:10.
[267] John 17:17; Ephesians 5:26; 2 Thessalonians 2:13.
[268] Romans 6:6,14.
[269] Romans 8:13; Galatians 5:24.
[270] Ephesians 3:16-19; Colossians 1:11;.
[271] 2 Corinthians 7:1; Hebrews 12:14.
[272] 1 Thessalonians 5:23.
[273] Romans 7:18,23; Philippians 3:12; 1 John 1:10.
[274] Galatians 5:17; 1 Peter 2:11.
[275] Romans 7:23.
[276] Romans 6:14; Ephesians 4:15-16; 1 John 5:4.
[277] 2 Corinthians 3:18; 2 Peter 3:18.
[278] 2 Corinthians 7:1.

Chapter XIV – Of Saving Faith.

I. The grace of faith, whereby the elect are enabled to believe to the saving of their souls,[279] is the work of the Spirit of Christ in their hearts;[280] and is ordinarily wrought by the ministry of the Word:[281] by which also, and by the administration of the sacraments, and prayer, it is increased and strengthened.[282]

II. By this faith, a Christian believeth to be true whatsoever is revealed in the Word, for the authority of God Himself speaking therein;[283] and acteth differently upon that which each particular passage thereof containeth; yielding obedience to the commands,[284] trembling at the threatenings,[285] and embracing the promises of God for this life, and that which is to come.[286] But the principal acts of saving faith are accepting, receiving, and resting upon Christ alone for justification, sanctification, and eternal life, by virtue of the covenant of grace.[287]

III. This faith is different in degrees, weak or strong;[288] may be often and many ways assailed, and weakened, but gets the victory;[289] growing up in many to the attainment of a full assurance through Christ,[290] who is both the author and finisher of our faith.[291]

Chapter XV – Of Repentance unto Life.

I. Repentance unto life is an evangelical grace,[292] the doctrine whereof is to be preached by every minister of the Gospel, as well as that of faith in Christ.[293]

II. By it, a sinner, out of the sight and sense not only of the danger, but also of the filthiness and odiousness of his sins, as contrary to the holy nature and righteous law of God; and upon the apprehension of his mercy in Christ to such as are penitent, so grieves for, and hates his sins, as to turn from them all unto God,[294] purposing and endeavouring to walk with Him in all the ways of His commandments.[295]

---

[279] Hebrews 10:39.
[280] 2 Corinthians 4:13; Ephesians 1:17-19, 2:8.
[281] Romans 10:14,17.
[282] Luke 17:5; Acts 20:32; Romans 1:16-17, 4:11; 1 Peter 2:2.
[283] John 4:42; Acts 24:14; 1 Thessalonians 2:13; 1 John 5:10.
[284] Romans 16:26.
[285] Isaiah 66:2.
[286] 1 Timothy 4:8; Hebrews 11:13.
[287] John 1:12; Acts 15:11, 16:31; Galatians 2:20.
[288] Matthew 6:30, 8:10; Romans 4:19-20; Hebrews 5:13-14.
[289] Luke 22:31-32; Ephesians 6:16; 1 John 5:4-5.
[290] Colossians 2:2; Hebrews 6:11-12, 10:22.
[291] Hebrews 12:2.
[292] Zechariah 12:10; Acts 11:18.
[293] Mark 1:15; Luke 24:47; Acts 20:21.
[294] Psalm 51:4, 119:128; Isaiah 30:22; Jeremiah 31:18-19; Ezekiel 18:30-31, 36:31; Joel 2:12-13; Amos 5:15; 2 Corinthians 7:11.
[295] 2 Kings 23:25; Psalm 119:6,59,106; Luke 1:6.

III. Although repentance be not to be rested in, as any satisfaction for sin, or any cause of the pardon thereof,[296] which is the act of God's free grace in Christ;[297] yet is it of such necessity to all sinners, that none may expect pardon without it.[298]

IV. As there is no sin so small, but it deserves damnation,[299] so there is no sin so great, that it can bring damnation upon those who truly repent.[300]

V. Men ought not to content themselves with a general repentance, but it is every man's duty to endeavour to repent of his particular sins, particularly.[301]

VI. As every man is bound to make private confession of his sins to God, praying for the pardon thereof;[302] upon which, and the forsaking of them, he shall find mercy:[303] so, he that scandalizeth his brother, or the Church of Christ, ought to be willing, by a private or public confession, and sorrow for his sin, to declare his repentance to those that are offended,[304] who are thereupon to be reconciled to him, and in love to receive him.[305]

Chapter XVI – Of Good Works.

I. Good works are only such as God hath commanded in His holy Word,[306] and not such as, without the warrant thereof, are devised by men, out of blind zeal, or upon any pretense of good intention.[307]

II. These good works, done in obedience to God's commandments, are the fruits and evidences of a true and lively faith:[308] and by them believers manifest their thankfulness,[309] strengthen their assurance,[310] edify their brethren,[311] adorn the profession of the Gospel,[312] stop the mouths of the adversaries,[313] and glorify God,[314] whose workmanship they are, created in Christ Jesus thereunto;[315] that, having their fruit unto holiness, they may have the end, eternal life.[316]

---

[296] Ezekiel 16:61-63, 36:31-32;.
[297] Hosea 14:2,4; Romans 3:24; Ephesians 1:7.
[298] Luke 13:3,5; Acts 17:30-31.
[299] Matthew 12:36; Romans 5:12,6:23.
[300] Isaiah 1:16,18, 55:7; Romans 8:1.
[301] Psalm 19:13; Luke 19:8; 1 Timothy 1:13,15.
[302] Psalm 32:5-6, 51:4-5,7,9,14.
[303] Proverbs 28:13; 1 John 1:9.
[304] Joshua 7:19; Psalm 51:1-19; Luke 17:3-4; James 5:16.
[305] 2 Corinthians 2:8.
[306] Micah 6:8; Romans 12:2; Hebrews 13:21.
[307] 1 Samuel 15:21-23; Isaiah 29:13; Matthew 15:9; John 16:2; Romans 10:2; 1 Peter 1:18.
[308] James 2:18,22.
[309] Psalm 116:12-13; 1 Peter 2:9.
[310] 2 Peter 1:5-10; 1 John 2:3,5.
[311] Matthew 5:16; 2 Corinthians 9:2.
[312] 1 Timothy 6:1; Titus 2:5,9-12.
[313] 1 Peter 2:15.
[314] John 15:8; Philippians 1:11; 1 Peter 2:12.
[315] Ephesians 2:10.
[316] Romans 6:22.

III. Their ability to do good works is not at all of themselves, but wholly from the Spirit of Christ.[317] And that they may be enabled thereunto, besides the graces they have already received, there is required an actual influence of the same Holy Spirit, to work in them to will and to do of His good pleasure:[318] yet are they not hereupon to grow negligent, as if they were not bound to perform any duty, unless upon a special motion of the Spirit; but they ought to be diligent in stirring up the grace of God that is in them.[319]

IV. They, who in their obedience attain to the greatest height which is possible in this life, are so far from being able to supererogate, and to do more than God requires, as that they fall short of much which in duty they are bound to do.[320]

V. We cannot, by our best works, merit pardon of sin, or eternal life at the hand of God, by reason of the great disproportion that is between them and the glory to come; and the infinite distance that is between us and God, whom, by them, we can neither profit, nor satisfy for the debt of our former sins,[321] but when we have done all we can, we have done but our duty, and are unprofitable servants;[322] and because, as they are good, they proceed from His Spirit;[323] and as they are wrought by us, they are defiled, and mixed with so much weakness and imperfection, that they cannot endure the severity of God's judgment.[324]

VI. Yet notwithstanding, the persons of believers being accepted through Christ, their good works also are accepted in Him,[325] not as though they were in this life wholly unblamable and unreproveable in God's sight;[326] but that He, looking upon them in His Son, is pleased to accept and reward that which is sincere, although accompanied with many weaknesses and imperfections.[327]

VII. Works done by unregenerate men, although for the matter of them they may be things which God commands, and of good use both to themselves and others:[328] yet, because they proceed not from a heart purified by faith;[329] nor are done in a right manner according to the Word;[330] nor to a right end, the glory of God;[331] they are therefore sinful, and cannot please God, or make a man meet to receive grace from God.[332] And yet, their neglect of them is more sinful, and displeasing unto God.[333]

---

[317] Ezekiel 36:26-27; John 15:4-5.
[318] 2 Corinthians 3:5; Philippians 2:13 4:13.
[319] Isaiah 64:7; Acts 26:6-7; Philippians 2:12; 2 Timothy 1:6; Hebrews 6:11-12; 2 Peter 1:3,5,10-11; Jude 20-21.
[320] Nehemiah 13:22; Job 9:2-3; Luke 17:10; Galatians 5:17.
[321] Job 22:2-3, 35:7-8; Psalm 16:2; Romans 3:20, 4:2,4,6, 8:18; Ephesians 2:8-9; Titus 3:5-7.
[322] Luke 17:10.
[323] Galatians 5:22-23.
[324] Psalm 130:3, 143:2; Isaiah 64:6; Romans 7:15,18; Galatians 5:17.
[325] Genesis 4:4; Exodus 28:38; Ephesians 1:6; Hebrews 11:4; 1 Peter 2:5.
[326] Job 9:20; Psalm 143:2.
[327] Matthew 25:21-23; 2 Corinthians 8:12; Hebrews 6:10, 13:20-21.
[328] 1 Kings 21:27,29; 2 Kings 10:30-31; Philippians 1:15-16,18.
[329] Genesis 4:5; Hebrews 11:4,6.
[330] Isaiah 1:12; 1 Corinthians 13:3.
[331] Matthew 6:2,5,16.
[332] Hosea 1:4; Amos 5:22-23; Haggai 2:14; Romans 9:16; Titus 1:15, 3:5.
[333] Job 21:14-15; Psalm 14:4, 36:3; Matthew 23:23, 25:41-43,45.

Chapter XVII – Of the Perseverance of the Saints.

I. They, whom God hath accepted in His Beloved, effectually called, and sanctified by His Spirit, can neither totally, nor finally, fall away from the state of grace: but shall certainly persevere therein to the end, and be eternally saved.[334]

II. This perseverance of the saints depends not upon their own free will, but upon the immutability of the decree of election, flowing from the free and unchangeable love of God the Father;[335] upon the efficacy of the merit and intercession of Jesus Christ;[336] the abiding of the Spirit, and of the seed of God within them;[337] and the nature of the covenant of grace:[338] from all which ariseth also the certainty and infallibility thereof.[339]

III. Nevertheless, they may, through the temptations of Satan and of the world, the prevalency of corruption remaining in them, and the neglect of the means of their preservation, fall into grievous sins;[340] and, for a time, continue therein:[341] whereby they incur God's displeasure,[342] and grieve His Holy Spirit,[343] come to be deprived of some measure of their graces and comforts,[344] have their hearts hardened,[345] and their consciences wounded,[346] hurt and scandalize others,[347] and bring temporal judgments upon themselves.[348]

Chapter XVIII – Of the Assurance of Grace and Salvation.

I. Although hypocrites and other unregenerate men may vainly deceive themselves with false hopes, and carnal presumptions of being in the favour of God, and estate of salvation;[349] which hope of theirs shall perish:[350] yet such as truly believe in the Lord Jesus, and love Him in sincerity, endeavouring to walk in all good conscience before Him, may, in this life, be certainly assured that they are in the state of grace,[351] and may rejoice in the hope of the glory of God, which hope shall never make them ashamed.[352]

II. This certainty is not a bare conjectural and probable persuasion, grounded upon a fallible hope;[353] but an infallible assurance of faith, founded upon the divine truth of the promises of salvation,[354] the inward

---

[334] John 10:28-29; Philippians 1:6; 1 Peter 1:5,9; 2 Peter 1:10; 1 John 3:9.
[335] Jeremiah 31:3; 2 Timothy 2:18-19.
[336] Luke 22:32; John 17:11,24; Romans 8:33-39; Hebrews 7:25, 9:12-15, 10:10,14, 13:20-21.
[337] John 14:16-17; 1 John 2:27, 3:9.
[338] Jeremiah 32:40.
[339] John 10:28; 2 Thessalonians 3:3; 1 John 2:19.
[340] Matthew 26:70,72,74.
[341] Psalm 51:1,14.
[342] 2 Samuel 11:27; Isaiah 64:5,7,9.
[343] Ephesians 4:30.
[344] Psalm 51:8,10,12; Song of Solomon 5:2-4,6; Revelation 2:4.
[345] Isaiah 63:17; Mark 6:52, 16:14.
[346] Psalm 32:3-4, 51:8.
[347] 2 Samuel 12:14.
[348] Psalm 89:31-32; 1 Corinthians 11:32.
[349] Deuteronomy 29:19; Job 8:13-14; Micah 3:11; John 8:41.
[350] Matthew 7:22-23.
[351] 1 John 2:3, 3:14,18-19,21,24, 5:13.
[352] Romans 5:2,5.
[353] Hebrews 6:11,19.
[354] Hebrews 6:17-18.

evidence of those graces unto which these promises are made,[355] the testimony of the Spirit of adoption witnessing with our spirits that we are the children of God:[356] which Spirit is the earnest of our inheritance, whereby we are sealed to the day of redemption.[357]

III. This infallible assurance doth not so belong to the essence of faith, but that a true believer may wait long, and conflict with many difficulties before he be partaker of it:[358] yet, being enabled by the Spirit to know the things which are freely given him of God, he may without extraordinary revelation, in the right use of ordinary means, attain thereunto.[359] And therefore it is the duty of everyone to give all diligence to make his calling and election sure;[360] that thereby his heart may be enlarged in peace and joy in the Holy Ghost, in love and thankfulness to God, and in strength and cheerfulness in the duties of obedience, the proper fruits of this assurance:[361] so far is it from inclining men to looseness.[362]

IV. True believers may have the assurance of their salvation divers ways shaken, diminished, and intermitted; as, by negligence in preserving of it, by falling into some special sin, which woundeth the conscience and grieveth the Spirit; by some sudden or vehement temptation, by God's withdrawing the light of His countenance, and suffering even such as fear Him to walk in darkness and to have no light:[363] yet are they never so utterly destitute of that seed of God, and life of faith, that love of Christ and the brethren, that sincerity of heart, and conscience of duty, out of which, by the operation of the Spirit, this assurance may, in due time, be revived;[364] and by the which, in the meantime, they are supported from utter despair.[365]

Chapter XIX – Of the Law of God.

I. God gave to Adam a law, as a covenant of works, by which He bound him and all his posterity to personal, entire, exact, and perpetual obedience; promised life upon the fulfilling, and threatened death upon the breach of it: and endued him with power and ability to keep it.[366]

II. This law, after his fall, continued to be a perfect rule of righteousness, and, as such, was delivered by God upon Mount Sinai, in ten commandments, and written in two tables:[367] the four first commandments containing our duty towards God; and the other six our duty to man.[368]

III. Beside this law, commonly called moral, God was pleased to give to the people of Israel, as a church under age, ceremonial laws, containing several typical ordinances, partly of worship, prefiguring Christ,

---

[355] 2 Corinthians 1:12; 2 Peter 1:4-5,10-11; 1 John 2:3, 3:14.
[356] Romans 8:15-16.
[357] 2 Corinthians 1:21-22; Ephesians 1:13-14, 4:30;.
[358] Psalm 77:1-12, 88:1-18; Isaiah 50:10; Mark 9:24; 1 John 5:13.
[359] 1 Corinthians 2:12; Ephesians 3:17-19; Hebrews 6:11-12; 1 John 4:13.
[360] 2 Peter 1:10.
[361] Psalm 4:6-7, 119:32; Romans 5:1-2,5, 14:17, 15:13; Ephesians 1:3-4.
[362] Psalm 130:4; Romans 6:1-2, 8:1,12; 2 Corinthians 7:1; Titus 2:11-12,14; 1 John 1:6-7, 2:1-2, 3:2-3.
[363] Psalm 31:22, 51:8,12,14, 77:1-10, 88:1-18; Song of Solomon 5:2-3,6; Isaiah 50:10; Matthew 26:69-72; Ephesians 4:30-31.
[364] Job 13:15; Psalm 51:8,12, 73:15; Isaiah 50:10; Luke 22:32; 1 John 3:9.
[365] Psalm 22:1, 88:1-18; Isaiah 54:7-10; Jeremiah 32:40; Micah 7:7-9.
[366] Genesis 1:26-27, 2:17; Job 28:28; Ecclesiastes 7:29; Romans 2:14-15, 5:12,19, 10:5; Galatians 3:10,12.
[367] Exodus 34:1; Deuteronomy 5:32, 10:4; Romans 13:8-9; James 1:25, 2:8,10-12.
[368] Matthew 22:37-40.

His graces, actions, sufferings, and benefits;[369] and partly holding forth divers instructions of moral duties.[370] All which ceremonial laws are now abrogated, under the New Testament.[371]

IV. To them also, as a body politic, He gave sundry judicial laws, which expired together with the State of that people; not obliging any other now, further than the general equity thereof may require.[372]

V. The moral law doth forever bind all, as well justified persons as others, to the obedience thereof;[373] and that, not only in regard of the matter contained in it, but also in respect of the authority of God the Creator, who gave it:[374] neither doth Christ, in the Gospel, any way dissolve, but much strengthen this obligation.[375]

VI. Although true believers be not under the law, as a covenant of works, to be thereby justified, or condemned;[376] yet is it of great use to them, as well as to others; in that, as a rule of life informing them of the will of God, and their duty, it directs, and binds them to walk accordingly;[377] discovering also the sinful pollutions of their nature, hearts, and lives;[378] so as, examining themselves thereby, they may come to further conviction of, humiliation for, and hatred against sin;[379] together with a clearer sight of the need they have of Christ, and the perfection of His obedience.[380] It is likewise of use to the regenerate, to restrain their corruptions, in that it forbids sin:[381] and the threatenings of it serve to show what even their sins deserve; and what afflictions, in this life, they may expect for them, although freed from the curse thereof threatened in the law.[382] The promises of it, in like manner, show them God's approbation of obedience, and what blessings they may expect upon the performance thereof;[383] although not as due to them by the law, as a covenant of works.[384] So as, a man's doing good, and refraining from evil, because the law encourageth to the one and deterreth from the other, is no evidence of his being under the law; and not under grace.[385]

VII. Neither are the forementioned uses of the law contrary to the grace of the Gospel, but do sweetly comply with it;[386] the Spirit of Christ subduing and enabling the will of man to do that, freely and cheerfully, which the will of God, revealed in the law, requireth to be done.[387]

---

[369] Galatians 4:1-3; Colossians 2:17; Hebrews 9:1-28, 10:1.
[370] 1 Corinthians 5:7; 2 Corinthians 6:17; Jude 23.
[371] Daniel 9:27; Ephesians 2:15-16; Colossians 2:14,16-17.
[372] Genesis 49:10; Exodus 21:1-36, 22:1-29; Matthew 5:17,38-39; 1 Corinthians 9:8-10; 1 Peter 2:13-14.
[373] Romans 13:8-10; Ephesians 6:2; 1 John 2:3-4,7-8.
[374] James 2:10-11.
[375] Matthew 5:17-19; Romans 3:31; James 2:8.
[376] Acts 13:39; Romans 6:14, 8:1; Galatians 2:16, 3:13, 4:4-5.
[377] Psalm 119:4-6; Romans 7:12,22,25; 1 Corinthians 7:19; Galatians 5:14,16,18-23.
[378] Romans 3:20, 7:7.
[379] Romans 7:9,14,24; James 1:23-25.
[380] Romans 7:24-25, 8:3-4; Galatians 3:24.
[381] Psalm 119:101,104,128; James 2:11.
[382] Ezra 9:13-14; Psalm 89:30-34.
[383] Leviticus 26:1-14; Psalm 19:11, 37:11; Matthew 5:5; 2 Corinthians 6:16; Ephesians 6:2-3.
[384] Luke 17:10; Galatians 2:16.
[385] Psalm 34:12-16; Romans 6:12,14; Hebrews 12:28-29; 1 Peter 3:8-12.
[386] Galatians 3:21.
[387] Jeremiah 31:33; Ezekiel 36:27; Hebrews 8:10.

Chapter XX – Of Christian Liberty, and Liberty of Conscience.

I. The liberty which Christ hath purchased for believers under the Gospel consists in their freedom from the guilt of sin, and condemning wrath of God, the curse of the moral law;[388] and, in their being delivered from this present evil world, bondage to Satan, and dominion of sin;[389] from the evil of afflictions, the sting of death, the victory of the grace, and everlasting damnation;[390] as also, in their free access to God,[391] and their yielding obedience unto Him, not out of slavish fear, but a child-like love and willing mind.[392] All which were common also to believers under the law.[393] But, under the New Testament, the liberty of Christians is further enlarged, in their freedom from the yoke of the ceremonial law, to which the Jewish Church was subjected;[394] and in greater boldness of access to the throne of grace,[395] and in fuller communications of the free Spirit of God, than believers under the law did ordinarily partake of.[396]

II. God alone is Lord of the conscience,[397] and hath left it free from the doctrines and commandments of men, which are in anything contrary to His Word; or beside it, if matters of faith or worship.[398] So that, to believe such doctrines, or to obey such commands, out of conscience,[399] is to betray true liberty of conscience: and the requiring of an implicit faith, and an absolute and blind obedience is to destroy liberty of conscience, and reason also.[400]

III. They who, upon pretense of Christian liberty, do practice any sin, or cherish any lust, do thereby destroy the end of Christian liberty, which is, that being delivered out of the hands of our enemies, we might serve the Lord, without fear, in holiness and righteousness before Him, all the days of our life.[401]

IV. And because the powers which God hath ordained, and the liberty which Christ hath purchased, are not intended by God to destroy, but mutually to uphold and preserve one another; they who, upon pretense of Christian liberty, shall oppose any lawful power, or the lawful exercise of it, whether it be civil or ecclesiastical, resist the ordinance of God.[402] And, for their publishing of such opinions, or maintaining of such practices, as are contrary to the light of nature, or to the known principles of Christianity(whether concerning faith, worship, or conversation), or to the power of godliness; or, such erroneous opinions or practices, as either in their own nature, or in the manner of publishing or maintaining them, are destructive to the external peace and order which Christ hath established in the Church, they may lawfully be called to account, and proceeded against by the censures of the Church.[403]

---

[388] Galatians 3:13; 1 Thessalonians 1:10; Titus 2:14.
[389] Acts 26:18; Romans 6:14; Galatians 1:4; Colossians 1:13.
[390] Psalm 119:71; Romans 8:1, 28; 1 Corinthians 15:54-57.
[391] Romans 5:1-2.
[392] Romans 8:14-15; 1 John 4:18.
[393] Galatians 3:9,14.
[394] Acts 15:10-11; Galatians 4:1-3,6-7, 5:1.
[395] Hebrews 4:14,16, 10:1:1,19-22.
[396] John 7:38-39; 2 Corinthians 3:13,17-18.
[397] Romans 14:4; James 4:12.
[398] Matthew 15:9, 23:8-10; Acts 4:19, 5:29; 1 Corinthians 7:23; 2 Corinthians 1:24;.
[399] Galatians 1:10, 2:4-5, 5:1; Colossians 2:20,22-23.
[400] Isaiah 8:20; Jeremiah 8:9; Hosea 5:11; John 4:22; Acts 17:11; Romans 10:17, 14:23; Revelation 13:12,16-17.
[401] Luke 1:74-75; John 8:34; Galatians 5:13; 1 Peter 2:16; 2 Peter 2:19.
[402] Matthew 12:25; Romans 13:1-8; Hebrews 13:17; 1 Peter 2:13-14,16.
[403] Matthew 18:15-17; Romans 1:32; 1 Corinthians 5:1,5,11,13; 2 Thessalonians 3:14; 1 Timothy 1:19-20, 6:3-5, Titus 1:10-11,13, 3:10; 2 John 10-11; Revelation 2:2,14-15,20, 3:9.

Chapter XXI – Of Religious Worship and the Sabbath-day.

I. The light of nature showeth that there is a God, who hath lordship and sovereignty over all, is good, and doth good unto all, and is therefore to be feared, loved, praised, called upon, trusted in, and served, with all the heart, and with all the soul, and with all the might.[404] But the acceptable way of worshipping the true God is instituted by Himself, and so limited by His own revealed will, that He may not be worshipped according to the imaginations and devices of men, or the suggestions of Satan, under any visible representation, or any other way not prescribed in the Holy Scripture.[405]

II. Religious worship is to be given to God, the Father, Son, and Holy Ghost; and to Him alone;[406] not to angels, saints, or any other creature:[407] and since the fall, not without a Mediator; nor in the mediation of any other but of Christ alone.[408]

III. Prayer, with thanksgiving, being one special part of religious worship,[409] is by God required of all men:[410] and that it may be accepted, it is to be made in the name of the Son,[411] by the help of His Spirit,[412] according to His will,[413] with understanding, reverence, humility, fervency, faith, love, and perseverance;[414] and, if vocal, in a known tongue.[415]

IV. Prayer is to be made for things lawful;[416] and for all sorts of men living, or that shall live hereafter:[417] but not for the dead,[418] nor for those of whom it may be known that they have sinned the sin unto death.[419]

V. The reading of the Scriptures with godly fear,[420] the sound preaching[421] and conscionable hearing of the Word, in obedience unto God, with understanding, faith and reverence;[422] singing of psalms with grace in the heart;[423] as also, the due administration and worthy receiving of the sacraments instituted by Christ; are all parts of the ordinary religious worship of God:[424] beside religious oaths,[425] vows,[426] solemn fastings,[427]

---

[404] Joshua 24:14; Psalm 18:3, 31:23, 62:8, 119:68; Jeremiah 10:7; Mark 12:33; Acts 17:24; Romans 1:20, 10:12.
[405] Exodus 20:4-6; Deuteronomy 4:15-20, 12:32; Matthew 4:9-10, 15:9; Acts 17:25; Colossians 2:23.
[406] Matthew 4:10; John 5:23; 2 Corinthians 13:14.
[407] Romans 1:25; Colossians 2:18, Revelation 19:10.
[408] John 14:6; Ephesians 2:18; Colossians 3:17; 1 Timothy 2:5.
[409] Philippians 4:6.
[410] Psalm 65:2.
[411] John 14:13-14; 1 Peter 2:5.
[412] Romans 8:26.
[413] 1 John 5:14.
[414] Genesis 18:27; Psalm 47:7; Ecclesiastes 5:1-2; Matthew 6:12,14-15; Mark 11:24; Ephesians 6:18; Colossians 4:2; Hebrews 12:28; James 1:6-7, 5:16.
[415] 1 Corinthians 14:14.
[416] 1 John 5:14.
[417] Ruth 4:12; 2 Samuel 7:29; John 17:20; 1 Timothy 2:1-2.
[418] 2 Samuel 12:21-23; Luke 16:25-26; Revelation 14:13.
[419] 1 John 5:16.
[420] Acts 15:21; Revelation 1:3.
[421] 2 Timothy 4:2.
[422] Isaiah 66:2; Matthew 13:19; Acts 10:33; Hebrews 4:2; James 1:22.
[423] Ephesians 5:19; Colossians 3:16; James 5:13.
[424] Matthew 28:19; Acts 2:42; 1 Corinthians 11:23-29.
[425] Deuteronomy 6:13; Nehemiah 10:29.
[426] Isaiah 19:21; Ecclesiastes 5:4-5.
[427] Esther 4:16; Joel 2:12; Matthew 9:15; 1 Corinthians 7:5.

and thanksgivings, upon special occasions,[428] which are, in their several times and seasons, to be used in a holy and religious manner.[429]

VI. Neither prayer, nor any other part of religious worship, is now under the Gospel either tied unto, or made more acceptable by any place in which it is performed, or towards which it is directed:[430] but God is to be worshipped everywhere,[431] in spirit and truth;[432] as in private families[433] daily,[434] and in secret each one by himself;[435] so, more solemnly, in the public assemblies, which are not carelessly or wilfully to be neglected, or forsaken, when God, by His Word or providence, calls thereunto.[436]

VII. As it is the law of nature, that, in general, a due proportion of time be set apart for the worship of God; so, in His Word, by a positive, moral, and perpetual commandment, binding all men, in all ages, He hath particularly appointed one day in seven, for a Sabbath, to be kept holy unto Him:[437] which, from the beginning of the world to the resurrection of Christ, was the last day of the week; and, from the resurrection of Christ, was changed into the first day of the week,[438] which, in Scripture, is called the Lord's Day,[439] and is to be continued to the end of the world, as the Christian Sabbath.[440]

VIII. This Sabbath is then kept holy unto the Lord, when men, after a due preparing of their hearts, and ordering of their common affairs beforehand, do not only observe an holy rest, all the day, from their own works, words, and thoughts about their worldly employments and recreations,[441] but also are taken up the whole time in the public and private exercises of His worship, and in the duties of necessity and mercy.[442]

Chapter XXII – Of Lawful Oaths and Vows.

I. A lawful oath is a part of religious worship,[443] wherein, upon just occasion, the person swearing solemnly calleth God to witness what he asserteth, or promiseth, and to judge him according to the truth or falsehood of what he sweareth.[444]

II. The name of God only is that by which men ought to swear; and therein it is to be used with all holy fear and reverence.[445] Therefore, to swear vainly or rashly, by that glorious and dreadful Name; or, to swear at all by any other thing, is sinful, and to be abhorred.[446] Yet, as in matters of weight and moment, an oath is

---

[428] Esther 9:22; Psalm 107:1-43.
[429] Hebrews 12:28.
[430] John 4:21.
[431] Malachi 1:11; 1 Timothy 2:8.
[432] John 4:23-24.
[433] Deuteronomy 6:6-7; 2 Samuel 6:18,20; Job 1:5; Jeremiah 10:25; Acts 10:2; 1 Peter 3:7.
[434] Matthew 6:11.
[435] Matthew 6:6; Ephesians 6:18.
[436] Proverbs 1:20-21,24, 8:34; Isaiah 56:6-7; Luke 4:16; Acts 2:42, 13:42; Hebrews 10:25.
[437] Exodus 20:8,10-11; Isaiah 56:2,4,6-7.
[438] Genesis 2:2-3; Acts 20:7; 1 Corinthians 16:1-2.
[439] Revelation 1:10.
[440] Exodus 20:8,10; Matthew 5:17-18.
[441] Exodus 16:23,25-26,29-30, 20:8, 31:15-17; Nehemiah 13:15-19,21-22; Isaiah 58:13.
[442] Isaiah 58:13; Matthew 12:1-13.
[443] Deuteronomy 10:20.
[444] Exodus 20:7; Leviticus 19:12; 2 Chronicles 6:22-23; 2 Corinthians 1:23.
[445] Deuteronomy 6:13.
[446] Exodus 20:7; Jeremiah 5:7; Matthew 5:34,37; James 5:12.

warranted by the Word of God, under the New Testament, as well as under the Old;[447] so a lawful oath, being imposed by lawful authority, in such matters ought to be taken.[448]

III. Whosoever taketh an oath ought duly to consider the weightiness of so solemn an act; and therein to avouch nothing, but what he is fully persuaded is the truth.[449] Neither may any man bind himself by oath to anything but what is good and just, and what he believeth so to be, and what he is able and resolved to perform.[450]

IV. An oath is to be taken in the plain and common sense of the words, without equivocation, or mental reservation.[451] It cannot oblige to sin: but in anything not sinful, being taken, it binds to performance, although to a man's own hurt.[452] Not is it to be violated, although made to heretics, or infidels.[453]

V. A vow is of the like nature with a promissory oath, and ought to be made with the like religious care, and to be performed with the like faithfulness.[454]

VI. It is not to be made to any creature, but to God alone:[455] and that it may be accepted, it is to be made voluntarily, out of faith, and conscience of duty, in way of thankfulness for mercy received, or for the obtaining of what we want; whereby we more strictly bind ourselves to necessary duties; or to other things, so far and so long as they may fitly conduce thereunto.[456]

VII. No man may vow to do anything forbidden in the Word of God, or what would hinder any duty therein commanded, or which is not in his own power, and for the performance whereof he hath no promise of ability from God.[457] In which respects, Popish monastical vows of perpetual single life, professed poverty, and regular obedience, are so far from being degrees of higher perfection, that they are superstitious and sinful snares, in which no Christian may entangle himself.[458]

Chapter XXIII – Of the Civil Magistrate.

I. God, the supreme Lord and King of all the world, hath ordained civil magistrates, to be, under Him, over the people, for His own glory, and the public good: and, to this end, hath armed them with the power of the sword, for the defense and encouragement of them that are good, and for the punishment of evil doers.[459]

II. It is lawful for Christians to accept and execute the office of a magistrate, when called thereunto;[460] in the managing whereof, as they ought especially to maintain piety, justice, and peace, according to the

---

[447] Isaiah 65:16; 2 Corinthians 1:23; Hebrews 6:16.
[448] 1 Kings 8:31; Nehemiah 13:25; Ezra 10:5.
[449] Exodus 20:7; Jeremiah 4:2.
[450] Genesis 24:2-3,5-9.
[451] Psalm 24:4; Jeremiah 4:2.
[452] 1 Samuel 25:22,32-34; Psalm 15:4.
[453] Joshua 9:18-19; 2 Samuel 21:1; Ezekiel 17:16,18-19.
[454] Psalm 61:8, 66:13-14; Ecclesiastes 5:4-6; Isaiah 19:21.
[455] Psalm 76:11; Jeremiah 44:25-26.
[456] Genesis 28:20-22; Deuteronomy 23:21-23; 1 Samuel 1:11; Psalm 50:14, 66:13-14, 132:2-5.
[457] Numbers 30:5,8,12-13; Mark 6:26; Acts 23:12,14.
[458] Matthew 19:11-12; 1 Corinthians 7:2,9,23; Ephesians 4:28; 1 Peter 4:2.
[459] Romans 13:1-4; 1 Peter 2:13-14.
[460] Proverbs 8:15-16; Romans 13:1-2,4.

wholesome laws of each commonwealth;[461] so for that end, they may lawfully now, under the New Testament, wage war, upon just and necessary occasion.[462]

III. The civil magistrate may not assume to themselves the administration of the Word and sacraments; or the power of the keys of the kingdom of heaven;[463] or, in the least, interfere in matters of faith. Yet, as nursing fathers, it is the duty of civil magistrates to protect the church of our common Lord, without giving the preference to any denomination of Christians above the rest, in such a manner that all ecclesiastical persons whatever shall enjoy the full, free, and unquestioned liberty of discharging every part of their sacred functions without violence or danger.[464] And, as Jesus Christ hath appointed a regular government and discipline in his Church, no law of any commonwealth should interfere with, let, or hinder, the due exercise thereof, among the voluntary members of any denomination of Christians, according to their own profession and belief.[465] It is the duty of civil magistrates to protect the person and good name of all their people, in such an effectual manner as that no person be suffered, either upon pretence of religion or of infidelity, to offer any indignity, violence, abuse, or injury to any other person whatsoever: and to take order, that all religious and ecclesiastical assemblies be held without molestation or disturbance.[466]

IV. It is the duty of people to pray for magistrates,[467] to honour their persons,[468] to pay them tribute or other dues,[469] to obey their lawful commands, and to be subject to their authority, for conscience' sake.[470] Infidelity, or difference in religion, doth not make void the magistrates' just and legal authority, nor free the people from their due obedience to them:[471] from which ecclesiastical persons are not exempted,[472] much less hath the Pope any power and jurisdiction over them in their dominions, or over any of their people; and, least of all, to deprive them of their dominions, or lives, if he shall judge them to be heretics, or upon any other pretense whatsoever.[473]

Chapter XXIV – Of Marriage and Divorce.

I. Marriage is to be between one man and one woman: neither is it lawful for any man to have more than one wife, nor for any woman to have more than one husband; at the same time.[474]

II. Marriage was ordained for the mutual help of husband and wife,[475] for the increase of mankind with a legitimate issue, and of the Church with an holy seed;[476] and for preventing of uncleanness.[477]

---

[461] Psalm 2:10-12, 82:3-4; 2 Samuel 23:3; 1 Timothy 2:2; 1 Peter 2:13.
[462] Matthew 8:9-10; Luke 3:14; Acts 10:1-2; Romans 13:4; Revelation 17:14,16.
[463] 2 Chronicles 26:18; Matthew 16:19, 18:17; Romans 10:15; 1 Corinthians 4:1-2, 12:28-29; Ephesians 4:11-12; Hebrews 5:4.
[464] Isaiah 49:23; Romans 13:1.
[465] Psalm 104:15; Acts 18:14-15.
[466] Romans 13:4; 1 Timothy 2:2.
[467] 1 Timothy 2:1-2.
[468] 1 Peter 2:17.
[469] Romans 13:6-7.
[470] Romans 13:5; Titus 3:1.
[471] 1 Peter 2:13-14,16.
[472] 1 Kings 2:35; Acts 25:9-11; Romans 13:1; 2 Peter 2:1,10-11; Jude 8-11.
[473] 2 Thessalonians 2:4; Revelation 13:15-17.
[474] Genesis 2:24; Proverbs 2:17; Matthew 19:5-6.
[475] Genesis 2:18.
[476] Malachi 2:15.
[477] 1 Corinthians 7:2,9.

III. It is lawful for all sorts of people to marry, who are able with judgment to give their consent.[478] Yet is it the duty of Christians to marry only in the Lord:[479] and therefore such as profess the true reformed religion should not marry with infidels, papists, or other idolaters: neither should such as are godly be unequally yoked, by marrying with such as are notoriously wicked in their life, or maintain damnable heresies.[480]

IV. Marriage ought not to be within the degrees of consanguinity or affinity forbidden by the Word;[481] nor can such incestuous marriages ever be made lawful by any law of man or consent of parties, so as those persons may live together as man and wife.[482]

V. Adultery or fornication committed after a contract, being detected before marriage, giveth just occasion to the innocent party to dissolve that contract.[483] In the case of adultery after marriage, it is lawful for the innocent party to sue out a divorce:[484] and, after the divorce, to marry another, as if the offending party were dead.[485]

VI. Although the corruption of man be such as is apt to study arguments unduly to put asunder those whom God hath joined together in marriage: yet nothing but adultery, or such wilful desertion as can no way be remedied by the Church or civil magistrate, is cause sufficient of dissolving the bond of marriage:[486] wherein, a public and orderly course of proceeding is to be observed; and the persons concerned in it not left to their own wills and discretion, in their own case.[487]

Chapter XXV – Of the Church.

I. The catholic or universal Church which is invisible, consists of the whole number of the elect, that have been, are, or shall be gathered into one, under Christ the Head thereof; and is the spouse, the body, the fullness of Him that filleth all in all.[488]

II. The visible Church, which is also catholic or universal under the Gospel (not confined to one nation as before under the law), consists of all those throughout the world that profess the true religion;[489] and of their children:[490] and is the kingdom of the Lord Jesus Christ,[491] the house and family of God,[492] out of which there is no ordinary possibility of salvation.[493]

---

[478] Genesis 24:57-58; 1 Corinthians 7:36-38; 1 Timothy 4:3; Hebrews 13:4.
[479] 1 Corinthians 7:39.
[480] Genesis 34:14; Exodus 34:16; Deuteronomy 7:3-4; 1 Kings 11:4; Nehemiah 13:25-27; Malachi 2:11-12; 2 Corinthians 6:14.
[481] Leviticus 18:1-30; Amos 2:7; 1 Corinthians 5:1.
[482] Leviticus 18:24-28; Mark 6:18.
[483] Matthew 1:18-20.
[484] Matthew 5:31-32.
[485] Matthew 19:9; Romans 7:2-3.
[486] Matthew 19:6,8-9; 1 Corinthians 7:15.
[487] Deuteronomy 24:1-4.
[488] Ephesians 1:10,22-23, 5:23,27,32; Colossians 1:18.
[489] Psalm 2:8; Romans 15:9-12; 1 Corinthians 1:2, 12:12-13; Revelation 7:9.
[490] Genesis 3:15, 17:7; Ezekiel 16:20-21; Acts 2:39; Romans 11:16; 1 Corinthians 7:14.
[491] Isaiah 9:7; Matthew 13:47.
[492] Ephesians 2:19, 3:15.
[493] Acts 2:47.

III. Unto this catholic visible Church Christ hath given the ministry, oracles, and ordinances of God, for the gathering and perfecting of the saints, in this life, to the end of the world: and doth by His own presence and Spirit, according to His promise, make them effectual thereunto.[494]

IV. This catholic Church hath been sometimes more, sometimes less visible.[495] And particular Churches, which are members thereof, are more or less pure, according as the doctrine of the Gospel is taught and embraced, ordinances administered, and public worship performed more or less purely in them.[496]

V. The purest Churches under heaven are subject both to mixture and error:[497] and some have so degenerated, as to become no Churches of Christ, but synagogues of Satan.[498] Nevertheless, there shall be always a Church on earth, to worship God according to His will.[499]

VI. There is no other head of the Church, but the Lord Jesus Christ;[500] nor can the Pope of Rome, in any sense, be head thereof.[501]

Chapter XXVI – Of the Communion of the Saints.

I. All saints, that are united to Jesus Christ their Head by His Spirit and by faith, have fellowship with Him in His grace, sufferings, death, resurrection, and glory:[502] and, being united to one another in love, they have communion in each other's gifts and graces,[503] and are obliged to the performance of such duties, public and private, as do conduce to their mutual good, both in the inward and outward man.[504]

II. Saints by profession are bound to maintain a holy fellowship and communion in the worship of God; and in performing such other spiritual services as tend to their mutual edification;[505] as also in relieving each other in outward things, according to their several abilities, and necessities. Which communion, as God offereth opportunity, is to be extended unto all those who, in every place, call upon the name of the Lord Jesus.[506]

III. This communion which the saints have with Christ, doth not make them, in any wise, partakers of the substance of His Godhead; or to be equal with Christ, in any respect: either of which to affirm is impious and blasphemous.[507] Nor doth their communion one with another, as saints, take away, or infringe the title or propriety which each man hath in his goods and possessions.[508]

---

[494] Isaiah 59:21; Matthew 28:19-20; 1 Corinthians 12:28; Ephesians 4:11-13.

[495] Romans 11:3-4; Revelation 12:6,14.

[496] 1 Corinthians 5:6-7; Revelation 2:1-29,3:1-22.

[497] Matthew 13:24-30,47; 1 Corinthians 13:12; Revelation 2:1-29, 3:1-22.

[498] Romans 11:18-22; Revelation 18:2.

[499] Psalm 72:17, 102:28; Matthew 16:18, 28:19-20.

[500] Ephesians 1:22; Colossians 1:18.

[501] Matthew 23:8-10; 2 Thessalonians 2:3-4,8-9; Revelation 13:6.

[502] John 1:3, 1:16; Romans 6:5-6; Ephesians 2:5-6, 3:16-19; Philippians 3:10; 2 Timothy 2:12.

[503] 1 Corinthians 3:21-23, 12:7; Ephesians 4:15-16; Colossians 2:19.

[504] Romans 1:11-12,14; Galatians 6:10; 1 Thessalonians 5:11,14; 1 John 3:16-18.

[505] Isaiah 2:3; Acts 2:42,46; 1 Corinthians 11:20; Hebrews 10:24-25.

[506] Acts 2:44-45, 11:29-30; 2 Corinthians 8:1,9;1 John 3:17.

[507] Psalm 45:7; Isaiah 42:8; 1 Corinthians 8:6; Colossians 1:18-19; 1 Timothy 6:15-16; Hebrews 1:8-9.

[508] Exodus 20:15; Acts 5:4; Ephesians 4:28.

Chapter XXVII – Of the Sacraments.

I. Sacraments are holy signs and seals of the covenant of grace,[509] immediately instituted by God,[510] to represent Christ and His benefits; and to confirm our interest in Him;[511] as also, to put a visible difference between those that belong unto the Church, and the rest of the world;[512] and solemnly to engage them to the service of God in Christ, according to His Word.[513]

II. There is in every sacrament a spiritual relation, or sacramental union, between the sign and the thing signified: whence it comes to pass, that the names and effects of the one are attributed to the other.[514]

III. The grace which is exhibited in or by the sacraments rightly used, is not conferred by any power in them; neither doth the efficacy of a sacrament depend upon the piety or intention of him that doth administer it:[515] but upon the work of the Spirit,[516] and the word of institution, which contains, together with a precept authorizing the use thereof, a promise of benefit to worthy receivers.[517]

IV. There are only two sacraments ordained by Christ our Lord in the Gospel; that is to say, Baptism and the Supper of the Lord: neither of which may be dispensed by any but by a minister of the Word lawfully ordained.[518]

V. The sacraments of the Old Testament, in regard to the spiritual things thereby signified and exhibited, were, for substance, the same with those of the New.[519]

Chapter XXVIII – Of Baptism.

I. Baptism is a sacrament of the New Testament, ordained by Jesus Christ,[520] not only for the solemn admission of the party baptized into the visible Church;[521] but also, to be unto him a sign and seal of the covenant of grace,[522] of his ingrafting into Christ,[523] of regeneration,[524] of remission of sins,[525] and of his giving up unto God through Jesus Christ, to walk in the newness of life.[526] Which sacrament is, by Christ's own appointment, to be continued in His Church until the end of the world.[527]

---

[509] Genesis 17:7,10; Romans 4:11.
[510] Matthew 28:19; 1 Corinthians 11:23.
[511] 1 Corinthians 10:16, 11:25-26; Galatians 3:17.
[512] Genesis 34:14; Exodus 12:48; Romans 15:8.
[513] Romans 6:3-4; 1 Corinthians 10:16,21.
[514] Genesis 17:10; Matthew 26:27-28; Titus 3:5.
[515] Romans 2:28-29; 1 Peter 3:21.
[516] Matthew 3:11; 1 Corinthians 12:13.
[517] Matthew 26:27-28, 28:19-20.
[518] Matthew 28:19; 1 Corinthians 4:1, 11:20,23; Hebrews 5:4.
[519] 1 Corinthians 10:1-4.
[520] Matthew 28:19.
[521] 1 Corinthians 12:13.
[522] Romans 4:11; Colossians 2:11-12.
[523] Romans 6:5; Galatians 3:27.
[524] Titus 3:5.
[525] Mark 1:4.
[526] Romans 6:3-4.
[527] Matthew 28:19-20.

II. The outward element to be used in this sacrament is water, wherewith the party is to be baptized, in the name of the Father, and of the Son, and of the Holy Ghost, by a minister of the Gospel, lawfully called thereunto.[528]

III. Dipping of the person into the water is not necessary; but Baptism is rightly administered by pouring or sprinkling water upon the person.[529]

IV. Not only those that do actually profess faith in and obedience unto Christ,[530] but also the infants of one or both believing parents, are to be baptized.[531]

V. Although it be a great sin to contemn or neglect this ordinance,[532] yet grace and salvation are not so inseparably annexed unto it, as that no person can be regenerated or saved without it;[533] or, that all that are baptized are undoubtedly regenerated.[534]

VI. The efficacy of Baptism is not tied to that moment of time wherein it is administered;[535] yet notwithstanding, by the right use of this ordinance, the grace promised is not only offered, but really exhibited and conferred, by the Holy Ghost, to such (whether of age or infants) as that grace belongeth unto, according to the counsel of God's own will, in His appointed time.[536]

VII. The sacrament of Baptism is but once to be administered unto any person.[537]

Chapter XXIX – Of the Lord's Supper.

I. Our Lord Jesus, in the night wherein He was betrayed, instituted the sacrament of His body and blood, called the Lord's Supper, to be observed in His Church, unto the end of the world, for the perpetual remembrance of the sacrifice of Himself in His death; the sealing all benefits thereof unto true believers, their spiritual nourishment and growth in Him, their further engagement in and to all duties which they owe unto Him; and to be a bond and pledge of their communion with Him, and with each other, as members of His mystical body.[538]

II. In this sacrament, Christ is not offered up to His Father; nor any real sacrifice made at all for remission of sins of the quick or dead;[539] but only a commemoration of that one offering up of Himself, by Himself, upon the cross, once for all: and a spiritual oblation of all possible praise unto God for the same:[540] so that

---

[528] Matthew 3:11, 28:19-20; John 1:33.

[529] Mark 7:4; Acts 2:41, 16:33; Hebrews 9:10,19-22.

[530] Mark 16:15-16; Acts 8:37-38.

[531] Genesis 17:7,9-10; Matthew 28:19; Mark 10:13-16; Luke 18:15; Acts 2:38-39; Romans 4:11-12; 1 Corinthians 7:14; Galatians 3:9,14; Colossians 2:11-12.

[532] Exodus 4:24-26; Luke 7:30.

[533] Acts 10:2,4,22,31,45,47; Romans 4:11.

[534] Acts 8:13,23.

[535] John 3:5,8.

[536] Acts 2:38-41; Galatians 3:27; Ephesians 5:25-26; Titus 3:5.

[537] Titus 3:5.

[538] 1 Corinthians 10:16-17,21, 11:23-26, 12:13.

[539] Hebrews 9:22,25-26,28.

[540] Matthew 26:26-27; 1 Corinthians 11:24-26.

the Popish sacrifice of the mass (as they call it) is most abominably injurious to Christ's one, only sacrifice, the alone propitiation for all the sins of His elect.[541]

III. The Lord Jesus hath, in this ordinance, appointed His ministers to declare His word of institution to the people; to pray, and bless the elements of bread and wine, and thereby to set them apart from a common to a holy use; and to take and break the bread, to take the cup, and (they communicating also themselves) to give both to the communicants;[542] but to none who are not then present in the congregation.[543]

IV. Private masses, or receiving this sacrament by a priest or any other alone;[544] as likewise, the denial of the cup to the people,[545] worshipping the elements, the lifting them up or carrying them about for adoration, and the reserving them for any pretended religious use; are all contrary to the nature of this sacrament, and to the institution of Christ.[546]

V. The outward elements in this sacrament, duly set apart to the uses ordained by Christ, have such relation to Him crucified, as that, truly, yet sacramentally only, they are sometimes called by the name of the things they represent, to wit, the body and blood of Christ;[547] albeit in substance and nature they still remain truly and only bread and wine, as they were before.[548]

VI. That doctrine which maintains a change of the substance of bread and wine into the substance of Christ's body and blood (commonly called transubstantiation) by consecration of a priest, or by any other way, is repugnant, not to Scripture alone, but even to common sense and reason; overthroweth the nature of the sacrament, and hath been, and is the cause of manifold superstitions; yea, of gross idolatries.[549]

VII. Worthy receivers outwardly partaking of the visible elements in this sacrament,[550] do then also, inwardly by faith, really and indeed, yet not carnally and corporally, but spiritually, receive and feed upon Christ crucified, and all benefits of His death: the body and blood of Christ being then, not corporally or carnally, in, with, or under the bread and wine; yet, as really, but spiritually, present to the faith of believers in that ordinance, as the elements themselves are to their outward senses.[551]

VIII. Although ignorant and wicked men receive the outward elements in this sacrament: yet they receive not the thing signified thereby, but by their unworthy coming thereunto are guilty of the body and blood of the Lord to their own damnation. Wherefore, all ignorant and ungodly persons, as they are unfit to enjoy communion with Him, so are they unworthy of the Lord's Table; and cannot, without great sin against Christ while they remain such, partake of these holy mysteries,[552] or be admitted thereunto.[553]

---

[541] Hebrews 7:23-24,27, 10:11-12,14,18.
[542] Matthew 26:26-28; Mark 14:22-24; Luke 22:19-20; 1 Corinthians 11:23-26.
[543] Acts. 20:7; 1 Corinthians 11:20.
[544] 1 Corinthians 10:16.
[545] Mark 14:23; 1 Corinthians 11:25-29.
[546] Matthew 15:9.
[547] Matthew 26:26-28.
[548] Matthew 26:29; 1 Corinthians 11:26-28.
[549] Luke 24:6,39; Acts 3:21; 1 Corinthians 11:24-26;.
[550] 1 Corinthians 11:28.
[551] 1 Corinthians 10:16.
[552] 1 Corinthians 11:27-29; 2 Corinthians 6:14-16.
[553] Matthew 7:6; 1 Corinthians 5:6-7,13; 2 Thessalonians 3:6,14-15.

Chapter XXX – Of Church Censures.

I. The Lord Jesus, as King and Head of His Church, hath therein appointed a government, in the hand of Church officers, distinct from the civil magistrate.[554]

II. To these officers the keys of the kingdom of heaven are committed: by virtue whereof, they have power respectively to retain, and remit sins; to shut that kingdom against the impenitent, both by the Word and censures; and to open it unto penitent sinners, by the ministry of the Gospel, and by absolution from censures, as occasion shall require.[555]

III. Church censures are necessary, for the reclaiming and gaining of offending brethren, for deterring of others from the like offences, for purging out of that leaven which might infect the whole lump, for vindicating the honour of Christ, and the holy profession of the Gospel, and for preventing the wrath of God, which might justly fall upon the Church, if they should suffer His covenant and the seals thereof to be profaned by notorious and obstinate offenders.[556]

IV. For the better attaining of these ends, the officers of the Church are to proceed by admonition; suspension from the sacrament of the Lord's Supper for a season; and by excommunication from the Church; according to the nature of the crime, and demerit of the person.[557]

Chapter XXXI – Of Synods and Councils.

I. For the better government, and further edification of the Church, there ought to be such assemblies as are commonly called synods or councils;[558] and it belongeth to the overseers and other rulers of the particular churches, by virtue of their office, and the power which Christ hath given them for edification and not for destruction, to appoint such assemblies;[559] and to convene together in them, as often as they shall judge it expedient for the good of the church.[560]

II. It belongeth to synods and councils, ministerially to determine controversies of faith and cases of conscience; to set down rules and directions for the better ordering of the public worship of God, and government of his Church; to receive complaints in cases of maladministration, and authoritatively to determine the same: which decrees and determinations, if consonant to the Word of God, are to be received with reverence and submission; not only for their agreement with the Word, but also for the power whereby they are made, as being an ordinance of God appointed thereunto in His Word.[561]

III. All synods or councils, since the Apostles' times, whether general or particular, may err; and many have erred. Therefore they are not to be made the rule of faith, or practice; but to be used as a help in both.[562]

---

[554] Isaiah 9:6-7; Matthew 28:18-20; Acts 20:17,28; 1 Corinthians 12:28; 1 Thessalonians 5:12; 1 Timothy 5:17; Hebrews 13:7,17,24.
[555] Matthew 16:19, 18:17-18; John 20:21-23; 2 Corinthians 2:6-8.
[556] Matthew 7:6; 1 Corinthians 11:27-34, 5:1-13; 1 Timothy 1:20, 5:20; Jude 23.
[557] Matthew 18:17; 1 Corinthians 5:4-5,13; 1 Thessalonians 5:12; 2 Thessalonians 3:6,14-15; Titus 3:10.
[558] Acts 15:2,4,6.
[559] Acts 15:1-29.
[560] Acts 15:22-23,25.
[561] Matthew 18:17-20; Acts 15:15,19,24,27-31, 16:4.
[562] Acts 17:11; 1 Corinthians 2:5; 2 Corinthians 1:24; Ephesians 2:20.

IV. Synods and councils are to handle, or conclude, nothing, but that which is ecclesiastical: and are not to intermeddle with civil affairs which concern the commonwealth; unless by way of humble petition, in cases extraordinary; or by way of advice, for satisfaction of conscience, if they be thereunto required by the civil magistrate.[563]

Chapter XXXII – Of the State of Man After Death, and of the Resurrection of the Dead.

I. The bodies of men, after death, return to dust and see corruption:[564] but their souls (which neither die nor sleep) having an immortal subsistence, immediately return to God who gave them:[565] the souls of the righteous, being then made perfect in holiness, are received into the highest heavens, where they behold the face of God, in light and glory, waiting for the full redemption of their bodies.[566] And the souls of the wicked are cast into hell, where they remain in torments and utter darkness, reserved to the judgment of the great day.[567] Beside these two places, for souls separated from their bodies, the Scripture acknowledgeth none.

II. At the last day, such as are found alive shall not die, but be changed:[568] and all the dead shall be raised up, with the selfsame bodies, and none other, although with different qualities, which shall be united again to their souls forever.[569]

III. The bodies of the unjust shall, by the power of Christ, be raised to dishonour: the bodies of the just, by His Spirit, unto honour; and be made conformable to His own glorious body.[570]

Chapter XXXIII – Of the Last Judgment.

I. God hath appointed a day, wherein He will judge the world in righteousness, by Jesus Christ,[571] to whom all power and judgment is given of the Father.[572] In which day, not only the apostate angels shall be judged,[573] but likewise all persons that have lived upon earth shall appear before the tribunal of Christ, to give an account of their thoughts, words, and deeds; and to receive according to what they have done in the body, whether good or evil.[574]

II. The end of God's appointing this day is for the manifestation of the glory of His mercy, in the eternal salvation of the elect; and of His justice, in the damnation of the reprobate who are wicked and disobedient.

---

[563] Luke 12:13-14; John 18:36.
[564] Genesis 3:19; Acts 13:36.
[565] Ecclesiastes 12:7; Luke 23:43.
[566] Acts 3:21; 2 Corinthians 5:1,6,8; Ephesians 4:10; Philippians 1:23; Hebrews 12:23.
[567] Luke 16:23-24; Acts 1:25; 1 Peter 3:19; Jude 6-7.
[568] 1 Corinthians 15:51-52; 1 Thessalonians 4:17.
[569] Job 19:26-27; 1 Corinthians 15:42-44.
[570] John 5:28-29; Acts 24:15; 1 Corinthians 15:43; Philippians 3:21.
[571] Acts 17:31.
[572] John 5:22,27.
[573] 1 Corinthians 6:3; 2 Peter 2:4; Jude 6.
[574] Ecclesiastes 12:14; Matthew 12:36-37; Romans 2:16, 14:10,12; 2 Corinthians 5:10.

For then shall the righteous go into everlasting life, and receive that fullness of joy and refreshing, which shall come from the presence of the Lord: but the wicked who know not God, and obey not the Gospel of Jesus Christ, shall be cast into eternal torments, and be punished with everlasting destruction from the presence of the Lord, and from the glory of His power.[575]

III. As Christ would have us to be certainly persuaded that there shall be a day of judgment, both to deter all men from sin, and for the greater consolation of the godly in their adversity;[576] so will He have that day unknown to men, that they may shake off all carnal security, and be always watchful, because they know not at what hour the Lord will come; and may be ever prepared to say, Come, Lord Jesus, come quickly, Amen.[577]

---

[575] Matthew 25:21,31-46; Acts 3:19; Romans 2:5-6, 9:22-23; 2 Thessalonians 1:7-10.
[576] Luke 21:27-28; Romans 8:23-25; 2 Corinthians 5:10-11; 2 Thessalonians 1:5-7; 2 Peter 3:11,14.
[577] Matthew 24:36,42-44; Mark 13:35-37; Luke 12:35-36; Revelation 22:20.

Children's Catechism

Questions 1 – 18

1. Q. Who made you?
   A. **God**

2. Q. What else did God make?
   A. **God made all things.**

3. Q. Why did God make you and all things?
   A. **For His own glory.**

4. Q. How can you glorify God?
   A. **By loving Him and doing what He commands.**

5. Q. Why are you to glorify God?
   A. **Because He made me and takes care of me.**

6. Q. Are there more Gods than one?
   A. **There is only one true God.**

7. Q. How many persons is this one true God?
   A. **Three.**

8. Q. Name these three persons.
   A. **The Father, the Son, and the Holy Spirit.**

9. Q. What is God?
   A. **God is a spirit and has no body as we do.**

10. Q. Where is God?
    A. **God is everywhere.**

11. Q. Can you see God?
    A. **No – I cannot see God, but He can always see me.**

12. Q. Does God know all things?
    A. **Yes – nothing can be hid from God.**

13. Q. Can God do all things?
    A. **Yes – God can do all His holy will.**

14. Q. Where do you learn how to love and obey God?
    A. **In the Bible alone.**

15. Q. Who wrote the Bible?
    A. **Chosen men who wrote by the inspiration of the Holy Spirit.**

16. Q. Who were our first parents?
    A. **Adam and Eve.**

17. Q. How did God make our first parents?
    A. **God made Adam's body out of the ground and Eve's body out of a rib from Adam.**

18. Q. What did God give Adam and Eve besides bodies?
    A. **He gave them spirits that will last forever.**

Questions 19 – 37

19. Q. Do you have a spirit as well as a body?
    A. **Yes – and my spirit is going to last forever.**

20. Q. How do you know your spirit will last forever?
    A. **Because the Bible tells me so.**

21. Q. In what conditions did God make Adam and Eve?
    A. **He made them holy and happy.**

22. Q. What is a sacred covenant?
    A. **A relationship that God sets up with us and guarantees by His Word.**

23. Q. What covenant did God make with Adam?
    A. **The covenant of life (or works).**

24. Q. What did God require Adam to do in the covenant of life?
    A. **To obey Him perfectly.**

25. Q. What did God promise in the covenant of life?
    A. **To reward Adam with life if he obeyed Him.**

26. Q. What did God threaten in the covenant of life?
    A. **To punish Adam with death if he disobeyed Him.**

27. Q. Did Adam keep the covenant of life?
    A. **No – he sinned against God.**

28. Q. What is sin?
    A. **Any thought, word or deed that breaks God's law by omission or commission.**

29. Q. What is a sin of omission?
    A. **Not being or doing what God requires.**

30. Q. What is a sin of commission?
    A. **Doing what God forbids.**

31. Q. What does every sin deserve?
    A. **The wrath and curse of God.**

32. Q. What was the sin of our first parents?
    A. **Eating the forbidden fruit.**

33. Q. Who tempted them to this sin?
    A. **Satan tempted Eve first, and then he used her to tempt Adam.**

34. Q. How did Adam and Eve change when they sinned?
    A. **Instead of being holy and happy, they became sinful and miserable.**

35. Q. Did Adam act for himself alone in the covenant of life?
    A. **No – he represented the whole human race.**

36. Q. What did Adam's sin do to you?
    A. **It made me guilty and sinful.**

37. Q. How sinful are you by nature?
    A. **I am corrupt in every part of my being.**

Questions 38 – 56

38. Q. Can you go to heaven with this sinful nature?
    A. **No – my heart must be changed before I can be fit for heaven.**

39. Q. What is the changing of your heart called?
    A. **The new birth, or regeneration.**

40. Q. Who is able to change your heart?
    A. **The Holy Spirit alone.**

41. Q. Can you be saved through the covenant of life?
    A. **No – because I broke it and am condemned by it.**

42. Q. How did you break the covenant of life?
    A. **Adam represented me, and so I fell with him in the first sin.**

43. Q. How, then, can you be saved?
    A. **By the Lord Jesus Christ in the covenant of grace.**

44. Q. Who was represented by Jesus in the covenant of grace?
    A. **His elect people.**

45. Q. How did Jesus fulfill the covenant of grace?
    A. **He kept the whole law for His people, and then was punished for all of their sins.**

46. Q. Did Jesus ever sin?
    A. **No – He lived a sinless life.**

47. Q. How could the Son of God suffer?
    A. **The Son of God became man so that He could obey and suffer.**

48. Q. For whom did Christ obey and suffer?
    A. **For all who were given to Him by the Father.**

49. Q. What kind of life did Christ live on earth?
    A. **A life of poverty and suffering.**

50. Q. What kind of death did Jesus die?
    A. **The painful and shameful death of the cross.**

51. Q. What is meant by the atonement?
    A. **Christ satisfied God's justice by His suffering and death in the place of sinners.**

52. Q. What did God the Father guarantee in the covenant of grace?
    A. **To justify and sanctify all those for whom Christ died.**

53. Q. How can God justify you?
    A. **By forgiving all my sins and declaring me to be righteous.**

54. Q. How can God sanctify you?
    A. **By making me holy in heart and conduct.**

55. Q. What must you do to be saved?
    A. **I must repent of my sins, believe in Christ, and live a new life.**

56. Q. How do you repent of your sins?
    A. **By being sorry enough for my sin and hate and forsake it.**

Questions 57 – 75

57. Q. Why must you hate and forsake your sins?
    A. **Because it displeases God.**

58. Q. What does it mean to believe in Christ?
    A. **To trust in Him alone for my salvation.**

59. Q. Can you repent and believe by your own power?
    A. **No – I cannot do anything good unless the Holy Spirit enables me.**

60. Q. How can you get the help of the Holy Spirit?
    A. **God will give the Holy Spirit to those who ask Him.**

61. Q. How long ago did Christ die?
    A. **About two thousand years ago.**

62. Q. How were sinners saved before Christ came?
    A. **By believing in a Messiah to come.**

63. Q. How did they show their faith?
    A. **By offering the sacrifices God required.**

64. Q. What did these sacrifices represent?
    A. **Christ, the Lamb of God, who would come to die for sinners.**

65. Q. How many offices did the Lord Jesus fulfill as the promised Messiah?
    A. **He fulfilled three offices.**

66. Q. What are they?
    A. **The offices of prophet, priest and King.**

67. Q. How is Christ your prophet?
    A. **He teaches me the will of God.**

68. Q. How is Christ your priest?
    A. **He died for my sins and prays for me.**

69. Q. How is Christ your King?
    A. **He rules over me and defends me.**

70. Q. Why do you need Christ as your prophet?
    A. **Because I am ignorant by nature.**

71. Q. Why do you need Christ as your priest?
    A. **Because I am guilty of breaking God's law.**

72. Q. Why do you need Christ as your King?
    A. **Because I am weak and helpless.**

73. Q. How many commandments did God write down on the stone tablets?
    A. **Ten Commandments.**

74. Q. What do the first four commandments teach you?
    A. **What it means to love God.**

75. Q. What do the last six commandments teach you?
    A. **What it means to love and serve my neighbor.**

Questions 76 – 90

76. Q. What is the sum of the Ten Commandments?
A. **To love God with all my heart, soul, strength and mind, and to love my neighbor as myself.**

77. Q. Who is your neighbor?
A. **Everybody is my neighbor.**

78. Q. Is God pleased if you love and obey Him?
A. **Yes – He loves those who love Him.**

79. Q. Is God displeased with those who refuse to love and obey Him?
A. **Yes – God is angry with the wicked every day.**

80. Q. What is the first commandment?
A. **"You shall have no other gods before me."**

81. Q. What does the first commandment teach you?
A. **To worship the true God and Him alone.**

82. Q. What is the second commandment?
A. **"You shall not make for yourself any carved image, or any likeness of anything that is in heaven above, or that is in the earth beneath, or that is in the water under the earth; you shall not bow down to them nor serve them. For I, the Lord your God, am a jealous God, visiting the iniquity of the fathers on the children to the third and fourth generations of those who hate me, but showing mercy to thousands, to those who love me and keep my commandments."**

83. Q. What does the second commandment teach you?
A. **To worship God only as He commands – without any statues or pictures.**

84. Q. What is the third commandment?
A. **"You shall not take the name of the Lord your God in vain, for the Lord will not hold him guiltless who takes His name in vain."**

85. Q. What does the third commandment teach you?
A. **To revere God's name, especially in keeping my vows.**

86. Q. What is the fourth commandment?
A. **"Remember the Sabbath day by keeping it holy. Six days you shall labor and do all your work. But on the seventh day is a Sabbath to the Lord your God. On it you shall not do any work, neither you, nor your son or daughter, nor your manservant or maidservant, nor your animals, nor the alien within your gates. For in six days the Lord made the heavens and the earth, the sea, and all that is in them, but He rested on the seventh day. Therefore the Lord blessed the Sabbath day and made it holy."**

87. Q. What does the fourth commandment teach you?
A. **To work six days and to keep a holy Sabbath.**

88. Q. What day of the week is the Christian Sabbath?
A. **The first day of the week, which is the Lord's Day.**

89. Q. Why is it called the Lord's Day?
A. **Because on that day our Lord rose from the dead.**

90. Q. How should you keep the Lord's Day?
A. **I should rest from my daily work and faithfully worship God.**

Questions 91 – 107

91. Q.   What is the fifth commandment?
      A.   **"Honor your father and your mother so that you may live long in the land the Lord you God is giving you."**

92. Q.   What does the fifth commandment teach you?
      A.   **To love and obey my parents and all others that God appoints to teach and govern me.**

93. Q.   What is the sixth commandment?
      A.   **"You shall not murder."**

94. Q.   What does the sixth commandment teach you?
      A.   **Not to take anyone's life unjustly.**

95. Q.   What is the seventh commandment?
      A.   **"You shall not commit adultery."**

96. Q.   What does the seventh commandment teach you?
      A.   **Not to have sex with anyone outside the bonds of holy marriage.**

97. Q.   What is the eighth commandment?
      A.   **"You shall not steal."**

98. Q.   What does the eighth commandment teach you?
      A.   **Not to take anything owned by another person.**

99. Q.   What is the ninth commandment?
      A.   **"You shall not give false testimony against your neighbor."**

100. Q.   What does the ninth commandment teach you?
      A.   **To tell the truth at all times.**

101. Q.   What is the tenth commandment?
      A.   **"You shall not covet your neighbor's house. You shall not covet your neighbor's wife, or his manservant or maidservant, his ox or donkey, or anything that belongs to your neighbor."**

102. Q.   What does the tenth commandment teach you?
      A.   **To be content with whatever God chooses to give me.**

103. Q.   Can you keep the Ten Commandments perfectly?
      A.   **No – since the fall of Adam, the only One who has been able to do this is Jesus.**

104. Q.   Of what use are the Ten Commandments to you?
      A.   **They teach me what is pleasing to God and how much I need a Savior.**

105. Q.   What is prayer?
      A.   **Prayer is asking God for the things He has promised in the Bible – and giving thanks for what He has given.**

106. Q.   In whose name are we to pray?
      A.   **In the name of Christ only.**

107. Q.   What did Christ give us to teach us about prayer?
      A.   **The Lord's Prayer.**

Questions 108 – 125

108. Q. What is the Lord's Prayer?
   A. **"Our Father who art in heaven, Hallowed be thy name. Thy kingdom come. Thy will be done on earth, as it is in heaven. Give us this day our daily bread. And forgive us our trespasses, as we forgive those who trespass against us. And lead us not into temptation, but deliver us from evil: For Thine is the kingdom, and the power, and the glory, forever. Amen."**

109. Q. How many things do we pray for in the Lord's Prayer?
   A. **Six.**

110. Q. What do we pray first?
   A. **"Hallowed be Thy name."**

111. Q. What does it mean to pray, "Hallowed by Thy name"?
   A. **We are asking God to enable us and all creation to honor His name.**

112. Q. What do we pray second?
   A. **"Thy kingdom come."**

113. Q. What does it mean to pray, "Thy kingdom come"?
   A. **We are asking God to bring more and more people to believe and obey His gospel.**

114. Q. What do we pray third?
   A. **"Thy will be done on earth as it is in heaven."**

115. Q. What does it mean to pray "Thy will be done on earth as it is in heaven"?
   A. **We are asking for God to make us able and willing to serve Him as the angels do in heaven.**

116. Q. What do we pray fourth?
   A. **"Give us this day our daily bread."**

117. Q. What does it mean to pray "Give us this day our daily bread"?
   A. **We are asking God to provide us with all that we really need.**

118. Q. What do we pray fifth?
   A. **"Forgive us our trespasses as we forgive those who trespass against us."**

119. Q. What does it mean to pray "Forgive us our trespasses as we forgive those who trespass against us"?
   A. **We are asking God to forgive our sins for Christ's sake and to make us willing to forgive others.**

120. Q. What do we pray sixth?
   A. **"And lead us not into temptation, but deliver us from evil."**

121. Q. What does it mean to pray, "And lead us not into temptation, but deliver us from evil"?
   A. **We are asking God to keep us from being tempted or to make us strong enough to resist if we are tempted.**

122. Q. How many sacraments are there?
   A. **Two.**

123. Q. What are they called?
   A. **Baptism and the Lord's Supper.**

124. Q. Who appointed these sacraments?
   A. **The Lord Jesus Christ.**

125. Q. Why did Christ appoint these sacraments?
   A. **To mark us off from the world and to give us comfort and strength.**

Questions 126 – 143

126. Q.   What sign is used in Baptism?
     A.   **Washing with water.**

127. Q.   What does this washing with water represent?
     A.   **Union with Christ by cleansing through His blood.**

128. Q.   In whose name are you baptized?
     A.   **In the name of the Father, and of the Son, and of the Holy Spirit.**

129. Q.   Who are to be baptized?
     A.   **Believers and their children.**

130. Q.   Why are we baptized even as little infants?
     A.   **Because God's command to Abraham is obeyed in our Baptism.**

131. Q.   What did Jesus say about little children?
     A.   **"Let the little children come to me, and do not hinder them, for the Kingdom of heaven belongs to such as these."**

132. Q.   What does your baptism call you to be?
     A.   **A true follower of Christ.**

133. Q.   What sign is used in the Lord's Supper?
     A.   **Eating bread and drinking wine in remembrance of the suffering and death of Jesus.**

134. Q.   What does the bread represent?
     A.   **Christ's body sacrificed for our sins.**

135. Q.   What does the wine represent?
     A.   **Christ's blood shed for our sins.**

136. Q.   Who may rightly partake of the Lord's Supper?
     A.   **Those who repent of their sins, believe in Christ, and live a new life.**

137. Q.   Did Christ remain in the tomb after He was buried?
     A.   **No – He came back out of the tomb on the third day.**

138. Q.   Where is Jesus now?
     A.   **At the right hand of the Father, praying for us.**

139. Q.   Will the Lord Jesus come again?
     A.   **Yes! He will return to judge the world at the last day.**

140. Q.   What will happen to us when we die?
     A.   **Our bodies will return to dust, while our spirits return to God.**

141. Q.   Will the bodies of all the dead be raised again?
     A.   **Yes – some will be raised to everlasting life and others to everlasting death.**

142. Q.   What will God do to unbelievers at the last day?
     A.   **He will cast them into the lake of fire, along with Satan and his angels.**

143. Q.   What will the lake of fire be like?
     A.   **It will be an awful place, where the lost will suffer for their sins forever.**

Questions 144 – 145

144. Q.   What will God do for believers at the last day?
    A.   **He will give them a home in the new heaven and the new earth.**

145. Q.   What will the new heaven and the new earth be like?
    A.   **It will be a glorious and happy place, where the saved will be with Jesus forever.**

<u>Notes</u>

Westminster Shorter Catechism
Questions 1 – 8

1.   Q.   What is the chief end of man?
       A.   **Man's chief end is to glorify God,[1] and to enjoy him forever.[2]**

2.   Q.   What rule hath God given to direct us how we may glorify and enjoy him?
       A.   **The Word of God, which is contained in the Scriptures of the Old and New Testaments,[3] is the only rule to direct us how we may glorify and enjoy him.[4]**

3.   Q.   What do the Scriptures principally teach?
       A.   **The Scriptures principally teach what man is to believe concerning God,[5] and what duty God requires of man.[6]**

4.   Q.   What is God?
       A.   **God is a Spirit,[7] infinite,[8] eternal,[9] and unchangeable[10] in his being,[11] wisdom,[12] power,[13] holiness,[14] justice,[15] goodness,[16] and truth.[17]**

5.   Q.   Are there more Gods than one?
       A.   **There is but one only,[18] the living and true God.[19]**

6.   Q.   How many persons are there in the Godhead?
       A.   **There are three persons in the Godhead; the Father, the Son, and the Holy Ghost;[20] and these three are one God, the same in substance, equal in power and glory.[21]**

7.   Q.   What are the decrees of God?
       A.   **The decrees of God are, his eternal purpose, according to the counsel of his will, whereby, for his own glory, he hath foreordained whatsoever comes to pass.[22]**

8.   Q.   How doth God execute his decrees?
       A.   **God executeth his decrees in the works of creation and providence.[23]**

---

[1] Psalm 86:9; Isaiah 60:21; Romans 11:36; 1 Corinthians 6:20, 10:31; Revelation 4:11.

[2] Psalm 16:5-11, 144:15; Isaiah 12:2; Luke 2:10; Philippians 4:4; Revelation 21:3-4.

[3] Matthew 19:4-5 with Genesis 2:24; Luke 24:27,44; 1 Corinthians 2:13, 14:37; 2 Peter 1:20-21, 3:2,15-16.

[4] Deuteronomy 4:2; Psalm 19:7-11; Isaiah 18:20; John 15:11, 20:30-31; Acts 17:11; 2 Timothy 3:15; 1 John 1:4.

[5] Genesis 1:1; John 5:39, 20:31; Romans 10:17; 2 Timothy 3:15.

[6] Deuteronomy 10:12-13; Joshua 1:8; Psalm 119:105; Micah 6:8; 2 Timothy 3:16-17.

[7] Deuteronomy 4:15-19; Luke 24:39; John 1:18, 4:24; Acts 17:29.

[8] 1 Kings 8:27; Psalm 139:7-10, 145:3, 147:5; Jeremiah 23:24; Romans 11:33-36.

[9] Deuteronomy 33:27; Psalm 90:2, 102:12,24-27; Revelation 1:4,8.

[10] Psalm 33:11; Malachi 3:6; Hebrews 1:12, 6:17-18, 13:8; James 1:17.

[11] Exodus 3:14; Psalm 115:2-3; 1 Timothy 1:17, 6:15-16.

[12] Psalm 104:24; Romans 11:33-34; Hebrews 4:13; 1 John 3:20.

[13] Genesis 17:1; Psalm 62:11; Jeremiah 32:17; Matthew 19:26; Revelation 1:8.

[14] Hebrews 1:13; 1 Peter 1:15-16; 1 John 3:3,5; Revelation 15:4.

[15] Genesis 18:25; Exodus 34:6; Deuteronomy 32:4; Psalm 96:13; Romans 3:5,26.

[16] Psalm 103:5, 107:8; Matthew 19:17; Romans 2:4.

[17] Exodus 34:6; Deuteronomy 32:4; Psalm 86:15, 117:2; Hebrews 6:18.

[18] Deuteronomy 6:4; Isaiah 44:6, 45:21-22; 1 Corinthians 8:4-6.

[19] Jeremiah 10:10; John 17:3; 1 Thessalonians 1:9; 1 John 5:20.

[20] Matthew 3:16-17, 28:19; 2 Corinthians 13:14; 1 Peter 1:2.

[21] Psalm 45:6; John 1:1, 17:5; Acts 5:3-4; Romans 9:5; Colossians 2:9; Jude 24-25.

[22] Psalm 33:11; Isaiah 14:24; Acts 2:23; Ephesians 1:11-12.

[23] Psalm 148:8; Isaiah 40:26; Daniel 4:35; Acts 4:24-28; Revelation 4:11.

Questions 9 – 17

9. Q. What is the work of creation?
   A. **The work of creation is, God's making all things of nothing, by the word of his power,[24] in the space of six days, and all very good.[25]**

10. Q. How did God create man?
    A. **God created man male and female, after his own image,[26] in knowledge,[27] righteousness, and holiness,[28] with dominion over the creatures.[29]**

11. Q. What are God's works of providence?
    A. **God's works of providence are, his most holy,[30] wise,[31] and powerful[32] preserving[33] and governing[34] all his creatures, and all their actions.[35]**

12. Q. What special act of providence did God exercise toward man in the estate wherein he was created?
    A. **When God had created man, he entered into a covenant of life with him, upon condition of perfect obedience; forbidding him to eat of the tree of the knowledge of good and evil, upon pain of death.[36]**

13. Q. Did our first parents continue in the estate wherein they were created?
    A. **Our first parents, being left to the freedom of their own will, fell from the estate wherein they were created, by sinning against God.[37]**

14. Q. What is sin?
    A. **Sin is any want of conformity unto, or transgression of, the law of God.[38]**

15. Q. What was the sin whereby our first parents fell from the estate wherein they were created?
    A. **The sin whereby our first parents fell from the estate wherein they were created, was their eating the forbidden fruit.[39]**

16. Q. Did all mankind fall in Adam's first transgression?
    A. **The covenant being made with Adam,[40] not only for himself, but for his posterity; all mankind, descending from him by ordinary generation, sinned in him, and fell with him, in his first transgression.[41]**

17. Q. Into what estate did the fall bring mankind?
    A. **The fall brought mankind into an estate of sin and misery.[42]**

---

[24] Genesis 1:1; Psalm 33:6,9; Hebrews 11:3.

[25] Genesis 1:31.

[26] Genesis 1:27.

[27] Colossians 3:10.

[28] Ephesians 4:24.

[29] Genesis 1:28; see Psalm 8.

[30] Psalm 145:17.

[31] Psalm 104:24.

[32] Hebrews 1:3

[33] Nehemiah 9:6.

[34] Ephesians 1:19-22.

[35] Psalm 36:6; Proverbs 16:33; Matthew 10:30.

[36] Genesis 2:16-17; James 2:10.

[37] Genesis 3:6-8, 13; 2 Corinthians 11:3.

[38] Leviticus 5:17; James 4:17; 1 John 3:4.

[39] Genesis 3:6.

[40] Genesis 2:16-17; James 2:10.

[41] Romans 5:12-21; 1 Corinthians 15:22.

[42] Genesis 3:16-19,23; Romans 3:16; 5:12; Ephesians 2:1.

Questions 19 – 25

19. Q. What is the misery of that estate whereinto man fell?
    A. **All mankind by their fall lost communion with God,[43] are under his wrath[44] and curse,[45] and so made liable to all miseries in this life,[46] to death[47] itself, and to the pains of hell forever.[48]**

20. Q. Did God leave all mankind to perish in the estate of sin and misery?
    A. **God having, out of his mere good pleasure, from all eternity, elected some to everlasting life,[49] did enter into a covenant of grace, to deliver them out of the estate of sin and misery, and to bring them into an estate of salvation by a Redeemer.[50]**

21. Q. Who is the Redeemer of God's elect?
    A. **The only Redeemer of God's elect is the Lord Jesus Christ,[51] who, being the eternal Son of God,[52] became man[53] and so was, and continueth to be, God and man in two distinct natures, and one person, forever.[54]**

22. Q. How did Christ, being the Son of God, become man?
    A. **Christ, the Son of God, became man, by taking to himself a true body, and a reasonable soul,[55] being conceived by the power of the Holy Ghost, in the womb of the virgin Mary, and born of her[56] yet without sin.[57]**

23. Q. What offices doth Christ execute as our Redeemer?
    A. **Christ, as our Redeemer, executeth the offices of a prophet,[58] of a priest,[59] and of a king,[60] both in his estate of humiliation and exaltation.**

24. Q. How doth Christ execute the office of a prophet?
    A. **Christ executeth the office of a prophet, in revealing to us, by his Word[61] and Spirit,[62] the will of God for our salvation.[63]**

25. Q. How doth Christ execute the office of a priest?
    A. **Christ executeth the office of a priest, in his once offering up of himself a sacrifice to satisfy divine justice,[64] and reconcile us to God;[65] and in making continual intercession for us.[66]**

---

[43] Genesis 3:8,24; John 8:34,42,44; Ephesians 2:12, 4:18.

[44] John 3:36; Romans 1:18; Ephesians 2:3, 5:6.

[45] Galatians 3:10; Revelation 22:3.

[46] Genesis 3:16-19; Job 5:7; Ecclesiastes 2:22-23; Romans 8:18-23.

[47] Ezekiel 18:4; Romans 5:12, 6:23.

[48] Matthew 25:41, 46; 2 Thessalonians 1:9; Revelation 14:9-11-11.

[49] Acts 13:48; Ephesians 1:4-5; 2 Thessalonians 2:13-14.

[50] Genesis 3:15; 17:7; Exodus 19:5-6; Jeremiah 31:31-34; Matthew 20:28; 1 Corinthians 11:25; Hebrews 9:15-17.

[51] John 14:6; Acts 4:12; 1 Timothy 2:5-6.

[52] Psalm 2:7; Matthew 3:17, 17:5; John 1:18.

[53] Isaiah 9:6; Matthew 1:23; John 1:14; Galatians 4:4.

[54] Acts 1:11; Hebrews 7:24-25.

[55] Philippians 2:7; Hebrews 2:14,17.

[56] Luke 1:27,31,35.

[57] 2 Corinthians 5:21; Hebrews 4:15, 7:26; 1 John 3:5.

[58] Deuteronomy 18:18; Acts 2:33, 3:22-23; Hebrews 1:1-2.

[59] Hebrews 4:14-15, 5:5-6.

[60] Isaiah 9:6-7; Luke 1:32-33; John 18:37; 1 Corinthians 15:25.

[61] Luke 4:18-19,21; Acts 1:1-2; Hebrews 2:3.

[62] John 15:26-27; Acts 1:8; 1 Peter 1:11.

[63] John 4:41-42, 20:30-31.

[64] Isaiah 53; Acts 8:32-35; Hebrews 9:26-28, 10:12.

[65] Romans 5:10-11; 2 Corinthians 5:18; Colossians 1:21-22.

[66] Romans 8:34; Hebrews 7:25, 9:24.

Questions 26 – 32

26. Q. How doth Christ execute the office of a king?
     A. **Christ executeth the office of a king, in subduing us to himself, in ruling and defending us,[67] and in restraining and conquering all his and our enemies.[68]**

27. Q. Wherein did Christ's humiliation consist?
     A. **Christ's humiliation consisted in his being born, and that in a low condition,[69] made under the law,[70] undergoing the miseries of this life,[71] the wrath of God,[72] and the cursed death of the cross;[73] in being buried, and continuing under the power of death for a time.[74]**

28. Q. Wherein consisteth Christ's exaltation?
     A. **Christ's exaltation consisteth in his rising again from the dead on the third day,[75] in ascending up into heaven,[76] in sitting at the right hand[77] of God the Father, and in coming to judge the world at the last day.[78]**

29. Q. How are we made partakers of the redemption purchased by Christ?
     A. **We are made partakers of the redemption purchased by Christ, by the effectual application of it to us by his Holy Spirit.[79]**

30. Q. How doth the Spirit apply to us the redemption purchased by Christ?
     A. **The Spirit applieth to us the redemption purchased by Christ, by working faith in us,[80] and thereby uniting us to Christ in our effectual calling.[81]**

31. Q. What is effectual calling?
     A. **Effectual calling is the work of God's Spirit, whereby, convincing us of our sin and misery, enlightening our minds in the knowledge of Christ,[82] and renewing our wills,[83] he doth persuade and enable us to embrace Jesus Christ,[84] freely offered to us in the gospel.[85]**

32. Q. What benefits do they that are effectually called partake of in this life?
     A. **They that are effectually called do in this life partake of justification, adoption, and sanctification, and the several benefits which in this life do either accompany or flow from them.[86]**

---

[67] Psalm 110:3; Matthew 28:18-20; John 17:2; Colossians 1:13.
[68] Psalm 2:6-9, 110:1-2; Matthew 12:28; 1 Corinthians 15:24-26; Colossians 2:15.
[69] Luke 2:7; 2 Corinthians 8:9; Galatians 4:4.
[70] Galatians 4:4.
[71] Isaiah 53:3; Luke 9:58; John 4:6, 11:35; Hebrews 2:18.
[72] Psalm 22:1; Isaiah 53:10; Matthew 27:46; 1 John 2:2.
[73] Galatians 3:13; Philippians 2:8.
[74] Matthew 12:40; 1 Corinthians 15:3-4.
[75] 1 Corinthians 15:4.
[76] Psalm 68:18; Acts 1:11; Ephesians 4:8.
[77] Psalm 110:1; Acts 2:33-34; Hebrews 1:3.
[78] Matthew 16:27; Acts 17:31.
[79] Titus 3:4-7.
[80] Romans 10:17; 1 Corinthians 2:12-16; Ephesians 2:8; Philippians 1:29.
[81] John 15:5; 1 Corinthians 1:9; Ephesians 3:17.
[82] Acts 26:18; 1 Corinthians 2:10,12; 2 Corinthians 4:6; Ephesians 1:17-18.
[83] Deuteronomy 30:6; Ezekiel 36:26-27; John 3:5; Titus 3:5.
[84] John 6:44-45; Acts 16:14.
[85] Isaiah 45:22; Matthew 11:28-30; Revelation 22:17.
[86] Romans 8:30; 1 Corinthians 1:30, 6:11; Ephesians 1:5.

Questions 34 – 41

34. Q.   What is adoption?
     A.   **Adoption is an act of God's free grace,[87] whereby we are received into the number, and have a right to all the privileges, of the sons of God.[88]**

35. Q.   What is sanctification?
     A.   **Sanctification is the work of God's free grace,[89] whereby we are renewed in the whole man after the image of God,[90] and are enabled more and more to die unto sin, and live unto righteousness.[91]**

36. Q.   What are the benefits which in this life do accompany or flow from justification, adoption, and sanctification?
     A.   **The benefits which in this life do accompany or flow from justification, adoption, and sanctification, are, assurance of God's love,[92] peace of conscience,[93] joy in the Holy Ghost,[94] increase of grace,[95] and perseverance Therein to the end.[96]**

37. Q.   What benefits do believers receive from Christ at death?
     A.   **The souls of believers are at their death made perfect in holiness,[97] and do immediately pass into glory;[98] and their bodies, being still united to Christ,[99] do rest in their graves till the resurrection.[100]**

38. Q.   What benefits do believers receive from Christ at the resurrection?
     A.   **At the resurrection, believers being raised up in glory,[101] shall be openly acknowledged and acquitted in the Day of Judgment,[102] and made perfectly blessed in the full enjoying of God[103] to all eternity.[104]**

39. Q.   What is the duty which God requireth of man?
     A.   **The duty which God requireth of man, is obedience to his revealed will.[105]**

40. Q.   What did God at first reveal to man for the rule of his obedience?
     A.   **The rule which God at first revealed to man for his obedience, was the moral law.[106]**

41. Q.   Wherein is the moral law summarily comprehended?
     A.   **The moral law is summarily comprehended in the Ten Commandments.[107]**

---

[87] 1 John 3:1.
[88] John 1:12; Romans 8:17.
[89] Ezekiel 36:27; Philippians 2:13; 2 Thessalonians 2:13.
[90] 2 Corinthians 5:17; Ephesians 4:23-24; 1 Thessalonians 5:23.
[91] Ezekiel 36:25-27; Romans 6:4,6,12-14; 2 Corinthians 7:1; 1 Peter 2:24.
[92] Romans 5:5.
[93] Romans 5:1.
[94] Romans 14:17.
[95] 2 Peter 3:18.
[96] Philippians 1:6; 1 Peter 1:5.
[97] Hebrews 12:23.
[98] Luke 23:43; 2 Corinthians 5:6,8; Philippians 1:23.
[99] 1 Thessalonians 4:14.
[100] Daniel 12:2; John 5:28-29; Acts 24:15.
[101] 1 Corinthians 15:42-43.
[102] Matthew 25:33-34,46.
[103] Romans 8:29; 1 John 3:2.
[104] Psalm 16:11; 1 Thessalonians 4:17.
[105] Deuteronomy 29:29; Micah 6:8; 1 John 5:2-3.
[106] Romans 2:14-15; 10:5.
[107] Deuteronomy 4:13; Matthew 19:17-19.

Questions 42 – 50

42. **Q.** What is the sum of the Ten Commandments?
    A. The sum of the Ten Commandments is, to love the Lord our God with all our heart, with all our soul, with all our strength, and with all our mind; and our neighbour as ourselves.[108]

43. **Q.** What is the preface to the Ten Commandments?
    A. The preface to the Ten Commandments is in these words, I am the Lord thy God, which have brought thee out of the land of Egypt, out of the house of bondage.[109]

44. **Q.** What doth the preface to the Ten Commandments teach us?
    A. The preface to the Ten Commandments teacheth us, That because God is the Lord, and our God, and Redeemer, therefore we are bound to keep all his commandments.[110]

45. **Q.** Which is the first commandment?
    A. The first commandment is, Thou shalt have no other gods before me.[111]

46. **Q.** What is required in the first commandment?
    A. The first commandment requireth us to know and acknowledge God to be the only true God, and our God; and to worship and glorify him accordingly.[112]

47. **Q.** What is forbidden in the first commandment?
    A. The first commandment forbiddeth the denying,[113] or not worshipping and glorifying the true God as God,[114] and our God;[115] and the giving of that worship and glory to any other, which is due to him alone.[116]

48. **Q.** What are we specially taught by these words, "before me," in the first commandment?
    A. These words, before me, in the first commandment teach us, that God, who seeth all things, taketh notice of, and is much displeased with, the sin of having any other God.[117]

49. **Q.** Which is the second commandment?
    A. The second commandment is, Thou shalt not make unto thee any graven image, or any likeness of anything that is in heaven above, or that is in the earth beneath, or that is in the water under the earth: thou shalt not bow down thy self to them, nor serve them: for I the Lord thy God am a jealous God, visiting the iniquity of the fathers upon the children unto the third and fourth generation of them that hate me; and showing mercy unto thousands of them that love me, and keep my commandments.[118]

50. **Q.** What is required in the second commandment?
    A. The second commandment requireth the receiving, observing, and keeping pure and entire, all such religious worship and ordinances as God hath appointed in his Word.[119]

---

[108] Matthew 22:37-40.
[109] Exodus 20:2; Deuteronomy 5:6.
[110] Luke 1:74-75; 1 Peter 1:14-19.
[111] Exodus 20:3; Deuteronomy 5:7.
[112] 1 Chronicles 28:9; Isaiah 45:20-25; Matthew 4:10.
[113] Psalm 14:1.
[114] Romans 1:20-21.
[115] Psalm 81:10-11.
[116] Ezekiel 8:16-18; Romans 1:25.
[117] Deuteronomy 30:17-18; Psalm 44:20-21; Ezekiel 8:12.
[118] Exodus 20:4-6; Deuteronomy 5:8-10.
[119] Deuteronomy 12:32; Matthew 28:20.

Questions 51 – 58

51. Q.   What is forbidden in the second commandment?
    A.   **The second commandment forbiddeth the worshipping of God by images,[120] or any other way not appointed in his Word.[121]**

52. Q.   What are the reasons annexed to the second commandment?
    A.   **The reasons annexed to the second commandment are, God's sovereignty over us,[122] his propriety in us,[123] and the zeal he hath to his own worship.[124]**

53. Q.   Which is the third commandment?
    A.   **The third commandment is, Thou shalt not take the name of the Lord thy God in vain; for the Lord will not hold him guiltless that taketh his name in vain.[125]**

54. Q.   What is required in the third commandment?
    A.   **The third commandment requireth the holy and reverend use of God's names, titles,[126] attributes,[127] ordinances,[128] Word,[129] and works.[130]**

55. Q.   What is forbidden in the third commandment?
    A.   **The third commandment forbiddeth all profaning or abusing of anything whereby God maketh himself known.[131]**

56. Q.   What is the reason annexed to the third commandment?
    A.   **The reason annexed to the third commandment is, that however the breakers of this commandment may escape punishment from men, yet the Lord our God will not suffer them to escape his righteous judgment.[132]**

57. Q.   Which is the fourth commandment?
    A.   **The fourth commandment is, Remember the Sabbath day, to keep it holy. Six days shalt thou labor, and do all thy work; but the seventh day is the Sabbath of the Lord thy God: in it thou shalt not do any work, thou, nor thy son, nor thy daughter, thy manservant, nor thy maidservant, nor thy cattle, nor thy stranger that is within thy gates. For in six days the Lord made heaven and earth, the sea, and all that in them is, and rested the seventh day: wherefore the Lord blessed the Sabbath day, and hallowed it.[133]**

58. Q.   What is required in the fourth commandment?
    A.   **The fourth commandment requireth the keeping holy to God such set times as he hath appointed in his Word; expressly one whole day in seven, to be a holy Sabbath to himself.[134]**

---

[120] Deuteronomy 4:15-19; Romans 1:22-23.
[121] Leviticus 10:1-2; Jeremiah 19:4-5; Colossians 2:18-23.
[122] Psalm 95:2-3,6-7; 96:9-10.
[123] Exodus 19:5; Psalm 45:11; Isaiah 54:5.
[124] Exodus 34:14; 1 Corinthians 10:22.
[125] Exodus 20:7; Deuteronomy 5:11.
[126] Deuteronomy 10:20; Psalm 29:2; Matthew 6:9.
[127] 1 Chronicles 29:10-13; Revelation 15:3-4.
[128] Acts 2:42; 1 Corinthians 11:27-28.
[129] Psalm 138:2; Revelation 22:18-19.
[130] Psalm 107:21-22; Revelation 4:11.
[131] Leviticus 19:12; Matthew 5:33-37; James 5:12.
[132] Deuteronomy 28:58-59; 1 Samuel 3:13; 4:11.
[133] Exodus 20:8-11; Deuteronomy 5:12-15.
[134] Exodus 31:13,16-17.

Questions 59 – 67

59. Q. Which day of the seven hath God appointed to be the weekly Sabbath?
    A. **From the beginning of the world to the resurrection of Christ, God appointed the seventh day of the week to be the weekly Sabbath;[135] and the first day of the week ever since, to continue to the end of the world, which is the Christian Sabbath.[136]**

60. Q. How is the Sabbath to be sanctified?
    A. **The Sabbath is to be sanctified by a holy resting all that day, even from such worldly employments and recreations as are lawful on other days;[137] and spending the whole time in the public and private exercises of God's worship,[138] except so much as is to be taken up in the works of necessity and mercy.[139]**

61. Q. What is forbidden in the fourth commandment?
    A. **The fourth commandment forbiddeth the omission or careless performance of the duties required, and the profaning the day by idleness, or doing that which is in itself sinful, or by unnecessary thoughts, words, or works, about our worldly employments or recreations.[140]**

62. Q. What are the reasons annexed to the fourth commandment?
    A. **The reasons annexed to the fourth commandment are, God's allowing us six days of the week for our own employments,[141] his challenging a special propriety in the seventh, his own example, and his blessing the Sabbath day.[142]**

63. Q. Which is the fifth commandment?
    A. **The fifth commandment is, Honour thy father and thy mother; that thy days may be long upon the land which the Lord thy God giveth thee.[143]**

64. Q. What is required in the fifth commandment?
    A. **The fifth commandment requireth the preserving the honor, and performing the duties, belonging to everyone in their several places and relations, as superiors, inferiors, or equals.[144]**

65. Q. What is forbidden in the fifth commandment?
    A. **The fifth commandment forbiddeth the neglecting of, or doing anything against, the honor and duty which belongeth to everyone in their several places and relations.[145]**

66. Q. What is the reason annexed to the fifth commandment?
    A. **The reason annexed to the fifth commandment is, a promise of long life and prosperity (as far as it shall serve for God's glory and their own good) to all such as keep this commandment.[146]**

67. Q. Which is the sixth commandment?
    A. **The sixth commandment is, Thou shalt not kill.[147]**

---

[135] Genesis 2:2-3; Exodus 20:11.
[136] Mark 2:27-28; Acts 20:7; 1 Corinthians 16:2; Revelation 1:10.
[137] Exodus 20:10; Nehemiah 13:15-22; Isaiah 58:13-14.
[138] Exodus 20:8; Leviticus 23:3; Luke 4:16; Acts 20:7.
[139] Matthew 12:1-13.
[140] Nehemiah 13:15-22; Isaiah 58:13-14; Amos 8:4-6.
[141] Exodus 20:9; 31:15; Leviticus 23:3.
[142] Genesis 2:2-3; Exodus 20:11, 31:17.
[143] Exodus 20:12; Deuteronomy 5:16.
[144] Romans 13:1,7; Ephesians 5:21-22,24, 6:1,4-5,9; 1 Peter 2:17.
[145] Matthew 15:4-6; Romans 13:8.
[146] Exodus 20:12; Deuteronomy 5:16; Ephesians 6:2-3.
[147] Exodus 20:13; Deuteronomy 5:17.

Questions 68 – 78

68. Q. What is required in the sixth commandment?
    A. **The sixth commandment requireth all lawful endeavors to preserve our own life, and the life of others.**[148]

69. Q. What is forbidden in the sixth commandment?
    A. **The sixth commandment forbiddeth the taking away of our own life, or the life of our neighbour, unjustly, or whatsoever tendeth thereunto.**[149]

70. Q. Which is the seventh commandment?
    A. **The seventh commandment is, Thou shalt not commit adultery.**[150]

71. Q. What is required in the seventh commandment?
    A. **The seventh commandment requireth the preservation of our own and our neighbor's chastity, in heart, speech, and behavior.**[151]

72. Q. What is forbidden in the seventh commandment?
    A. **The seventh commandment forbiddeth all unchaste thoughts, words, and actions.**[152]

73. Q. Which is the eighth commandment?
    A. **The eighth commandment is, Thou shalt not steal.**[153]

74. Q. What is required in the eighth commandment?
    A. **The eighth commandment requireth the lawful procuring and furthering the wealth and outward estate of ourselves and others.**[154]

75. Q. What is forbidden in the eighth commandment?
    A. **The eighth commandment forbiddeth whatsoever doth, or may, unjustly hinder our own, or our neighbor's, wealth or outward estate.**[155]

76. Q. Which is the ninth commandment?
    A. **The ninth commandment is, Thou shalt not bear false witness against thy neighbour.**[156]

77. Q. What is required in the ninth commandment?
    A. **The ninth commandment requireth the maintaining and promoting of truth between man and man, and of our own and our neighbor's good name,**[157] **especially in witness bearing.**[158]

78. Q. What is forbidden in the ninth commandment?
    A. **The ninth commandment forbiddeth whatsoever is prejudicial to truth, or injurious to our own, or our neighbor's, good name.**[159]

---

[148] Ephesians 5:28-29.
[149] Genesis 9:6; Matthew 5:22; 1 John 3:15.
[150] Exodus 20:14; Deuteronomy 5:18.
[151] 1 Corinthians 7:2-3,5; 1 Thessalonians 4:3-5.
[152] Matthew 5:28; Ephesians 5:3-4.
[153] Exodus 20:15; Deuteronomy 5:19.
[154] Leviticus 25:35; Ephesians 4:28b; Philippians 2:4.
[155] Proverbs 28:19ff; Ephesians 4:28a; 2 Thessalonians 3:10; 1 Timothy 5:8.
[156] Exodus 20:16; Deuteronomy 5:20.
[157] Zechariah 8:16; Acts 25:10; 2 John 12.
[158] Proverbs 14:5,25.
[159] Leviticus 19:16; Psalm 15:3; Proverb 6:16-19; Luke 3:14.

Questions 79 – 86

79. Q. Which is the tenth commandment?
    A. **The tenth commandment is, Thou shalt not covet thy neighbor's house, thou shalt not covet thy neighbor's wife, nor his manservant, nor his maidservant, nor his ox, nor his ass, nor anything that is thy neighbor's.**[160]

80. Q. What is required in the tenth commandment?
    A. **The tenth commandment requireth full contentment with our own condition,[161] with a right and charitable frame of spirit toward our neighbour, and all that is his.**[162]

81. Q. What is forbidden in the tenth commandment?
    A. **The tenth commandment forbiddeth all discontentment with our own estate,[163] envying or grieving at the good of our neighbour, and all inordinate motions and affections to anything that is his.**[164]

82. Q. Is any man able perfectly to keep the commandments of God?
    A. **No mere man, since the fall, is able in this life perfectly to keep the commandments of God, but doth daily break them in thought, word, and deed.**[165]

83. Q. Are all transgressions of the law equally heinous?
    A. **Some sins in themselves, and by reason of several aggravations, are more heinous in the sight of God than others.**[166]

84. Q. What doth every sin deserve?
    A. **Every sin deserveth God's wrath and curse, both in this life, and that which is to come.**[167]

85. Q. What doth God require of us, that we may escape his wrath and curse, due to us for sin?
    A. **To escape the wrath and curse of God, due to us for sin, God requireth of us faith in Jesus Christ, repentance unto life,[168] with the diligent use of all the outward means whereby Christ communicateth to us the benefits of redemption.**[169]

86. Q. What is faith in Jesus Christ?
    A. **Faith in Jesus Christ is a saving grace,[170] whereby we receive and rest upon him alone for salvation, as he is offered to us in the gospel.**[171]

---

[160] Exodus 20:17; Deuteronomy 5:21.
[161] Psalm 34:1; Philippians 4:11; 1 Timothy 6:6; Hebrews 13:5.
[162] Luke 15:6,9,11-32; Romans 12:15; Philippians 2:4.
[163] 1 Corinthians 10:10; James 3:14-16.
[164] Galatians 5:26; Colossians 3:5.
[165] Genesis 8:21; Romans 3:9ff,23.
[166] Ezekiel 8:6,13,15; Matthew 11:20-24; John 19:11.
[167] Matthew 25:41; Galatians 3:10; Ephesians 5:6; James 2:10.
[168] Mark 1:15; Acts 20:21.
[169] Acts 2:38; 1 Corinthians 11:24-25; Colossians 3:16.
[170] Ephesians 2:8-9; cf. Romans 4:16.
[171] John 20:30-31; Galatians 2:15-16; Philippians 3:3-11.

Questions 87 – 94

87.   Q.   What is repentance unto life?
     A.   **Repentance unto life is a saving grace,[172] whereby a sinner, out of a true sense of his sin, and apprehension of the mercy of God in Christ,[173] doth, with grief and hatred of his sin, turn from it unto God,[174] with full purpose of, and endeavour after, new obedience.[175]**

88.   Q.   What are the outward and ordinary means whereby Christ communicateth to us the benefits of redemption?
     A.   **The outward and ordinary means whereby Christ communicateth to us the benefits of redemption are, his ordinances, especially the Word, sacraments, and prayer; all which are made effectual to the elect for salvation.[176]**

89.   Q.   How is the Word made effectual to salvation?
     A.   **The Spirit of God maketh the reading, but especially the preaching of the Word, an effectual means of convincing and converting sinners, and of building them up in holiness and comfort, through faith, unto salvation.[177]**

90.   Q.   How is the Word to be read and heard, that it may become effectual to salvation?
     A.   **That the Word may become effectual to salvation, we must attend thereunto with diligence, preparation, and prayer;[178] receive it with faith and love, lay it up in our hearts, and practice it in our lives.[179]**

91.   Q.   How do the sacraments become effectual means of salvation?
     A.   **The sacraments become effectual means of salvation, not from any virtue in them, or in him that doth administer them; but only by the blessing of Christ, and the working of his Spirit in them that by faith receive them.[180]**

92.   Q.   What is a sacrament?
     A.   **A sacrament is an holy ordinance instituted by Christ;[181] wherein, by sensible signs, Christ, and the benefits of the new covenant, are represented, sealed, and applied to believers.[182]**

93.   Q.   Which are the sacraments of the New Testament?
     A.   **The sacraments of the New Testament are, Baptism,[183] and the Lord's Supper.[184]**

94.   Q.   What is Baptism?
     A.   **Baptism is a sacrament, wherein the washing with water in the name of the Father, and of the Son, and of the Holy Ghost,[185] doth signify and seal our ingrafting into Christ, and partaking of the benefits of the covenant of grace, and our engagement to be the Lord's.[186]**

---

[172] Acts 11:18; 2 Timothy 2:25.
[173] Psalm 51:1-4; Joel 2:13; Luke 15:7,10; Acts 2:37.
[174] Jeremiah 31:18-19; Luke 1:16-17; 1 Thessalonians 1:9.
[175] 2 Chronicles 7:14; Psalm 119:57-64; Matthew 3:8; 2 Corinthians 7:10.
[176] Matthew 28:18-20; Acts 21:41-42.
[177] Nehemiah 8:8-9; Acts 20:32; Romans 10:14-17; 2 Timothy 3:15-17.
[178] Deuteronomy 6:6ff; Psalm 119:18; 1 Peter 2:1-2.
[179] Psalm 119:11; 2 Thessalonians 2:10; Hebrews 4:2; James 1:22-25.
[180] 1 Corinthians 3:7; cf. 1 Corinthians 1:12-17.
[181] Matthew 26:26-28, 28:19; Mark 14:22-25; Luke 22:19-20; 1 Corinthians 1:22-26.
[182] Galatians 3:27; 1 Corinthians 10:16-17.
[183] Matthew 28:19.
[184] 1 Corinthians 11:23-26.
[185] Matthew 28:19.
[186] Acts 2:38-42; 22:16; Romans 6:3-4; Galatians 3:26-27; 1 Peter 3:21.

Questions 95 – 101

95. Q. To whom is Baptism to be administered?
    A. **Baptism is not to be administered to any that are out of the visible church, till they profess their faith in Christ, and obedience to him;[187] but the infants of such as are members of the visible church are to be baptized.[188]**

96. Q. What is the Lord's Supper?
    A. **The Lord's Supper is a sacrament, wherein, by giving and receiving bread and wine, according to Christ's appointment, his death is showed forth;[189] and the worthy receivers are, not after a corporal and carnal manner, but by faith, made partakers of his body and blood, with all his benefits, to their spiritual nourishment, and growth in grace.[190]**

97. Q. What is required for the worthy receiving of the Lord's Supper?
    A. **It is required of them that would worthily partake of the Lord's Supper, that they examine themselves of their knowledge to discern the Lord's body, of their faith to feed upon him, of their repentance, love, and new obedience; lest, coming unworthily, they eat and drink judgment to themselves.[191]**

98. Q. What is prayer?
    A. **Prayer is an offering up of our desires unto God,[192] for things agreeable to his will,[193] in the name of Christ,[194] with confession of our sins,[195] and thankful acknowledgement of his mercies.[196]**

99. Q. What rule hath God given for our direction in prayer?
    A. **The whole Word of God is of use to direct us in prayer;[197] but the special rule of direction is that form of prayer which Christ taught his disciples, commonly called The Lord's Prayer.[198]**

100. Q. What doth the preface of the Lord's Prayer teach us?
    A. **The preface of the Lord's Prayer, which is, Our Father which art in heaven, teacheth us to draw near to God with all holy reverence[199] and confidence,[200] as children to a father,[201] able and ready to help us;[202] and that we should pray with and for others.[203]**

101. Q. What do we pray for in the first petition?
    A. **In the first petition, which is, Hallowed be thy name, we pray, that God would enable us, and others, to glorify him in all that whereby he maketh himself known;[204] and that he would dispose all things to his own glory.[205]**

---

[187] Acts. 2:41; 8:12,36,38; 18:8.
[188] Genesis 17:7,9-11; Acts 2:38-39, 16:32-33; Colossians 2:11-12.
[189] Luke 22:19-20; 1 Corinthians 11:23-26.
[190] 1 Corinthians 10:16-17.
[191] 1 Corinthians 11:27-32.
[192] Psalm 10:17, 62:8; Matthew 7:7-8.
[193] 1 John 5:14.
[194] John 16:23-24.
[195] Psalm 32:5-6; Daniel 9:4-19; 1 John 1:9.
[196] Psalm 103:1-5,136; Philippians 4:6.
[197] 1 John 5:14.
[198] Matthew 6:9-13.
[199] Psalm 95:6.
[200] Ephesians 3:12.
[201] Matthew 7:9-11, cf. Luke 11:11-13; Romans 8:15.
[202] Ephesians 3:20.
[203] Ephesians 6:18; 1 Timothy 2:1-2.
[204] Psalm 67:1-3, 99:3, 100:3-4.
[205] Romans 11:33-36; Revelation 4:11.

Questions 102 – 107

102. Q.   What do we pray for in the second petition?
   A.   **In the second petition, which is, Thy kingdom come, we pray, that Satan's kingdom may be destroyed;[206] and that the kingdom of grace may be advanced,[207] ourselves and others brought into it, and kept in it;[208] and that the kingdom of glory may be hastened.[209]**

103. Q.   What do we pray for in the third petition?
   A.   **In the third petition, which is, Thy will be done in earth, as it is in heaven, we pray, that God, by his grace, would make us able and willing to know, obey, and submit to his will in all things,[210] as the angels do in heaven.[211]**

104. Q.   What do we pray for in the fourth petition?
   A.   **In the fourth petition, which is, Give us this day our daily bread, we pray that of God's free gift we may receive a competent portion of the good things of this life, and enjoy his blessing with them.[212]**

105. Q.   What do we pray for in the fifth petition?
   A.   **In the fifth petition, which is, And forgive us our debts, as we forgive our debtors, we pray that God, for Christ's sake, would freely pardon all our sins;[213] which we are the rather encouraged to ask, because by his grace we are enabled from the heart to forgive others.[214]**

106. Q.   What do we pray for in the sixth petition?
   A.   **In the sixth petition, which is, And lead us not into temptation, but deliver us from evil, we pray, that God would either keep us from being tempted to sin,[215] or support and deliver us when we are tempted.[216]**

107. Q.   What doth the conclusion of the Lord's Prayer teach us?
   A.   **The conclusion of the Lord's Prayer, which is, For Thine is the kingdom, and the power, and the glory, forever, Amen. teacheth us to take our encouragement in prayer from God only,[217] and in our prayers to praise him, ascribing kingdom, power, and glory to him;[218] and, in testimony of our desire, and assurance to be heard, we say, Amen.[219]**

---

[206] Matthew 12:25-28; Romans 16:20; 1 John 3:8.

[207] Psalm 72:8-11; Matthew 24:14; 1 Corinthians 15:24-25.

[208] Psalm 119:5; Luke 22:32; 2 Thessalonians 3:1-5.

[209] Revelation 22:20.

[210] Psalm 19:14, 119; 1 Thessalonians 5:23; Hebrews 13:20-21.

[211] Psalm 103:20-21; Hebrews 1:14.

[212] Proverbs 30:8-9; Matthew 6:31-34; Philippians 4:11,19; 1 Timothy 6:6-8.

[213] Psalm 51:1-2,7,9; Daniel 9:17-19; 1 John 1:7.

[214] Matthew 18:21-35; Ephesians 4:32; Colossians 3:13.

[215] Psalm 19:13; Matthew 26:41; John 17:15.

[216] Luke 22:31-32; 1 Corinthians 10:13; 2 Corinthians 12:7-9; Hebrews 2:18.

[217] Daniel 9:4,7-9,16-19; Luke 18:1,7-8.

[218] 1 Chronicles 29:10-13; 1 Timothy 1:17; Revelation 5:11-13.

[219] 1 Corinthians 14:16; Revelation 22:20.

Notes

Westminster Larger Catechism
Questions 1 – 6

1. Q. What is the chief and highest end of man?
    A. **Man's chief and highest end is to glorify God,[1] and fully to enjoy him forever.[2]**

2. Q. How doth it appear that there is a God?
    A. **The very light of nature in man, and the works of God, declare plainly that there is a God;[3] but his word and Spirit only do sufficiently and effectually reveal him unto men for their salvation.[4]**

3. Q. What is the Word of God?
    A. **The holy Scriptures of the Old and New Testament are the Word of God,[5] the only rule of faith and obedience.[6]**

4. Q. How doth it appear that the Scriptures are the Word of God?
    A. **The Scriptures manifest themselves to be the Word of God, by their majesty[7] and purity;[8] by the consent of all the parts,[9] and the scope of the whole, which is to give all glory to God;[10] by their light and power to convince and convert sinners, to comfort and build up believers unto salvation:[11] but the Spirit of God bearing witness by and with the Scriptures in the heart of man, is alone able fully to persuade it that they are the very word of God.[12]**

5. Q. What do the Scriptures principally teach?
    A. **The Scriptures principally teach, what man is to believe concerning God, and what duty God requires of man.[13]**

What Man Ought to Believe Concerning God

6. Q. What do the Scriptures make known of God?
    A. **The Scriptures make known what God is,[14] the persons in the Godhead,[15] his decrees,[16] and the execution of his decrees.[17]**

---

[1] Romans 11:36; 1 Corinthians 10:31.

[2] Psalm 73:24-28; John 17:21-23.

[3] Psalm 19:1-3; Acts 17:28; Romans 1:19-20.

[4] Isaiah 59:21; 1 Corinthians 2:9-10; 2 Timothy 3:15-17.

[5] 2 Timothy 3:16; 2 Peter 1:19-21.

[6] Isaiah 8:20; Luke 16: 29,31; Galatians 1:8-9; Ephesians 2:20; 2 Timothy 3:15-16; Revelation 22:18-19.

[7] Psalm 119:18,129; Hosea 8:12; 1 Corinthians 2:6-7,13.

[8] Psalm 12:6, 119:140.

[9] Acts 10:43, 26:22.

[10] Romans 3:19,27.

[11] Psalm 19:7-9; Acts 18:28, 20:32; Romans 15:4; Hebrews 4:12; James 1:18.

[12] John 16:13-14, 20:31; 1 John 2:20,27.

[13] 2 Timothy 1:13.

[14] Hebrews 11:6.

[15] 1 John 5:7.

[16] Acts 15:14-15,18.

[17] Acts 4:27-28.

Questions 7 – 12

7. Q. What is God?
    A. **God is a Spirit,[18] in and of himself infinite in being,[19] glory,[20] blessedness,[21] and perfection;[22] all-sufficient,[23] eternal,[24] unchangeable,[25] incomprehensible,[26] every where present,[27] almighty,[28] knowing all things,[29] most wise,[30] most holy,[31] most just,[32] most merciful and gracious, long-suffering, and abundant in goodness and truth.[33]**

8. Q. Are there more Gods than one?
    A. **There is but one only, the living and true God.[34]**

9. Q. How many persons are there in the Godhead?
    A. **There be three persons in the Godhead, the Father, the Son, and the Holy Ghost; and these three are one true, eternal God, the same in substance, equal in power and glory; although distinguished by their personal properties.[35]**

10. Q. What are the personal properties of the three persons in the Godhead?
    A. **It is proper to the Father to beget the Son,[36] and to the Son to be begotten of the Father,[37] and to the Holy Ghost to proceed from the Father and the Son from all eternity.[38]**

11. Q. How does it appear that the Son and the Holy Ghost are God equal with the Father?
    A. **The Scriptures manifest that the Son and the Holy Ghost are God equal with the Father, ascribing unto them such names,[39] attributes,[40] works,[41] and worship,[42] as are proper to God only.**

12. Q. What are the decrees of God?
    A. **God's decrees are the wise, free, and holy acts of the counsel of his will,[43] whereby, from all eternity, he hath, for his own glory, unchangeably foreordained whatsoever comes to pass in time,[44] especially concerning angels and men.**

---

[18] John 4:24.

[19] Exodus 3:14; Job 11:7-9.

[20] Acts 7:2.

[21] 1 Timothy 6:15.

[22] Matthew 5:48.

[23] Genesis 17:1.

[24] Psalm 90:2.

[25] Malachi 3:6; James 1:17.

[26] 1 Kings 8:27.

[27] Psalm 139:1-13.

[28] Revelation 4:8.

[29] Hebrews 4:13.

[30] Romans 16:27.

[31] Isaiah 6:3; Revelation 15:4.

[32] Deuteronomy 32:4.

[33] Exodus 34:6.

[34] Deuteronomy 6:4; Jeremiah 10:10; 1 Corinthians 8:4,6.

[35] Matthew 3:16-17, 28:19; John 10:30; 2 Corinthians 13:14; 1 John 5:7.

[36] Hebrews 1:5-6,8.

[37] John 1:14,18.

[38] John 15:26; Galatians 4:6.

[39] Isaiah 6:3,5,8; John 12:41; Acts 5:3-4, 28:25; 1 John 5:20.

[40] Isaiah 9:6; John 1:1, 2:24-25; 1 Corinthians 2:10-11.

[41] Genesis 1:2; Colossians 1:16.

[42] Matthew 28:19; 2 Corinthians 13:14.

[43] Romans 9:14-15,18, 11:33; Ephesians 1:11.

[44] Psalm 33:11; Romans 9:22-23; Ephesians 1:4,11.

Questions 13 – 17

13. Q. What hath God especially decreed concerning angels and men?
    A. God, by an eternal and immutable decree, out of his mere love, for the praise of his glorious grace, to be manifested in due time, hath elected some angels to glory;[45] and in Christ hath chosen some men to eternal life, and the means thereof:[46] and also, according to his sovereign power, and the unsearchable counsel of his own will, (whereby he extendeth or withholdeth favor as he pleaseth,) hath passed by and foreordained the rest to dishonor and wrath, to be for their sin inflicted, to the praise of the glory of his justice.[47]

14. Q. How doth God execute his decrees?
    A. God executeth his decrees in the works of creation and providence, according to his infallible foreknowledge, and the free and immutable counsel of his own will.[48]

15. Q. What is the work of creation?
    A. The work of creation is that wherein God did in the beginning, by the word of his power, make of nothing the world, and all things therein, for himself, within the space of six days, and all very good.[49]

16. Q. How did God create angels?
    A. God created all the angels[50] spirits,[51] immortal,[52] holy,[53] excelling in knowledge,[54] mighty in power,[55] to execute his commandments, and to praise his name,[56] yet subject to change.[57]

17. Q. How did God create man?
    A. After God had made all other creatures, he created man male and female;[58] formed the body of the man of the dust of the ground,[59] and the woman of the rib of the man,[60] endued them with living, reasonable, and immortal souls;[61] made them after his own image,[62] in knowledge,[63] righteousness, and holiness;[64] having the law of God written in their hearts,[65] and power to fulfill it,[66] and dominion over the creatures;[67] yet subject to fall.[68]

---

[45] 1 Timothy 5:21.
[46] Ephesians 1:4-6; 2 Thessalonians 2:13-14.
[47] Matthew 11:25-26; Romans 9:17-18,21-22; 2 Timothy 2:20; 1 Peter 2:8; Jude 4.
[48] Ephesians 1:11.
[49] Genesis 1:1-31; Proverbs 16:4; Hebrews 11:3.
[50] Colossians 1:16.
[51] Psalm 104:4.
[52] Matthew 22:30.
[53] Matthew 25:31.
[54] 2 Samuel 14:17; Matthew 24:36.
[55] 2 Thessalonians 1:7.
[56] Psalm 103:20-21.
[57] 2 Peter 2:4.
[58] Genesis 1:27.
[59] Genesis 2:7.
[60] Genesis 2:22.
[61] Genesis 2:7; Job 35:11; Ecclesiastes 12:7; Matthew 10:28; Luke 23:43.
[62] Genesis 1:27.
[63] Colossians 3:10.
[64] Ephesians 4:24.
[65] Romans 2:14-15.
[66] Ecclesiastes 7:29.
[67] Genesis 1:28.
[68] Genesis 3:6; Ecclesiastes 7:29.

Questions 18 – 23

18. Q. What are God's works of providence?
    A. **God's works of providence are his most holy,[69] wise,[70] and powerful preserving[71] and governing[72] all his creatures; ordering them, and all their actions,[73] to his own glory.[74]**

19. Q. What is God's providence towards the angels?
    A. **God by his providence permitted some of the angels, willfully and irrecoverably, to fall into sin and damnation,[75] limiting and ordering that, and all their sins, to his own glory;[76] and established the rest in holiness and happiness;[77] employing them all,[78] at his pleasure, in the administrations of his power, mercy, and justice.[79]**

20. Q. What was the providence of God toward man in the estate in which he was created?
    A. **The providence of God toward man in the estate in which he was created, was the placing him in paradise, appointing him to dress it, giving him liberty to eat of the fruit of the earth;[80] putting the creatures under his dominion,[81] and ordaining marriage for his help;[82] affording him communion with himself;[83] instituting the Sabbath;[84] entering into a covenant of life with him, upon condition of personal, perfect, and perpetual obedience,[85] of which the tree of life was a pledge;[86] and forbidding to eat of the tree of knowledge of good and evil, upon the pain of death.[87]**

21. Q. Did man continue in that estate wherein God at first created him?
    A. **Our first parents being left to the freedom of their own will, through the temptation of Satan, transgressed the commandment of God in eating the forbidden fruit; and thereby fell from the estate of innocency wherein they were created.[88]**

22. Q. Did all mankind fall in that first transgression?
    A. **The covenant being made with Adam as a public person, not for himself only, but for his posterity, all mankind descending from him by ordinary generation,[89] sinned in him, and fell with him in that first transgression.[90]**

23. Q. Into what estate did the fall bring mankind?
    A. **The fall brought mankind into an estate of sin and misery.[91]**

---

[69] Psalm 145:17.
[70] Psalm 104:24; Isaiah 28:29.
[71] Hebrews 1:3.
[72] Psalm 103:19.
[73] Genesis 45:7; Matthew 10:29-31.
[74] Isaiah 63:14; Romans 11:36.
[75] John 8:44; Hebrews 2:16; 2 Peter 2:4; Jude 6.
[76] Job 1:12; Matthew 8:31.
[77] Mark 8:38; 1 Timothy 5:21; Hebrews 12:22.
[78] Psalm 104:4.
[79] 2 Kings 19:35; Hebrews 1:14.
[80] Genesis 2:8,15-16.
[81] Genesis 1:28.
[82] Genesis 2:18.
[83] Genesis 1:26-29, 3:8.
[84] Genesis 2:3.
[85] Romans 10:5; Galatians 3:12.
[86] Genesis 2:9.
[87] Genesis 2:17.
[88] Genesis 3:6-8,13; Ecclesiastes 7:29; 2 Corinthians 11:3.
[89] Acts 17:26.
[90] Genesis 2:16-17; Romans 5:12-20; 1 Corinthians 15:21-22.
[91] Romans 5:12, 3:23.

Questions 24 – 29

24. Q. What is sin?
    A. Sin is any want of conformity unto, or transgression of, any law of God, given as a rule to the reasonable creature.[92]

25. Q. Wherein consisteth the sinfulness of that estate whereinto man fell?
    A. The sinfulness of that estate whereinto man fell, consisteth in the guilt of Adam's first sin,[93] the want of that righteousness wherein he was created, and the corruption of his nature, whereby he is utterly indisposed, disabled, and made opposite unto all that is spiritually good, and wholly inclined to all evil, and that continually;[94] which is commonly called original sin, and from which do proceed all actual transgressions.[95]

26. Q. How is original sin conveyed from our first parents unto their posterity?
    A. Original sin is conveyed from our first parents unto their posterity by natural generation, so as all that proceed from them in that way are conceived and born in sin.[96]

27. Q. What misery did the fall bring upon mankind?
    A. The fall brought upon mankind the loss of communion with God,[97] his displeasure and curse; so as we are by nature children of wrath,[98] bond slaves to Satan,[99] and justly liable to all punishments in this world, and that which is to come.[100]

28. Q. What are the punishments of sin in this world?
    A. The punishments of sin in this world are either inward, as blindness of mind,[101] a reprobate sense,[102] strong delusions,[103] hardness of heart,[104] horror of conscience,[105] and vile affections;[106] or outward, as the curse of God upon the creatures of our sakes,[107] and all other evils that befall us in our bodies, names, estates, relations, and employments;[108] together with death itself.[109]

29. Q. What are the punishments of sin in the world to come?
    A. The punishments of sin in the world to come, are everlasting separation from the comfortable presence of God, and most grievous torments in soul and body, without intermission, in hell-fire forever.[110]

---

[92] Galatians 3:10,12; 1 John 3:4.
[93] Romans 5:12,19.
[94] Genesis 6:5; Romans 3:10-19, 5:6, 8:7-8; Ephesians 2:1-3.
[95] Matthew 15:19; James 1:14-15.
[96] Job 14:4; Psalm 51:5; John 3:6.
[97] Genesis 3:8,10,24.
[98] Ephesians 2:2-3.
[99] 2 Timothy 2:26.
[100] Genesis 2:17; Lamentations 3:39; Matthew 25:41,46; Romans 6:23; Jude 7.
[101] Ephesians 4:18.
[102] Romans 1:28.
[103] 2 Thessalonians 2:11.
[104] Romans 2:5.
[105] Genesis 4:13; Isaiah 33:14; Matthew 27:4.
[106] Romans 1:26.
[107] Genesis 3:17.
[108] Deuteronomy 28:15-18.
[109] Romans 6:21,23.
[110] Mark 9:43-44,46,48; Luke 16:24; 2 Thessalonians 1:9.

Questions 30 – 34

30. Q. Doth God leave all mankind to perish in the estate of sin and misery?
    A. **God doth not leave all men to perish in the estate of sin and misery,**[111] **into which they fell by the breach of the first covenant, commonly called the covenant of works;**[112] **but of his mere love and mercy delivereth his elect out of it, and bringeth them into an estate of salvation by the second covenant, commonly called the covenant of grace.**[113]

31. Q. With whom was the covenant of grace made?
    A. **The covenant of grace was made with Christ as the second Adam, and in him with all the elect as his seed.**[114]

32. Q. How is the grace of God manifested in the second covenant?
    A. **The grace of God is manifested in the second covenant, in that he freely provideth and offereth to sinners a Mediator,**[115] **and life and salvation by him;**[116] **and requiring faith as the condition to interest them in him,**[117] **promiseth and giveth his Holy Spirit**[118] **to all his elect, to work in them that faith,**[119] **with all other saving graces;**[120] **and to enable them unto all holy obedience,**[121] **as the evidence of the truth of their faith**[122] **and thankfulness to God,**[123] **and as the way which he hath appointed them to salvation.**[124]

33. Q. Was the covenant of grace always administered after one and the same manner?
    A. **The covenant of grace was not always administered after the same manner, but the administrations of it under the Old Testament were different from those under the New.**[125]

34. Q. How was the covenant of grace administered under the Old Testament?
    A. **The covenant of grace was administered under the Old Testament, by promises,**[126] **prophecies,**[127] **sacrifices,**[128] **circumcision,**[129] **the Passover,**[130] **and other types and ordinances, which did all fore-signify Christ then to come, and were for that time sufficient to build up the elect in faith in the promised Messiah,**[131] **by whom they then had full remission of sin, and eternal salvation.**[132]

---

[111] 1 Thessalonians 5:9.
[112] Galatians 3:10,12.
[113] Romans 3:20-22; Galatians 3:21; Titus 3:4-7.
[114] Isaiah 53:10-11; Romans 5:15-21; Galatians 3:16.
[115] Genesis 3:15; John 6:27.
[116] 1 John 5:11-12.
[117] John 1:12, 3:16.
[118] Proverbs 1:23.
[119] 2 Corinthians 4:13.
[120] Galatians 5:22-23.
[121] Ezekiel 36:27.
[122] James 2:18,22.
[123] 2 Corinthians 5:14-15.
[124] Ephesians 2:18.
[125] 2 Corinthians 3:6-9.
[126] Romans 15:8.
[127] Acts 3:20,24.
[128] Hebrews 10:1.
[129] Romans 4:11.
[130] 1 Corinthians 5:7.
[131] Hebrews 8:1,9-10, 11:13.
[132] Galatians 3:7-9,14.

Questions 35 – 39

35. Q. How is the covenant of grace administered under the New Testament?

A. **Under the New Testament, when Christ the substance was exhibited, the same covenant of grace was and still is to be administered in the preaching of the Word,[133] and the administration of the sacraments of Baptism[134] and the Lord's Supper;[135] in which grace and salvation are held forth in more fulness, evidence, and efficacy, to all nations.[136]**

36. Q. Who is the mediator of the covenant of grace?

A. **The only Mediator of the covenant of grace is the Lord Jesus Christ,[137] who, being the eternal Son of God, of one substance and equal with the Father,[138] in the fullness of time became man,[139] and so was and continues to be God and man, in two entire distinct natures, and one person, forever.[140]**

37. Q. How did Christ, being the Son of God, become man?

A. **Christ the Son of God became man, by taking to himself a true body, and a reasonable soul,[141] being conceived by the power of the Holy Ghost in the womb of the Virgin Mary, of her substance, and born of her,[142] yet without sin.[143]**

38. Q. Why was it requisite that the mediator should be God?

A. **It was requisite that the Mediator should be God, that he might sustain and keep the human nature from sinking under the infinite wrath of God, and the power of death,[144] give worth and efficacy to his sufferings, obedience, and intercession;[145] and to satisfy God's justice,[146] procure his favour,[147] purchase a peculiar people,[148] give his Spirit to them,[149] conquer all their enemies,[150] and bring them to everlasting salvation.[151]**

39. Q. Why was it requisite that the mediator should be man?

A. **It was requisite that the Mediator should be man, that he might advance our nature,[152] perform obedience to the law,[153] suffer and make intercession for us in our nature,[154] have a fellow-feeling of our infirmities;[155] that we might receive the adoption of sons,[156] and have comfort and access with boldness unto the throne of grace.[157]**

---

[133] Mark 16:15.
[134] Matthew 28:19-20.
[135] 1 Corinthians 11:23-25.
[136] Matthew 28:19; 2 Corinthians 3:6-9; Hebrews 8:6, 10-11.
[137] 1 Timothy 2:5.
[138] John 1:1,14, 10:30; Philippians 2:6.
[139] Galatians 4:4.
[140] Luke 1:35; Romans 9:5; Colossians 2:9; Hebrews 7:24-25.
[141] John 1:14; Matthew 26:38.
[142] Luke 1:27,31,35,42; Galatians 4:4.
[143] Hebrews 4:15, 7:26.
[144] Acts 2:24-25; Romans 1:4, 4:25; Hebrews 9:14.
[145] Acts 20:28; Hebrews 7:25-28, 9:14.
[146] Romans 3:24-26.
[147] Matthew 3:17; Ephesians 1:6.
[148] Titus 2:13-14.
[149] Galatians 4:6.
[150] Luke 1:68-69,71,74.
[151] Hebrews 5:8-9, 9:11-15.
[152] Hebrews 2:16.
[153] Galatians 4:4.
[154] Hebrews 2:14, 7:24-25.
[155] Hebrews 4:15.
[156] Galatians 4:5.
[157] Hebrews 4:16.

Questions 40 – 45

40. Q. Why was it requisite that the mediator should be God and man in one person?
    A. **It was requisite that the Mediator, who was to reconcile God and man, should himself be both God and man, and this in one person, that the proper works of each nature might be accepted of God for us,[158] and relied on by us as the works of the whole person.[159]**

41. Q. Why was our mediator called Jesus?
    A. **Our Mediator was called Jesus, because he saveth his people from their sins.[160]**

42. Q. Why was our mediator called Christ?
    A. **Our Mediator was called Christ, because he was anointed with the Holy Ghost above measure,[161] and so set apart, and fully furnished with all authority and ability,[162] to execute the offices of prophet,[163] priest,[164] and king of his church,[165] in the estate both of his humiliation and exaltation.**

43. Q. How doth Christ execute the office of a prophet?
    A. **Christ executeth the office of a prophet, in his revealing to the church,[166] in all ages, by his Spirit and Word,[167] in divers ways of administration,[168] the whole will of God,[169] in all things concerning their edification and salvation.[170]**

44. Q. How doth Christ execute the office of a priest?
    A. **Christ executeth the office of a priest, in his once offering himself a sacrifice without spot to God,[171] to be reconciliation for the sins of his people;[172] and in making continual intercession for them.[173]**

45. Q. How doth Christ execute the office of a king?
    A. **Christ executeth the office of a king, in calling out of the world a people to himself,[174] and giving them officers,[175] laws,[176] and censures, by which he visibly governs them;[177] in bestowing saving grace upon his elect,[178] rewarding their obedience,[179] and correcting them for their sins,[180] preserving and supporting them under all their temptations and sufferings,[181] restraining and overcoming all their enemies,[182] and**

---

[158] Matthew 1:21,23, 3:17; Hebrews 9:14.

[159] 1 Peter 2:6.

[160] Matthew 1:21.

[161] Psalm 45:7; John 3:34.

[162] Matthew 28:18-20; John 6:27.

[163] Luke 4:18,21; Acts 3:21-22.

[164] Hebrews 4:14-15, 5:5-7.

[165] Psalm 2:6; Isaiah 9:6-7; Matthew 21:5; Philippians 2:8-11.

[166] John 1:18.

[167] 1 Peter 1:10-12.

[168] Hebrews 1:1-2.

[169] John 15:15.

[170] John 20:31; Acts 20:23; Ephesians 4:11-13.

[171] Hebrews 9:14,28.

[172] Hebrews 2:17.

[173] Hebrews 7:25.

[174] Genesis 49:10; Psalm 110:3; Acts 15:14-16.

[175] 1 Corinthians 12:28; Ephesians 4:11-12.

[176] Isaiah 33:22.

[177] Matthew 18:17-18; 1 Corinthians 5:4-5.

[178] Acts 5:31.

[179] Revelation 2:10, 22:12.

[180] Revelation 3:19.

[181] Isaiah 63:9.

[182] Psalm 110:1-2; 1 Corinthians 15:25.

powerfully ordering all things for his own glory,[183] and their good;[184] and also in taking vengeance on the rest, who know not God, and obey not the gospel.[185]

Questions 45 (cont.) – 50

46. Q. What was the estate of Christ's humiliation?
    A. **The estate of Christ's humiliation was that low condition, wherein he for our sakes, emptying himself of his glory, took upon him the form of a servant, in his conception and birth, life, death, and after his death, until his resurrection.[186]**

47. Q. How did Christ humble himself in his conception and birth?
    A. **Christ humbled himself in his conception and birth, in that, being from all eternity the Son of God, in the bosom of the Father, he was pleased in the fullness of time to become the son of man, made of a woman of low estate, and to be born of her; with divers circumstances of more than ordinary abasement.[187]**

48. Q. How did Christ humble himself in his life?
    A. **Christ humbled himself in his life, by subjecting himself to the law,[188] which he perfectly fulfilled;[189] and by conflicting with the indignities of the world,[190] temptations of Satan,[191] and infirmities in his flesh, whether common to the nature of man, or particularly accompanying that his low condition.[192]**

49. Q. How did Christ humble himself in his death?
    A. **Christ humbled himself in his death, in that having been betrayed by Judas,[193] forsaken by his disciples,[194] scorned and rejected by the world,[195] condemned by Pilate, and tormented by his persecutors;[196] having also conflicted with the terrors of death, and the powers of darkness, felt and borne the weight of God's wrath,[197] he laid down his life an offering for sin,[198] enduring the painful, shameful, and cursed death of the cross.[199]**

50. Q. Wherein consisted Christ's humiliation after his death?
    A. **Christ's humiliation after his death consisted in his being buried,[200] and continuing in the state of the dead, and under the power of death till the third day;[201] which hath been otherwise expressed in these words, He descended into hell.**

---

[183] Romans 14:10-11.
[184] Romans 8:28.
[185] Psalm 2:8-9; 2 Thessalonians 1:8-9.
[186] Luke 1:31; Acts 2:24; 2 Corinthians 8:9; Philippians 2:6-8.
[187] John 1:14,18; Luke 2:7; Galatians 4:4.
[188] Galatians 4:4.
[189] Matthew 5:17; Romans 5:19.
[190] Psalm 22:6; Hebrews 12:2-3.
[191] Matthew 4:1-12; Luke 4:13.
[192] Isaiah 52:13-14; Hebrews 2:17-18, 4:15.
[193] Matthew 27:4.
[194] Matthew 26:56.
[195] Isaiah 53:2-3.
[196] Matthew 27:26-50; John 19:34.
[197] Matthew 27:46; Luke 22:44.
[198] Isaiah 53:10.
[199] Galatians 3:13; Philippians 2:8; Hebrews 12:2.
[200] 1 Corinthians 15:3-4.
[201] Psalm 16:10; Matthew 12:40; Acts 2:24-27,31.

Questions 51 – 53

51. Q. What was the estate of Christ's exaltation?

A. The estate of Christ's exaltation comprehendeth his resurrection,[202] ascension,[203] sitting at the right hand of the Father,[204] and his coming again to judge the world.[205]

52. Q. How was Christ exalted in his resurrection?

A. Christ was exalted in his resurrection, in that, not having seen corruption in death, (of which it was not possible for him to be held),[206] and having the very same body in which he suffered, with the essential properties thereof,[207] (but without mortality, and other common infirmities belonging to this life), really united to his soul,[208] he rose again from the dead the third day by his own power;[209] whereby he declared himself to be the Son of God,[210] to have satisfied divine justice,[211] to have vanquished death, and him that had the power of it,[212] and to be Lord of quick and dead:[213] all which he did as a public person,[214] the head of his church,[215] for their justification,[216] quickening in grace,[217] support against enemies,[218] and to assure them of their resurrection from the dead at the last day.[219]

53. Q. How was Christ exalted in his ascension?

A. Christ was exalted in his ascension, in that having after his resurrection often appeared unto and conversed with his apostles, speaking to them of the things pertaining to the kingdom of God,[220] and giving them commission to preach the gospel to all nations,[221] forty days after his resurrection, he, in our nature, and as our head,[222] triumphing over enemies,[223] visibly went up into the highest heavens, there to receive gifts for men,[224] to raise up our affections thither,[225] and to prepare a place for us,[226] where he himself is, and shall continue till his second coming at the end of the world.[227]

---

[202] 1 Corinthians 15:4
[203] Mark 16:19.
[204] Ephesians 1:20.
[205] Acts 1:11, 17:31.
[206] Acts 2:24,27.
[207] Luke 24:39.
[208] Romans 6:9; Revelation 1:18.
[209] John 10:18.
[210] Romans 1:4.
[211] Romans 8:34.
[212] Hebrews 2:14.
[213] Romans 14:9.
[214] 1 Corinthians 15:21-22.
[215] Ephesians 1:20-23; Colossians 1:18.
[216] Romans 4:25.
[217] Ephesians 2:1,5-6; Colossians 2:12.
[218] 1 Corinthians 15:25-27.
[219] 1 Corinthians 15:20.
[220] Acts 1:2-3.
[221] Matthew 28:19-20.
[222] Hebrews 6:20.
[223] Ephesians 4:8.
[224] Psalm 68:18; Acts 1:9-11; Ephesians 4:10.
[225] Colossians 3:1-2.
[226] John 14:3.
[227] Acts 3:21.

Questions 54 – 58

54. Q. How is Christ exalted in his sitting at the right hand of God?
    A. **Christ is exalted in his sitting at the right hand of God, in that as God-man he is advanced to the highest favour with God the Father,[228] with all fulness of joy,[229] glory,[230] and power over all things in heaven and earth;[231] and does gather and defend his church, and subdue their enemies; furnisheth his ministers and people with gifts and graces,[232] and maketh intercession for them.[233]**

55. Q. How doth Christ make intercession?
    A. **Christ maketh intercession, by his appearing in our nature continually before the Father in heaven,[234] in the merit of his obedience and sacrifice on earth,[235] declaring his will to have it applied to all believers;[236] answering all accusations against them,[237] and procuring for them quiet of conscience, notwithstanding daily failings,[238] access with boldness to the throne of grace,[239] and acceptance of their persons[240] and services.[241]**

56. Q. How is Christ to be exalted in his coming again to judge the world?
    A. **Christ is to be exalted in his coming again to judge the world, in that he, who was unjustly judged and condemned by wicked men,[242] shall come again at the last day in great power,[243] and in the full manifestation of his own glory, and of his Father's, with all his holy angels,[244] with a shout, with the voice of the archangel, and with the trumpet of God,[245] to judge the world in righteousness.[246]**

57. Q. What benefits hath Christ procured by his mediation?
    A. **Christ, by his mediation, hath procured redemption,[247] with all other benefits of the covenant of grace.[248]**

58. Q. How do we come to be made partakers of the benefits which Christ hath procured?
    A. **We are made partakers of the benefits which Christ hath procured, by the application of them unto us,[249] which is the work especially of God the Holy Ghost.[250]**

---

[228] Philippians 2:9.

[229] Psalm 16:11; Acts 2:28.

[230] John 17:5.

[231] Ephesians 1:22; 1 Peter 3:22.

[232] Psalm 110:1; Ephesians 4:10-12.

[233] Romans 8:34.

[234] Hebrews 9:12,24.

[235] Hebrews 1:3.

[236] John 3:16, 17:9,20,24.

[237] Romans 8:33-34.

[238] Romans 5:1-2; 1 John 2:1-2.

[239] Hebrews 4:16.

[240] Ephesians 1:6.

[241] 1 Peter 2:5.

[242] Acts 3:14-15.

[243] Matthew 24:30.

[244] Matthew 25:31; Luke 9:26.

[245] 1 Thessalonians 4:16.

[246] Acts 17:31.

[247] Hebrews 9:12.

[248] 2 Corinthians 1:20.

[249] John 1:11-12.

[250] Titus 3:5-6.

Questions 59 – 65

59. **Q.** Who are made partakers of redemption through Christ?
    A. **Redemption is certainly applied, and effectually communicated, to all those for whom Christ hath purchased it;[251] who are in time by the Holy Ghost enabled to believe in Christ according to the gospel.[252]**

60. **Q.** Can they who have never heard the gospel, and so know not Jesus Christ, nor believe in him, be saved by their living according to the light of nature?
    A. **They who, having never heard the gospel,[253] know not Jesus Christ,[254] and believe not in him, cannot be saved,[255] be they never so diligent to frame their lives according to the light of nature,[256] or the laws of that religion which they profess;[257] neither is there salvation in any other, but in Christ alone,[258] who is the Savior only of his body the church.[259]**

61. **Q.** Are all they saved who hear the gospel, and live in the church?
    A. **All that hear the gospel, and live in the visible church, are not saved; but they only who are true members of the church invisible.[260]**

62. **Q.** What is the visible church?
    A. **The visible church is a society made up of all such as in all ages and places of the world do profess the true religion,[261] and of their children.[262]**

63. **Q.** What are the special privileges of the visible church?
    A. **The visible church hath the privilege of being under God's special care and government;[263] of being protected and preserved in all ages, notwithstanding the opposition of all enemies;[264] and of enjoying the communion of saints, the ordinary means of salvation,[265] and offers of grace by Christ to all the members of it in the ministry of the gospel, testifying, that whosoever believes in him shall be saved,[266] and excluding none that will come unto him.[267]**

64. **Q.** What is the invisible church?
    A. **The invisible church is the whole number of the elect, that have been, are, or shall be gathered into one under Christ the head.[268]**

65. **Q.** What special benefits do the members of the invisible church enjoy by Christ?
    A. **The members of the invisible church by Christ enjoy union and communion with him in grace and glory.[269]**

---

[251] John 6:37,39, 10:15-16; Ephesians 1:13-14.

[252] 2 Corinthians 4:13; Ephesians 2:8.

[253] Romans 10:14.

[254] John 1:10-12; Ephesians 2:12; 2 Thessalonians 1:8-9.

[255] Mark 16:16; John 8:24.

[256] 1 Corinthians 1:20-24.

[257] John 4:22; Romans 9:31-32; Philippians 3:4-9.

[258] Acts 4:12.

[259] Ephesians 5:23.

[260] Matthew 22:14, 7:21; John 12:38-40; Romans 9:6, 11:7.

[261] Psalm 2:8, 22:27-31, 45:17; Isaiah 59:21; Matthew 28:19-20; Romans 15:9-12; 1 Corinthians 1:2, 12:13; Revelation 7:9.

[262] Genesis 17:7; Acts 2:39; Romans 11:16; 1 Corinthians 7:14.

[263] Isaiah 9:5-6; 1 Timothy 4:10.

[264] Psalm 115:1-2,9; Isaiah 31:4-5; Zechariah 12:2-4,8-9.

[265] Acts 2:39,42.

[266] Psalm 147:19-20; Mark 16:15-16; Romans 9:4; Ephesians 4:11-12.

[267] John 6:37.

[268] John 10:16, 11:52; Ephesians 1:10, 1:22-23.

[269] John 17:21,24; Ephesians 2:5-6.

Questions 66 – 70

66. Q. What is that union which the elect have with Christ?
    A. The union which the elect have with Christ is the work of God's grace,[270] whereby they are spiritually and mystically, yet really and inseparably, joined to Christ as their head and husband;[271] which is done in their effectual calling.[272]

67. Q. What is effectual calling?
    A. Effectual calling is the work of God's almighty power and grace,[273] whereby (out of his free and special love to his elect, and from nothing in them moving him thereunto)[274] he doth, in his accepted time, invite and draw them to Jesus Christ, by his Word and Spirit;[275] savingly enlightening their minds,[276] renewing and powerfully determining their wills,[277] so as they (although in themselves dead in sin) are hereby made willing and able freely to answer his call, and to accept and embrace the grace offered and conveyed therein.[278]

68. Q. Are the elect only effectually called?
    A. All the elect, and they only, are effectually called:[279] although others may be, and often are, outwardly called by the ministry of the Word,[280] and have some common operations of the Spirit;[281] who, for their willful neglect and contempt of the grace offered to them, being justly left in their unbelief, do never truly come to Jesus Christ.[282]

69. Q. What is the communion in grace which the members of the invisible church have with Christ?
    A. The communion in grace which the members of the invisible church have with Christ, is their partaking of the virtue of his mediation, in their justification,[283] adoption,[284] sanctification, and whatever else, in this life, manifests their union with him.[285]

70. Q. What is justification?
    A. Justification is an act of God's free grace unto sinners,[286] in which he pardoneth all their sins, accepteth and accounteth their persons righteous in his sight;[287] not for any thing wrought in them, or done by them,[288] but only for the perfect obedience and full satisfaction of Christ, by God imputed to them,[289] and received by faith alone.[290]

---

[270] Ephesians 1:22, 2:6-7.
[271] John 10:28; 1 Corinthians 6:17; Ephesians 5:23,30.
[272] 1 Corinthians 1:9; 1 Peter 5:10.
[273] John 5:25; Ephesians 1:18-20; 2 Timothy 1:8-9.
[274] Romans 9:11; Ephesians 2:4-5,7-9; Titus 3:4-5.
[275] John 6:44; 2 Corinthians 5:20, 6:1-2; 2 Thessalonians 2:13-14.
[276] Acts 26:18; 1 Corinthians 2:10,12.
[277] Ezekiel 11:19, 36:26-27; John 6:45.
[278] Deuteronomy 30:6; Ephesians 2:5; Philippians 2:13.
[279] Acts 13:48.
[280] Matthew 22:14.
[281] Matthew 7:22; Hebrews 6:4-6.
[282] Psalm 81:11-12; John 6:64-65, 12:38-40; Acts 28:25-27.
[283] Romans 8:30.
[284] Ephesians 1:5.
[285] 1 Corinthians 1:30.
[286] Romans 3:22,24-25, 4:5.
[287] Romans 3:22,24-25,27-28; 2 Corinthians 5:19,21.
[288] Ephesians 1:7; Titus 3:5,7.
[289] Romans 5:17-19, 4:6-8.
[290] Acts 10:43; Galatians 2:16; Philippians 3:9.

Questions 71 – 74

71. Q. How is justification an act of God's free grace?
    A. Although Christ, by his obedience and death, did make a proper, real, and full satisfaction to God's justice in the behalf of them that are justified;[291] yet in as much as God accepteth the satisfaction from a surety, which he might have demanded of them, and did provide this surety, his own only Son,[292] imputing his righteousness to them,[293] and requiring nothing of them for their justification but faith,[294] which also is his gift,[295] their justification is to them of free grace.[296]

72. Q. What is justifying faith?
    A. Justifying faith is a saving grace,[297] wrought in the heart of a sinner by the Spirit[298] and Word of God,[299] whereby he, being convinced of his sin and misery, and of the disability in himself and all other creatures to recover him out of his lost condition,[300] not only assenteth to the truth of the promise of the gospel,[301] but receiveth and resteth upon Christ and his righteousness, therein held forth, for pardon of sin,[302] and for the accepting and accounting of his person righteous in the sight of God for salvation.[303]

73. Q. How doth faith justify a sinner in the sight of God?
    A. Faith justifies a sinner in the sight of God, not because of those other graces which do always accompany it, or of good works that are the fruits of it,[304] nor as if the grace of faith, or any act thereof, were imputed to him for his justification;[305] but only as it is an instrument by which he receiveth and applieth Christ and his righteousness.[306]

74. Q. What is adoption?
    A. Adoption is an act of the free grace of God,[307] in and for his only Son Jesus Christ,[308] whereby all those that are justified are received into the number of his children,[309] have his name put upon them,[310] the Spirit of his Son given to them,[311] are under his fatherly care and dispensations,[312] admitted to all the liberties and privileges of the sons of God, made heirs of all the promises, and fellow-heirs with Christ in glory.[313]

---

[291] Romans 5:8-10,19.

[292] Isaiah 53:4-6,10-12; Daniel 9:24,26; Matthew 20:28; Romans 8:32; 1 Timothy 2:5-6; Hebrews 7:22, 10:10; 1 Peter 1:18-19.

[293] 2 Corinthians 5:21.

[294] Romans 3:24-25.

[295] Ephesians 2:8.

[296] Ephesians 1:17.

[297] Hebrews 10:39.

[298] 2 Corinthians 4:13; Ephesians 1:17-19.

[299] Romans 10:14-17.

[300] John 16:8-9; Acts 2:37, 4:12, 16:30; Romans 6:6; Ephesians 2:1.

[301] Ephesians 1:13.

[302] John 1:12; Acts 16:31, 10:43.

[303] Acts 15:11; Philippians 3:9.

[304] Romans 3:28; Galatians 3:11.

[305] Romans 4:5, 10:10.

[306] John 1:12; Galatians 1:16; Philippians 3:9.

[307] 1 John 3:1.

[308] Galatians 4:4-5; Ephesians 1:5.

[309] John 1:12.

[310] 2 Corinthians 6:18; Revelation 3:12.

[311] Galatians 4:6.

[312] Psalm 103:13; Proverbs 14:26; Matthew 6:32.

[313] Romans 8:17; Hebrews 6:12.

Questions 75 – 78

75. Q. What is sanctification?
    A. Sanctification is a work of God's grace, whereby they whom God hath, before the foundation of the world, chosen to be holy, are in time, through the powerful operation of his Spirit[314] applying the death and resurrection of Christ unto them,[315] renewed in their whole man after the image of God;[316] having the seeds of repentance unto life, and all other saving graces, put into their hearts,[317] and those graces so stirred up, increased, and strengthened,[318] as that they more and more die unto sin, and rise unto newness of life.[319]

76. Q. What is repentance unto life?
    A. Repentance unto life is a saving grace,[320] wrought in the heart of a sinner by the Spirit[321] and Word of God,[322] whereby, out of the sight and sense, not only of the danger,[323] but also of the filthiness and odiousness of his sins,[324] and upon the apprehension of God's mercy in Christ to such as are penitent,[325] he so grieves for[326] and hates his sins,[327] as that he turns from them all to God,[328] purposing and endeavouring constantly to walk with him in all the ways of new obedience.[329]

77. Q. Wherein do justification and sanctification differ?
    A. Although sanctification be inseparably joined with justification,[330] yet they differ, in that God in justification imputeth the righteousness of Christ;[331] in sanctification of his Spirit infuseth grace, and enableth to the exercise thereof;[332] in the former, sin is pardoned;[333] in the other, it is subdued:[334] the one doth equally free all believers from the revenging wrath of God, and that perfectly in this life, that they never fall into condemnation[335] the other is neither equal in all,[336] nor in this life perfect in any,[337] but growing up to perfection.[338]

78. Q. Whence ariseth the imperfection of sanctification in believers?
    A. The imperfection of sanctification in believers ariseth from the remnants of sin abiding in every part of them, and the perpetual lustings of the flesh against the spirit; whereby they are often foiled with

---

[314] 1 Corinthians 6:11; Ephesians 1:4; 2 Thessalonians 2:13.
[315] Romans 6:4-6.
[316] Ephesians 4:23-24.
[317] Acts 11:18; 1 John 3:9.
[318] Ephesians 3:16-19; Colossians 1:10-11; Hebrews 6:11-12; Jude 20.
[319] Romans 6:4,6,14; Galatians 5:24.
[320] 2 Timothy 2:25.
[321] Zechariah 12:10.
[322] Acts 11:18,20-21,.
[323] Ezekiel 18:28,30,32; Hosea 2:6-7; Luke 15:17-18.
[324] Isaiah 30:22; Ezekiel 36:31.
[325] Joel 2:12-13.
[326] Jeremiah 31:18-19.
[327] 2 Corinthians 7:11.
[328] 1 Kings 8:47-48; Ezekiel 14:6; Acts 26:18.
[329] 2 Kings 23:25; Psalm 119:6,59,128; Luke 1:6.
[330] 1 Corinthians 1:30, 6:11.
[331] Romans 4:6,8.
[332] Ezekiel 36:27.
[333] Romans 3:24-25.
[334] Romans 6:6,14.
[335] Romans 8:33-34.
[336] Hebrews 5:12-14; 1 John 2:12-14.
[337] 1 John 1:8,10.
[338] 2 Corinthians 7:1; Philippians 3:12-14.

temptations, and fall into many sins,[339] are hindered in all their spiritual services,[340] and their best works are imperfect and defiled in the sight of God.[341]

Questions 78 (cont.) – 83

79. Q. May not true believers, by reason of their imperfections, and the many temptations and sins they are overtaken with, fall away from the state of grace?

A. **True believers, by reason of the unchangeable love of God,[342] and his decree and covenant to give them perseverance,[343] their inseparable union with Christ,[344] his continual intercession for them,[345] and the Spirit and seed of God abiding in them,[346] can neither totally nor finally fall away from the state of grace,[347] but are kept by the power of God through faith unto salvation.[348]**

80. Q. Can true believers be infallibly assured that they are in the estate of grace, and that they shall persevere therein unto salvation?

A. **Such as truly believe in Christ, and endeavour to walk in all good conscience before him,[349] may, without extraordinary revelation, by faith grounded upon the truth of God's promises, and by the Spirit enabling them to discern in themselves those graces to which the promises of life are made,[350] and bearing witness with their spirits that they are the children of God,[351] be infallibly assured that they are in the estate of grace, and shall persevere therein unto salvation.[352]**

81. Q. Are all true believers at all times assured of their present being in the estate of grace, and that they shall be saved?

A. **Assurance of grace and salvation not being of the essence of faith,[353] true believers may wait long before they obtain it;[354] and, after the enjoyment thereof, may have it weakened and intermitted, through manifold distempers, sins, temptations, and desertions;[355] yet they are never left without such a presence and support of the Spirit of God as keeps them from sinking into utter despair.[356]**

82. Q. What is the communion in glory which the members of the invisible church have with Christ?

A. **The communion in glory which the members of the invisible church have with Christ, is in this life,[357] immediately after death,[358] and at last perfected at the resurrection and Day of Judgment.[359]**

83. Q. What is the communion in glory with Christ which the members of the invisible church enjoy in this life?

A. **The members of the invisible church have communicated to them in this life the firstfruits of glory with Christ, as they are members of him their head, and so in him are interested in that glory which he is fully**

---

[339] Mark 14:66; Romans 7:18,23; Galatians 2:11-12.

[340] Hebrews 12:1.

[341] Exodus 28:38; Isaiah 64:6.

[342] Jeremiah 31:3.

[343] 2 Samuel 23:5; 2 Timothy 2:19; Hebrews 13:20-21.

[344] 1 Corinthians 1:8-9.

[345] Luke 22:32; Hebrews 7:25.

[346] 1 John 2:27, 3:9.

[347] Jeremiah 32:40; John 10:28.

[348] 1 Peter 1:5.

[349] 1 John 2:3.

[350] 1 Corinthians 2:12; Hebrews 6:11-12; 1 John 3:14,18-19,21,24, 4:13,16.

[351] Romans 8:16.

[352] 1 John 5:13.

[353] Ephesians 1:13.

[354] Psalm 88:1-3,6-7,9-10,13-15; Isaiah 50:10.

[355] Psalm 22:1, 31:22, 51:8,12, 77:1-12; Song of Solomon 5:2-3,6.

[356] Psalm 73:15,23; Isaiah 54:7-10; 1 John 3:9.

[357] 2 Corinthians 3:18.

[358] Luke 23:43.

[359] 1 Thessalonians 4:17.

possessed of;[360] and, as an earnest thereof, enjoy the sense of God's love,[361] peace of conscience, joy in the Holy Ghost, and hope of glory;[362] as, on the contrary, sense of God's revenging wrath, horror of conscience, and a fearful expectation of judgment, are to the wicked the beginning of their torments which they shall endure after death.[363]

Questions 83 (cont.) – 87

84. **Q.** Shall all men die?

A. Death being threatened as the wages of sin,[364] it is appointed unto all men once to die;[365] for that all have sinned.[366]

85. **Q.** Death being the wages of sin, why are not the righteous delivered from death, seeing all their sins are forgiven in Christ?

A. The righteous shall be delivered from death itself at the last day, and even in death are delivered from the sting and curse of it;[367] so that, although they die, yet it is out of God's love,[368] to free them perfectly from sin and misery,[369] and to make them capable of further communion with Christ in glory, which they then enter upon.[370]

86. **Q.** What is the communion in glory with Christ which the members of the invisible church enjoy immediately after death?

A. The communion in glory with Christ, which the members of the invisible church enjoy immediately after death is, in that their souls are then made perfect in holiness,[371] and received into the highest heavens,[372] where they behold the face of God in light and glory,[373] waiting for the full redemption of their bodies,[374] which even in death continue united to Christ,[375] and rest in their graves as in their beds,[376] till at the last day they be again united to their souls.[377] Whereas the souls of the wicked are at their death cast into hell, where they remain in torments and utter darkness, and their bodies kept in their graves, as in their prisons, till the resurrection and judgment of the great day.[378]

87. **Q.** What are we to believe concerning the resurrection?

A. We are to believe that at the last day there shall be a general resurrection of the dead, both of the just and unjust:[379] when they that are then found alive shall in a moment be changed; and the selfsame bodies of the dead which were laid in the grave, being then again united to their souls forever, shall be raised up by the power of Christ.[380] The bodies of the just, by the Spirit of Christ, and by virtue of his resurrection

---

[360] Ephesians 2:5-6.

[361] Romans 5:5; 2 Corinthians 1:22.

[362] Romans 5:1-2, 14:17.

[363] Genesis 4:13; Matthew 27:4; Mark 9:44; Romans 2:9; Hebrews 10:27.

[364] Romans 6:23.

[365] Hebrews 9:27.

[366] Romans 5:12.

[367] 1 Corinthians 15:26,55-57; Hebrews 2:15.

[368] 2 Kings 22:20; Isaiah 57:1-2.

[369] Ephesians 5:27; Revelation 14:13.

[370] Luke 23:43; Philippians 1:23.

[371] Hebrews 12:23.

[372] Acts 3:21; 2 Corinthians 5:1,6,8; Ephesians 4:10; Philippians 1:23.

[373] 1 Corinthians 13:12; 1 John 3:2.

[374] Psalm 16:9; Romans 8:23.

[375] 1 Thessalonians 4:14.

[376] Isaiah 57:2.

[377] Job 19:26-27.

[378] Luke 16:23-24; Acts 1:25; Jude 6-7.

[379] Acts 24:15.

[380] John 5:28-29; 1 Corinthians 15:51-53; 1 Thessalonians 4:15-17.

as their head, shall be raised in power, spiritual, incorruptible, and made like to his glorious body;[381] and the bodies of the wicked shall be raised up in dishonour by him, as an offended judge.[382]

Questions 87 (cont.) – 91

88. Q. What shall immediately follow after the resurrection?
    A. Immediately after the resurrection shall follow the general and final judgment of angels and men;[383] the day and hour whereof no man knoweth, that all may watch and pray, and be ever ready for the coming of the Lord.[384]

89. Q. What shall be done to the wicked at the Day of Judgment?
    A. At the Day of Judgment, the wicked shall be set on Christ's left hand,[385] and, upon clear evidence, and full conviction of their own consciences,[386] shall have the fearful but just sentence of condemnation pronounced against them;[387] and thereupon shall be cast out from the favourable presence of God, and the glorious fellowship with Christ, his saints, and all his holy angels, into hell, to be punished with unspeakable torments, both of body and soul, with the devil and his angels forever.[388]

90. Q. What shall be done to the righteous at the Day of Judgment?
    A. At the day of judgment, the righteous, being caught up to Christ in the clouds,[389] shall be set on his right hand, and there openly acknowledged and acquitted,[390] shall join with him in the judging of reprobate angels and men,[391] and shall be received into heaven,[392] where they shall be fully and forever freed from all sin and misery;[393] filled with inconceivable joys,[394] made perfectly holy and happy both in body and soul, in the company of innumerable saints and holy angels,[395] but especially in the immediate vision and fruition of God the Father, of our Lord Jesus Christ, and of the Holy Spirit, to all eternity.[396] And this is the perfect and full communion, which the members of the invisible church shall enjoy with Christ in glory, at the resurrection and Day of Judgment.

Having Seen What the Scriptures Principally Teach Us to Believe Concerning God, It Follows to Consider What They Require as the Duty of Man

91. Q. What is the duty which God requireth of man?
    A. The duty which God requireth of man, is obedience to his revealed will.[397]

---

[381] 1 Corinthians 15:21-23,42-44; Philippians 3:21.
[382] Matthew 25:33; John 5:27-29.
[383] Matthew 25:46; 2 Peter 2:4,6-7,14-15.
[384] Matthew 24:36,42,44.
[385] Matthew 25:33.
[386] Romans 2:15-16.
[387] Matthew 25:41-43.
[388] Luke 16:26; 2 Thessalonians 1:8-9.
[389] 1 Thessalonians 4:17.
[390] Matthew 25:33, 10:32.
[391] 1 Corinthians 6:2-3.
[392] Matthew 25:34,46.
[393] Ephesians 5:27; Revelation 14:13.
[394] Psalm 16:11.
[395] Hebrews 12:22-23.
[396] 1 Corinthians 13:12; 1 Thessalonians 4:17-18; 1 John 3:2.
[397] 1 Samuel 15:22; Micah 6:8; Romans 12:1-2.

Questions 92 – 97

92. Q. What did God first reveal unto man as the rule of his obedience?
    A. The rule of obedience revealed to Adam in the estate of innocence, and to all mankind in him, besides a special command not to eat of the fruit of the tree knowledge of good and evil, was the moral law.[398]

93. Q. What is the moral law?
    A. The moral law is the declaration of the will of God to mankind, directing and binding every one to personal, perfect, and perpetual conformity and obedience thereunto, in the frame and disposition of the whole man, soul and body,[399] and in performance of all those duties of holiness and righteousness which he oweth to God and man:[400] promising life upon the fulfilling, and threatening death upon the breach of it.[401]

94. Q. Is there any use of the moral law since the fall?
    A. Although no man, since the fall, can attain to righteousness and life by the moral law:[402] yet there is great use thereof, as well common to all men, as peculiar either to the unregenerate, or the regenerate.[403]

95. Q. Of what use is the moral law to all men?
    A. The moral law is of use to all men, to inform them of the holy nature and the will of God,[404] and of their duty, binding them to walk accordingly;[405] to convince them of their disability to keep it, and of the sinful pollution of their nature, hearts, and lives:[406] to humble them in the sense of their sin and misery,[407] and thereby help them to a clearer sight of the need they have of Christ,[408] and of the perfection of his obedience.[409]

96. Q. What particular use is there of the moral law to unregenerate men?
    A. The moral law is of use to unregenerate men, to awaken their consciences to flee from wrath to come,[410] and to drive them to Christ;[411] or, upon their continuance in the estate and way of sin, to leave them inexcusable,[412] and under the curse thereof.[413]

97. Q. What special use is there of the moral law to the regenerate?
    A. Although they that are regenerate, and believe in Christ, be delivered from the moral law as a covenant of works,[414] so as thereby they are neither justified[415] nor condemned;[416] yet, besides the general uses thereof common to them with all men, it is of special use, to show them how much they are bound to Christ for his fulfilling it, and enduring the curse thereof in their stead, and for their good;[417] and thereby

---

[398] Genesis 1:26-27, 2:17; Romans 2:14-15, 10:5.
[399] Deuteronomy 5:1-3,31,33; Luke 10:26-27; 1 Thessalonians 5:23.
[400] Luke 1:75; Acts 24:16.
[401] Romans 10:5; Galatians 3:10, 3:12.
[402] Romans 8:3.
[403] 1 Timothy 1:8.
[404] Leviticus 11:44-45, 20:7-8; Romans 8:12.
[405] Micah 6:8; James 2:10-11.
[406] Psalm 19:11-12; Romans 3:20, 7:7.
[407] Romans 3:9,23.
[408] Galatians 3:21-22.
[409] Romans 10:4.
[410] 1 Timothy 1:9-10.
[411] Galatians 3:10.
[412] Romans 1:20, 2:15.
[413] Galatians 3:10.
[414] Romans 6:14, 7:4,6; Galatians 4:4-5.
[415] Romans 3:20.
[416] Romans 8:1; Galatians 5:23.
[417] Romans 7:24-25, 8:3-4; Galatians 3:13-14.

to provoke them to more thankfulness,[418] and to express the same in their greater care to conform themselves thereunto as the rule of their obedience.[419]

Questions 97 (cont.) – 99

98. Q. Wherein is the moral law summarily comprehended?

A. **The moral law is summarily comprehended in the ten commandments, which were delivered by the voice of God upon Mount Sinai, and written by him in two tables of stone;[420] and are recorded in the twentieth chapter of Exodus. The four first commandments containing our duty to God, and the other six our duty to man.[421]**

99. Q. What rules are to be observed for the right understanding of the Ten Commandments?

A. **For the right understanding of the Ten Commandments, these rules are to be observed:**

1. That the law is perfect, and bindeth everyone to full conformity in the whole man unto the righteousness thereof, and unto entire obedience forever; so as to require the utmost perfection of every duty, and to forbid the least degree of every sin.[422]

2. That it is spiritual, and so reacheth the understanding, will, affections, and all other powers of the soul; as well as words, works, and gestures.[423]

3. That one and the same thing, in divers respects, is required or forbidden in several commandments.[424]

4. That as, where a duty is commanded, the contrary sin is forbidden;[425] and, where a sin is forbidden, the contrary duty is commanded:[426] so, where a promise is annexed, the contrary threatening is included;[427] and, where a threatening is annexed, the contrary promise is included.[428]

5. That what God forbids, is at no time to be done;[429] what he commands, is always our duty;[430] and yet every particular duty is not to be done at all times.[431]

6. That under one sin or duty, all of the same kind are forbidden or commanded; together with all the causes, means, occasions, and appearances thereof, and provocations thereunto.[432]

7. That what is forbidden or commanded to ourselves, we are bound, according to our places to endeavour that it may be avoided or performed by others, according to the duty of their places.[433]

---

[418] Luke 1:68-69,74-75; Colossians 1:12-14.
[419] Romans 7:22, 12:2; Titus 2:11-14.
[420] Exodus 34:1-4; Deuteronomy 10:4.
[421] Matthew 22:37-40.
[422] Psalm 19:7; Matthew 5:21-22; James 2:10.
[423] Deuteronomy 6:5; Matthew 22:37-39, 5:21-22,27-28,33-34,37-39,43-44; Romans 7:14.
[424] Proverbs 1:19; Amos 8:5; Colossians 3:5; 1 Timothy 6:10.
[425] Deuteronomy 6:13; Isaiah 58:13; Matthew 4:9-10, 15:4-6.
[426] Matthew 5:21-25; Ephesians 4:28.
[427] Exodus 20:12; Proverbs 30:17.
[428] Exodus 20:7; Psalm 15:1,4-5, 24:4-5; Jeremiah 18:7-8.
[429] Job 13:7-8, 36:21; Romans 3:8; Hebrews 11:25.
[430] Deuteronomy 4:8-9.
[431] Matthew 12:7.
[432] Matthew 5:21-22,27-28, 15:4-6; Galatians 5:26; Colossians 3:21; 1 Thessalonians 5:22; Jude 23; Hebrews 10:24-25.
[433] Genesis 18:19; Exodus 20:10; Leviticus 19:17; Deuteronomy 6:6-7; Joshua 14:15.

8. That in what is commanded to others, we are bound, according to our places and callings, to be helpful to them;[434] and to take heed of partaking with others in what is forbidden them.[435]

Questions 99 (cont.) – 104

100. Q. What special things are we to consider in the Ten Commandments?
   A. **We are to consider, in the Ten Commandments, the preface, the substance of the commandments themselves, and several reasons annexed to some of them, the more to enforce them.**

101. Q. What is the preface to the Ten Commandments?
   A. **The preface to the Ten Commandments is contained in these words, I am the Lord thy God, which have brought thee out of the land of Egypt, out of the house of bondage.[436] Wherein God manifesteth his sovereignty, as being JEHOVAH, the eternal, immutable, and almighty God;[437] having his being in and of himself,[438] and giving being to all his words[439] and works:[440] and that he is a God in covenant, as with Israel of old, so with all his people;[441] who, as he brought them out of their bondage in Egypt, so he delivereth us from our spiritual thraldom;[442] and that therefore we are bound to take him for our God alone, and to keep all his commandments.[443]**

102. Q. What is the sum of the four commandments which contain our duty to God?
   A. **The sum of the four commandments containing our duty to God is, to love the Lord our God with all our heart, and with all our soul, and with all our strength, and with all our mind.[444]**

103. Q. Which is the first commandment?
   A. **The first commandment is, Thou shalt have no other gods before me.[445]**

104. Q. What are the duties required in the first commandment?
   A. **The duties required in the first commandment are, the knowing and acknowledging of God to be the only true God, and our God;[446] and to worship and glorify him accordingly,[447] by thinking,[448] meditating,[449] remembering,[450] highly esteeming,[451] honouring,[452] adoring,[453] choosing,[454] loving[455]**

---

[434] 2 Corinthians 1:24.
[435] Ephesians 5:11; 1 Timothy 5:22.
[436] Exodus 20:2.
[437] Isaiah 44:6.
[438] Exodus 3:14.
[439] Exodus 6:3.
[440] Acts 17:24,28.
[441] Genesis 17:7; Romans 3:29.
[442] Luke 1:74-75.
[443] Leviticus 18:30, 19:37; 1 Peter 1:15,17-18.
[444] Luke 10:27.
[445] Exodus 20:3.
[446] Deuteronomy 26:7; 1 Chronicles 28:9; Isaiah 43:10; Jeremiah 14:22.
[447] Psalm 29:2, 95:6-7; Matthew 4:10;.
[448] Malachi 3:16.
[449] Psalm 63:6.
[450] Ecclesiastes 12:1.
[451] Psalm 71:19.
[452] Malachi 1:6.
[453] Isaiah 45:23.
[454] Joshua 24:15,22.
[455] Deuteronomy 6:5.

desiring,[456] fearing of him;[457] believing him;[458] trusting[459] hoping,[460] delighting,[461] rejoicing in him;[462] being zealous for him;[463] calling upon him, giving all praise and thanks,[464] and yielding all obedience and submission to him with the whole man;[465] being careful in all things to please him,[466] and sorrowful when in any thing he is offended;[467] and walking humbly with him.[468]

Questions 104 (cont.) – 105

105. Q. What are the sins forbidden in the first commandment?

A. The sins forbidden in the first commandment are, atheism, in denying or not having a God;[469] idolatry, in having or worshipping more gods than one, or any with or instead of the true God;[470] the not having and avouching him for God, and our God;[471] the omission or neglect of anything due to him, required in this commandment;[472] ignorance,[473] forgetfulness,[474] misapprehensions,[475] false opinions,[476] unworthy and wicked thoughts of him;[477] bold and curious searching into his secrets;[478] all profaneness,[479] hatred of God;[480] self-love,[481] self-seeking,[482] and all other inordinate and immoderate setting of our mind, will, or affections upon other things, and taking them off from him in whole or in part;[483] vain credulity,[484] unbelief,[485] heresy,[486] misbelief,[487] distrust,[488] despair,[489] incorrigibleness,[490] and insensibleness under

---

[456] Psalm 73:25.

[457] Isaiah 8:13.

[458] Exodus 14:31.

[459] Isaiah 26:4.

[460] Psalm 130:7.

[461] Psalm 37:4.

[462] Psalm 32:11.

[463] Numbers 25:11; Romans 12:11.

[464] Philippians 4:6.

[465] Jeremiah 7:23; James 4:7.

[466] 1 John 3:22.

[467] Psalm 119:136; Jeremiah 31:18.

[468] Micah 6:8.

[469] Psalm 14:1; Ephesians 2:12.

[470] Jeremiah 2:27-28; 1 Thessalonians 1:9.

[471] Psalm 81:11.

[472] Isaiah 43:2,23-24.

[473] Jeremiah 4:22; Hosea 4:1,6.

[474] Jeremiah 2:32.

[475] Acts 17:23,29.

[476] Isaiah 40:18.

[477] Psalm 50:21.

[478] Deuteronomy 29:29.

[479] Titus 1:16; Hebrews 12:16.

[480] Romans 1:30.

[481] 2 Timothy 3:2.

[482] Philippians 2:21.

[483] 1 Samuel 2:29; Colossians 2:2,5; 1 John 2:15-16.

[484] 1 John 4:1.

[485] Hebrews 3:12.

[486] Galatians 5:20; Titus 3:10.

[487] Acts 26:9.

[488] Psalm 78:22.

[489] Genesis 4:13.

[490] Jeremiah 5:3.

judgments,[491] hardness of heart,[492] pride,[493] presumption,[494] carnal security,[495] tempting of God;[496] using unlawful means,[497] and trusting in lawful means;[498] carnal delights and joys;[499] corrupt, blind, and indiscreet zeal;[500] lukewarmness,[501] and deadness in the things of God;[502] estranging ourselves, and apostatizing from God;[503] praying, or giving any religious worship, to saints, angels, or any other creatures;[504] all compacts and consulting with the devil,[505] and hearkening to his suggestions;[506] making men the lords of our faith and conscience;[507] slighting and despising God and his commands;[508] resisting and grieving of his Spirit,[509] discontent and impatience at his dispensations, charging him foolishly for the evils he inflicts on us;[510] and ascribing the praise of any good we either are, have or can do, to fortune,[511] idols,[512] ourselves,[513] or any other creature.[514]

Questions 105 (cont.) – 107

106. Q. What are we specially taught by these words, before me, in the first commandment?
    A. These words before me or before my face, in the first commandment, teach us, that God, who seeth all things, taketh special notice of, and is much displeased with, the sin of having any other God: that so it may be an argument to dissuade from it, and to aggravate it as a most impudent provocation:[515] as also to persuade us to do as in his sight, whatever we do in his service.[516]

107. Q. Which is the second commandment?
    A. The second commandment is, Thou shalt not make unto thee any graven image, or any likeness of anything that is in heaven above, or that is in the earth beneath, or that is in the water under the earth. Thou shalt not bow down thyself to them, nor serve them: for I the Lord thy God am a jealous God, visiting the iniquity of the fathers upon the children unto the third and fourth generation of them that hate me; and showing mercy unto thousands of them that love me, and keep my commandments.[517]

---

[491] Isaiah 42:25.
[492] Romans 2:5.
[493] Jeremiah 13:15.
[494] Psalm 10:13.
[495] Zephaniah 1:12.
[496] Matthew 4:7.
[497] Romans 3:8.
[498] Jeremiah 17:5.
[499] 2 Timothy 3:4.
[500] Luke 9:54-55; John 16:2; Romans 10:2; Galatians 4:17.
[501] Revelation 3:16.
[502] Revelation 2:1.
[503] Isaiah 1:4-5; Ezekiel 14:5.
[504] Hosea 4:12; Matthew 4:10; Acts 10:25-26; Romans 1:25, 10:13-14; Colossians 2:18; Revelation 19:10.
[505] Leviticus 20:6; 1 Samuel 28:7,11; 1 Chronicles 10:13-14.
[506] Acts 5:3.
[507] Matthew 23:9; 2 Corinthians 1:24.
[508] Deuteronomy 32:15; 2 Samuel 12:9; Proverbs 13:13.
[509] Acts 7:51; Ephesians 4:30.
[510] Job 1:22; Psalm 73:2-3,13-15,22.
[511] 1 Samuel 6:7-9.
[512] Daniel 5:23.
[513] Deuteronomy 8:17; Daniel 4:30.
[514] Habakkuk 1:16.
[515] Psalm 44:20-21; Ezekiel 8:5-6.
[516] 1 Chronicles 28:9.
[517] Exodus 20:4-6.

Questions 108 – 109

108. Q. What are the duties required in the second commandment?

A. **The duties required in the second commandment are, the receiving, observing, and keeping pure and entire, all such religious worship and ordinances as God hath instituted in his Word;[518] particularly prayer and thanksgiving in the name of Christ;[519] the reading, preaching, and hearing of the Word;[520] the administration and receiving of the sacraments;[521] church government and discipline;[522] the ministry and maintainance thereof;[523] religious fasting;[524] swearing by the name of God;[525] and vowing unto him;[526] as also the disapproving, detesting, opposing all false worship;[527] and, according to each one's place and calling, removing it, and all monuments of idolatry.[528]**

109. Q. What sins are forbidden in the second commandment?

A. **The sins forbidden in the second commandment are, all devising,[529] counselling,[530] commanding,[531] using,[532] and anywise approving, any religious worship not instituted by God himself;[533] tolerating a false religion; the making any representation of God, of all or of any of the three persons, either inwardly in our mind, or outwardly in any kind of image or likeness of any creature whatsoever;[534] all worshipping of it,[535] or God in it or by it;[536] the making of any representation of feigned deities,[537] and all worship of them, or service belonging to them,[538] all superstitious devices,[539] corrupting the worship of God,[540] adding to it, or taking from it,[541] whether invented and taken up of ourselves,[542] or received by tradition from others,[543] though under the title of antiquity,[544] custom,[545] devotion,[546] good intent, or any other**

---

[518] Deuteronomy 32:46-47; Matthew 28:20; Acts 2:42; 1 Timothy 6:13-14.

[519] Ephesians 5:20; Philippians 4:6.

[520] Deuteronomy 17:18-19; Acts 10:33, 15:21; 2 Timothy 4:2; James 1:21-22.

[521] Matthew 28:19; 1 Corinthians 11:23-30.

[522] Matthew 16:19, 18:15-17; 1 Corinthians 5:1-13, 12:28.

[523] 1 Corinthians 9:7-15; Ephesians 4:11-12; 1 Timothy 5:17-18.

[524] Joel 2:12,18; 1 Corinthians 7:5.

[525] Deuteronomy 6:13.

[526] Psalm 76:11.

[527] Psalm 16:4; Acts 17:16-17.

[528] Deuteronomy 7:5; Isaiah 30:22.

[529] Numbers 15:39.

[530] Deuteronomy 13:6-8.

[531] Hosea 5:11; Micah 6:16.

[532] 1 Kings 11:33, 12:33.

[533] Deuteronomy 12:30-32.

[534] Deuteronomy 4:15-19; Acts 17:29; Romans 1:21-23,25.

[535] Daniel 3:18; Galatians 4:8.

[536] Exodus 32:5.

[537] Exodus 32:8.

[538] 1 Kings 18:26,28; Isaiah 65:11.

[539] Acts 17:22; Colossians 2:21-23.

[540] Malachi 1:7-8,14.

[541] Deuteronomy 4:2.

[542] Psalm 106:39.

[543] Matthew 15:9.

[544] 1 Peter 1:18.

[545] Jeremiah 44:17.

[546] Isaiah 65:3-5; Galatians 1:13-14.

pretence whatsoever;[547] simony;[548] sacrilege;[549] all neglect,[550] contempt,[551] hindering,[552] and opposing the worship and ordinances which God hath appointed.[553]

Questions 110 (cont.) – 112

110. Q. What are the reasons annexed to the second commandment, the more to enforce it?
    A. The reasons annexed to the second commandment, the more to enforce it, contained in these words, For I the Lord thy God am a jealous God, visiting the iniquity of the fathers upon the children unto the third and fourth generation of them that hate me; and showing mercy unto thousands of them that love me, and keep my commandments;[554] are, besides God's sovereignty over us, and propriety in us,[555] his fervent zeal for his own worship,[556] and his revengeful indignation against all false worship, as being a spiritual whoredom;[557] accounting the breakers of this commandment such as hate him, and threatening to punish them unto divers generations;[558] and esteeming the observers of it such as love him and keep his commandments, and promising mercy to them unto many generations.[559]

111. Q. Which is the third commandment?
    A. The third commandment is, Thou shalt not take the name of the Lord thy God in vain: for the Lord will not hold him guiltless that taketh his name in vain.[560]

112. Q. What is required in the third commandment?
    A. The third commandment requires, That the name of God, his titles, attributes,[561] ordinances,[562] the Word,[563] sacraments,[564] prayer,[565] oaths,[566] vows,[567] lots,[568] his works,[569] and whatsoever else there is whereby he makes himself known, be holily and reverently used in thought,[570] meditation,[571] word,[572]

---

[547] 1 Samuel 13:11-12, 15:21.
[548] Acts 8:18.
[549] Malachi 3:8; Romans 2:22.
[550] Exodus 4:24-26.
[551] Malachi 1:7,13; Matthew 22:5.
[552] Matthew 23:13.
[553] Acts 13:44-45; 1 Thessalonians 2:15-16.
[554] Exodus 20:5-6.
[555] Psalm 45:11; Revelation 15:3-4.
[556] Exodus 34:13-14.
[557] Deuteronomy 32:16-20; 1 Corinthians 10:20-22.
[558] Hosea 2:2-4.
[559] Deuteronomy 5:29.
[560] Exodus 20:7.
[561] Deuteronomy 28:58; Psalm 29:2, 68:4; Matthew 11:9; Revelation 15:3-4.
[562] Ecclesiastes 5:1; Malachi 1:14.
[563] Psalm 138:2.
[564] 1 Corinthians 11:24-25,28-29.
[565] 1 Timothy 2:8.
[566] Jeremiah 4:2.
[567] Ecclesiastes 5:2,4-6.
[568] Acts 1:24,26.
[569] Job 36:24.
[570] Malachi 3:16.
[571] Psalm 8:1,3-4,9.
[572] Psalm 105:2,5; Colossians 3:17.

and writing;[573] by an holy profession,[574] and answerable conversation,[575] to the glory of God,[576] and the good of ourselves,[577] and others.[578]

Questions 112 (cont.) – 113

113. Q. What are the sins forbidden in the third commandment?

A. The sins forbidden in the third commandment are, the not using of God's name as is required;[579] and the abuse of it in an ignorant,[580] vain,[581] irreverent, profane,[582] superstitious[583] or wicked mentioning or otherwise using his titles, attributes,[584] ordinances,[585] or works,[586] by blasphemy,[587] perjury;[588] all sinful cursings,[589] oaths,[590] vows,[591] and lots;[592] violating of our oaths and vows, if lawful;[593] and fulfilling them, if of things unlawful;[594] murmuring and quarrelling at,[595] curious prying into,[596] and misapplying of God's decrees[597] and providences;[598] misinterpreting,[599] misapplying,[600] or any way perverting the Word, or any part of it;[601] to profane jests,[602] curious or unprofitable questions, vain janglings, or the maintaining of false doctrines;[603] abusing it, the creatures, or anything contained under the name of God, to charms,[604] or sinful lusts and practices;[605] the maligning,[606] scorning,[607] reviling,[608] or any wise opposing of God's truth, grace, and ways;[609] making profession of religion in hypocrisy, or for sinister

---

[573] Psalm 102:18.
[574] Micah 4:5; 1 Peter 3:15.
[575] Philippians 1:27.
[576] 1 Corinthians 10:31.
[577] Jeremiah 32:39.
[578] 1 Peter 2:12.
[579] Malachi 2:2.
[580] Acts 17:23.
[581] Proverbs 30:9.
[582] Malachi 1:6-7,12, 3:14.
[583] 1 Samuel 4:3-5; Jeremiah 7:4,9-10,14,31; Colossians 2:20-22.
[584] Exodus 5:2; 2 Kings 18:30,35; Psalm 139:20.
[585] Psalm 50:16-17.
[586] Isaiah 5:12.
[587] Leviticus 24:11; 2 Kings 19:22.
[588] Zechariah 5:4, 8:17.
[589] 1 Samuel 17:43; 2 Samuel 16:5.
[590] Jeremiah 5:7, 23:10.
[591] Deuteronomy 23:18; Acts 23:12,14.
[592] Esther 3:7, 9:24; Psalm 22:18.
[593] Psalm 24:4; Ezekiel 17:16,18-19.
[594] 1 Samuel 25:22,32-34; Mark 6:26.
[595] Romans 9:14,19-20.
[596] Deuteronomy 29:29.
[597] Romans 3:5,7, 6:1.
[598] Psalm 39:1-13; Ecclesiastes 8:11, 9:3.
[599] Matthew 5:21-22.
[600] Ezekiel 13:22.
[601] Matthew 22:24-31, 25:28-30; 2 Peter 3:16.
[602] Isaiah 22:13; Jeremiah 23:34,36,38.
[603] 1 Timothy 1:4,6-7, 6:4-5,20; 2 Timothy 2:14; Titus 3:9.
[604] Deuteronomy 18:10-14; Acts 19:13.
[605] 1 Kings 21:9-10; Romans 13:13-14; 2 Timothy 4:3-4; Jude 4.
[606] Acts 13:45; 1 John 3:12.
[607] Psalm 1:1; 2 Peter 3:3.
[608] 1 Peter 4:4.
[609] Acts 13:45-46,50, 4:18, 19:9; 1 Thessalonians 2:16; Hebrews 10:29.

ends;[610] being ashamed of it,[611] or a shame to it, by unconformable,[612] unwise,[613] unfruitful,[614] and offensive walking,[615] or backsliding from it.[616]

Questions 113 (cont.) – 117

114. Q. What reasons are annexed to the third commandment?
    A. The reasons annexed to the third commandment, in these words, The Lord thy God, and, For the Lord will not hold him guiltless that taketh his name in vain,[617] are, because he is the Lord and our God, therefore his name is not to be profaned, or any way abused by us;[618] especially because he will be so far from acquitting and sparing the transgressors of this commandment, as that he will not suffer them to escape his righteous judgment;[619] albeit many such escape the censures and punishments of men.[620]

115. Q. Which is the fourth commandment?
    A. The fourth commandment is, Remember the Sabbath day, to keep it holy. Six days shalt thou labour, and do all thy work; but the seventh day is the Sabbath of the Lord thy God: in it thou shalt not do any work, thou, nor thy son, nor thy daughter, thy man-servant, nor thy maid-servant, nor thy cattle, nor thy stranger that is within thy gates. For in six days the Lord made heaven and earth, the sea, and all that in them is, and rested in the seventh day: wherefore the Lord blessed the Sabbath-day and hallowed it.[621]

116. Q. What is required in the fourth commandment?
    A. The fourth commandment requireth of all men the sanctifying or keeping holy to God such set times as he hath appointed in his Word, expressly one whole day in seven; which was the seventh from the beginning of the world to the resurrection of Christ, and the first day of the week ever since, and so to continue to the end of the world; which is the Christian Sabbath,[622] and in the New Testament called The Lord's Day.[623]

117. Q. How is the Sabbath or the Lord's Day to be sanctified?
    A. The Sabbath or Lord's Day is to be sanctified by an holy resting all the day,[624] not only from such works as are at all times sinful, but even from such worldly employments and recreations as are on other days lawful;[625] and making it our delight to spend the whole time (except so much of it as is to be taken up in works of necessity and mercy[626]) in the public and private exercises of God's worship:[627] and, to that end, we are to prepare our hearts, and with such foresight, diligence, and moderation, to dispose and seasonally dispatch our worldly business, that we may be the more free and fit for the duties of that day.[628]

---

[610] Matthew 23:14, 6:1-2,5,16; 2 Timothy 3:5.

[611] Mark 8:38.

[612] Psalm 73:14-15.

[613] 1 Corinthians 6:5-6; Ephesians 5:15-17.

[614] Isaiah 5:4; 2 Peter 1:8-9.

[615] Romans 2:23-24.

[616] Galatians 3:1,3; Hebrews 6:6.

[617] Exodus 20:7.

[618] Leviticus 19:12.

[619] Deuteronomy 28:58-59; Ezekiel 36:21-23; Zechariah 5:2-4.

[620] 1 Samuel 2:12,17,22,24, 3:13.

[621] Exodus 20:8-11.

[622] Genesis 2:2-3; Deuteronomy 5:12-14; Isaiah 56:2,4,6-7; Matthew 5:17-18; 1 Corinthians 16:1-2.

[623] Revelation 1:10.

[624] Exodus 20:8,10.

[625] Exodus 16:25-28; Nehemiah 13:15-22; Jeremiah 17:21-22.

[626] Matthew 12:1-13.

[627] Psalm 92:1-15; Isaiah 58:13, 66:23; Acts 20:7; 1 Corinthians 16:1-2.

[628] Exodus 16:22,25-26,29, 20:8; Nehemiah 13:19; Luke 23:54,56.

Questions 118 – 121

118. Q. Why is the charge of keeping the Sabbath more specially directed to governors of families, and other superiors?

A. **The charge of keeping the Sabbath is more specially directed to governors of families, and other superiors, because they are bound not only to keep it themselves, but to see that it be observed by all those that are under their charge; and because they are prone ofttimes to hinder them by employments of their own.[629]**

119. Q. What are the sins forbidden in the fourth commandment?

A. **The sins forbidden in the fourth commandment are, all omissions of the duties required,[630] all careless, negligent, and unprofitable performing of them, and being weary of them;[631] all profaning the day by idleness, and doing that which is in itself sinful;[632] and by all needless works, words, and thoughts, about our worldly employments and recreations.[633]**

120. Q. What are the reasons annexed to the fourth commandment, the more to enforce it?

A. **The reasons annexed to the fourth commandment, the more to enforce it, are taken from the equity of it, God allowing us six days of seven for our own affairs, and reserving but one for himself in these words, Six days shalt thou labour, and do all thy work:[634] from God's challenging a special propriety in that day, The seventh day is the Sabbath of the Lord thy God:[635] from the example of God, who in six days made heaven and earth, the sea, and all that in them is, and rested the seventh day: and from that blessing which God put upon that day, not only in sanctifying it to be a day for his service, but in ordaining it to be a means of blessing to us in our sanctifying it; Wherefore the Lord blessed the Sabbath day, and hallowed it.[636]**

121. Q. Why is the word Remember set in the beginning of the fourth commandment?

A. **The word Remember is set in the beginning of the fourth commandment,[637] partly, because of the great benefit of remembering it, we being thereby helped in our preparation to keep it,[638] and, in keeping it, better to keep all the rest of the commandments,[639] and to continue a thankful remembrance of the two great benefits of creation and redemption, which contain a short abridgment of religion;[640] and partly, because we are very ready to forget it,[641] for that there is less light of nature for it,[642] and yet it restraineth our natural liberty in things at other times lawful;[643] that it cometh but once in seven days, and many worldly businesses come between, and too often take off our minds from thinking of it, either to prepare for it, or to sanctify it;[644] and that Satan with his instruments labours much to blot out the glory, and even the memory of it, to bring in all irreligion and impiety.[645]**

---

[629] Exodus 20:10, 23:12; Joshua 24:15; Nehemiah 13:15,17; Jeremiah 17:20-22.

[630] Ezekiel 22:26.

[631] Ezekiel 33:30-32; Amos 8:5; Malachi 1:13; Acts 20:7,9.

[632] Ezekiel 23:38.

[633] Isaiah 58:13; Jeremiah 17:24,27.

[634] Exodus 20:9.

[635] Exodus 20:10.

[636] Exodus 20:11.

[637] Exodus 20:8.

[638] Exodus 16:23; Nehemiah 13:19; Mark 15:42; Luke 23:54,56.

[639] Psalm 92:1-15; Ezekiel 20:12,19-20.

[640] Genesis 2:2-3; Psalm 118:22,24; Acts 4:10-11; Revelation 1:10.

[641] Ezekiel 22:26.

[642] Nehemiah 9:14.

[643] Exodus 34:21.

[644] Deuteronomy 5:14-15; Amos 8:5.

[645] Nehemiah 13:15-22; Jeremiah 17:21-23; Lamentations 1:7.

Questions 122 – 127

122. Q. What is the sum of the six commandments which contain our duty to man?
     A. **The sum of the six commandments which contain our duty to man, is, to love our neighbour as ourselves,[646] and to do to others what we would have them to do to us.[647]**

123. Q. Which is the fifth commandment?
     A. **The fifth commandment is, Honour thy father and thy mother: that thy days may be long upon the land which the Lord thy God giveth thee.[648]**

124. Q. Who are meant by father and mother in the fifth commandment?
     A. **By father and mother, in the fifth commandment, are meant, not only natural parents,[649] but all superiors in age[650] and gifts;[651] and especially such as, by God's ordinance, are over us in place of authority, whether in family,[652] church,[653] or commonwealth.[654]**

125. Q. Why are superiors styled Father and Mother?
     A. **Superiors are styled father and mother, both to teach them in all duties toward their inferiors, like natural parents, to express love and tenderness to them, according to their several relations;[655] and to work inferiors to a greater willingness and cheerfulness in performing their duties to their superiors, as to their parents.[656]**

126. Q. What is the general scope of the fifth commandment?
     A. **The general scope of the fifth commandment is, the performance of those duties which we mutually owe in our several relations, as inferiors, superiors, or equals.[657]**

127. Q. What is the honor that inferiors owe to their superiors?
     A. **The honour which inferiors owe to their superiors is, all due reverence in heart,[658] word,[659] and behaviour;[660] prayer and thanksgiving for them;[661] imitation of their virtues and graces;[662] willing obedience to their lawful commands and counsels;[663] due submission to their corrections;[664] fidelity to,[665] defence,[666] and maintenance of their persons and authority, according to their several ranks, and the**

---

[646] Matthew 22:39.

[647] Matthew 7:12.

[648] Exodus 20:12.

[649] Proverbs 23:22,25; Ephesians 6:1-2.

[650] 1 Timothy 5:1-2.

[651] Genesis 4:20-22, 45:8.

[652] 2 Kings 5:13.

[653] 2 Kings 2:12, 13:14; Galatians 4:19.

[654] Isaiah 49:23.

[655] Numbers 11:11-12; Ephesians 6:4; 2 Corinthians 12:14; 1 Thessalonians 2:7-8,11.

[656] 2 Kings 5:13; 1 Corinthians 4:14-16.

[657] Romans 12:10; Ephesians 5:21; 1 Peter 2:17.

[658] Leviticus 19:3; Malachi 1:6.

[659] Proverbs 31:28; 1 Peter 3:6.

[660] Leviticus 19:32; 1 Kings 2:19.

[661] 1 Timothy 2:1-2.

[662] Philippians 3:17; Hebrews 13:7.

[663] Exodus 18:19,24; Proverbs 4:3-4, 23:22; Romans 13:1-5; Ephesians 6:1-2,6-7; Hebrews 13:17; 1 Peter 2:13-14.

[664] Hebrews 12:9; 1 Peter 2:18-20.

[665] Titus 2:9-10.

[666] 1 Samuel 26:15-16; 2 Samuel 18:3; Esther 6:2.

nature of their places;[667] bearing with their infirmities, and covering them in love,[668] that so they may be an honour to them and to their government.[669]

Questions 127 (cont.) – 130

128. Q.   What are the sins of inferiors against their superiors?
     A.   The sins of inferiors against their superiors are, all neglect of the duties required toward them;[670] envying at,[671] contempt of,[672] and rebellion[673] against, their persons[674] and places,[675] in their lawful counsels,[676] commands, and corrections;[677] cursing, mocking[678] and all such refractory and scandalous carriage, as proves a shame and dishonour to them and their government.[679]

129. Q.   What is required of superiors towards their inferiors?
     A.   It is required of superiors, according to that power they receive from God, and that relation wherein they stand, to love,[680] pray for,[681] and bless their inferiors;[682] to instruct,[683] counsel, and admonish them;[684] countenancing,[685] commending,[686] and rewarding such as do well;[687] and discountenancing,[688] reproving, and chastising such as do ill;[689] protecting,[690] and providing for them all things necessary for soul[691] and body:[692] and by grave, wise, holy, and exemplary carriage, to procure glory to God,[693] honour to themselves,[694] and so to preserve that authority which God hath put upon them.[695]

130. Q.   What are the sins of superiors?
     A.   The sins of superiors are, besides the neglect of the duties required of them,[696] and inordinate seeking of themselves,[697] their own glory,[698] ease, profit, or pleasure;[699] commanding things unlawful,[700] or not in

---

[667] Genesis 45:11, 47:12; Matthew 22:21; Romans 13:6-7; Galatians 6:6; 1 Timothy 5:17-18.
[668] Genesis 9:23; Proverbs 23:22; 1 Peter 2:18.
[669] Psalm 127:3-5; Proverbs 31:23.
[670] Matthew 15:4-6.
[671] Numbers 11:28-29.
[672] 1 Samuel 8:7; Isaiah 3:5.
[673] 2 Samuel 15:1-12.
[674] Exodus 21:15.
[675] 1 Samuel 10:27.
[676] 1 Samuel 2:25.
[677] Deuteronomy 21:18-21.
[678] Proverbs 30:11,17.
[679] Proverbs 19:26.
[680] Colossians 3:19; Titus 2:4.
[681] 1 Samuel 12:23; Job 1:5.
[682] Genesis 49:28; 1 Kings 8:55-56; Hebrews 7:7.
[683] Deuteronomy 6:6-7.
[684] Ephesians 6:4.
[685] 1 Peter 3:7.
[686] Romans 13:3; 1 Peter 2:14.
[687] Esther 6:3.
[688] Romans 13:3-4.
[689] Proverbs 29:15; 1 Peter 2:14.
[690] Job 29:13-16; Isaiah 1:10,17.
[691] Ephesians 6:4.
[692] 1 Timothy 5:8.
[693] 1 Timothy 4:12; Titus 2:3-5.
[694] 1 Kings 3:28.
[695] Titus 2:15.
[696] Ezekiel 34:2-4.
[697] Philippians 2:21.
[698] John 5:44, 7:18.
[699] Deuteronomy 17:17; Isaiah 56:10-11.
[700] Daniel 3:4-6; Acts 4:17-18.

the power of inferiors to perform;[701] counseling,[702] encouraging,[703] or favouring them in that which is evil;[704] dissuading, discouraging, or discountenancing them in that which is good;[705] correcting them unduly;[706] careless exposing, or leaving them to wrong, temptation, and danger;[707] provoking them to wrath;[708] or any way dishonouring themselves, or lessening their authority, by an unjust, indiscreet, rigorous, or remiss behaviour.[709]

Questions 130 (cont.) – 135

131. Q. What are the duties of equals?
A. The duties of equals are, to regard the dignity and worth of each other,[710] in giving honour to go one before another;[711] and to rejoice in each others' gifts and advancement, as their own.[712]

132. Q. What are the sins of equals?
A. The sins of equals are, besides the neglect of the duties required,[713] the undervaluing of the worth,[714] envying the gifts,[715] grieving at the advancement of prosperity one of another;[716] and usurping pre-eminence one over another.[717]

133. Q. What is the reason annexed to the fifth commandment, the more to enforce it?
A. The reason annexed to the fifth commandment, in these words, That thy days may be long upon the land which the Lord thy God giveth thee,[718] is an express promise of long life and prosperity, as far as it shall serve for God's glory and their own good, to all such as keep this commandment.[719]

134. Q. Which is the sixth commandment?
A. The sixth commandment is, Thou shalt not kill.[720]

135. Q. What are the duties required in the sixth commandment?
A. The duties required in the sixth commandment are all careful studies, and lawful endeavors, to preserve the life of ourselves[721] and others[722] by resisting all thoughts and purposes,[723] subduing all passions,[724] and avoiding all occasions,[725] temptations,[726] and practices, which tend to the unjust taking away the life

---

[701] Exodus 5:10-18; Matthew 23:2,4.
[702] Matthew 14:8; Mark 6:24.
[703] 2 Samuel 13:28.
[704] 1 Samuel 3:13.
[705] Exodus 5:17; John 7:46-49; Colossians 3:21.
[706] Deuteronomy 25:3; Hebrews 12:10; 1 Peter 2:18-20.
[707] Genesis 38:11,26; Acts 18:17.
[708] Ephesians 6:4.
[709] Genesis 9:21; 1 Samuel 2:29-31; 1 Kings 1:6, 12:13-16.
[710] 1 Peter 2:17.
[711] Romans 12:10.
[712] Romans 12:15-16; Philippians 2:3-4.
[713] Romans 13:8.
[714] 2 Timothy 3:3.
[715] Acts 7:9; Galatians 5:26.
[716] Numbers 12:2; Esther 6:12-13.
[717] Luke 22:24; 3 John 9.
[718] Exodus 20:12.
[719] Deuteronomy 5:16; 1 Kings 8:25; Ephesians 6:2-3.
[720] Exodus 20:13.
[721] Ephesians 5:28-29.
[722] 1 Kings 18:4.
[723] Jeremiah 26:15-16; Acts 23:12,16-17,21,27.
[724] Ephesians 4:26-27.
[725] Deuteronomy 22:8; 2 Samuel 2:22.
[726] Proverbs 1:10-11,15-16; Matthew 4:6-7.

of any;[727] by just defence thereof against violence,[728] patient bearing of the hand of God,[729] quietness of mind,[730] cheerfulness of spirit;[731] a sober use of meat,[732] drink,[733] physic,[734] sleep,[735] labour,[736] and recreations;[737] by charitable thoughts,[738] love,[739] compassion,[740] meekness, gentleness, kindness;[741] peaceable,[742] mild and courteous speeches and behaviour;[743] forbearance, readiness to be reconciled, patient bearing and forgiving of injuries, and requiting good for evil;[744] comforting and succouring the distressed and protecting and defending the innocent.[745]

Questions 135 (cont.) – 136

136. Q. What are the sins forbidden in the sixth commandment?

A. The sins forbidden in the sixth commandment are, all taking away the life of ourselves,[746] or of others,[747] except in case of public justice,[748] lawful war,[749] or necessary defence;[750] the neglecting or withdrawing the lawful and necessary means of preservation of life;[751] sinful anger,[752] hatred,[753] envy,[754] desire of revenge;[755] all excessive passions,[756] distracting cares;[757] immoderate use of meat, drink,[758] labor,[759] and recreations;[760] provoking words,[761] oppression,[762] quarreling,[763] striking, wounding,[764] and whatsoever else tends to the destruction of the life of any.[765]

---

[727] Genesis 37:21-22; 1 Samuel 24:12, 26:9-11.
[728] Psalm 82:4; Proverbs 24:11-12; 1 Samuel 14:45.
[729] Hebrews 12:9; James 5:7-11.
[730] Psalm 37:8-11; 1 Thessalonians 4:11; 1 Peter 3:3-4.
[731] Proverbs 17:22.
[732] Proverbs 25:16,27.
[733] 1 Timothy 5:23.
[734] Isaiah 38:21.
[735] Psalm 127:2.
[736] Proverbs 16:20; Ecclesiastes 5:12; 2 Thessalonians 3:10,12.
[737] Ecclesiastes 3:4,11.
[738] 1 Samuel 19:4-5, 22:13-14.
[739] Romans 13:10.
[740] Luke 10:33-34.
[741] Colossians 3:12-13.
[742] James 3:17.
[743] Judges 8:1-3; Proverbs 15:1; 1 Peter 3:8-11.
[744] Matthew 5:24; Romans 12:17; Ephesians 5:2,32.
[745] Job 31:19-20; Proverbs 31:8-9; Matthew 25:35-36; 1 Thessalonians 5:14.
[746] Acts 16:28.
[747] Genesis 9:6.
[748] Numbers 35:31,33.
[749] Deuteronomy 20:1; Jeremiah 48:10.
[750] Exodus 22:2-3.
[751] Ecclesiastes 6:1-2; Matthew 25:42-43; James 2:15-16.
[752] Matthew 5:22.
[753] Leviticus 19:17; 1 John 3:15.
[754] Proverbs 14:30.
[755] Romans 12:19.
[756] Ephesians 4:31.
[757] Matthew 6:31,34.
[758] Luke 21:34; Romans 13:13.
[759] Ecclesiastes 12:12, 2:22-23.
[760] Isaiah 5:12.
[761] Proverbs 12:18, 15:1;.
[762] Exodus 1:14; Ezekiel 18:18.
[763] Proverbs 23:29; Galatians 5:15.
[764] Numbers 35:16-18,21.
[765] Exodus 21:18-36.

Questions 137 – 139

137. Q.   Which is the seventh commandment?
     A.   The seventh commandment is, Thou shalt not commit adultery.[766]

138. Q.   What are the duties required in the seventh commandment?
     A.   The duties required in the seventh commandment are, chastity in body, mind, affections,[767] words,[768] and behavior;[769] and the preservation of it in ourselves and others;[770] watchfulness over the eyes and all the senses;[771] temperance,[772] keeping of chaste company,[773] modesty in apparel;[774] marriage by those that have not the gift of continency,[775] conjugal love,[776] and cohabitation;[777] diligent labor in our callings;[778] shunning all occasions of uncleanness, and resisting temptations thereunto.[779]

139. Q.   What are the sins forbidden in the seventh commandment?
     A.   The sins forbidden in the seventh commandment, besides the neglect of the duties required,[780] are, adultery, fornication,[781] rape, incest,[782] sodomy, and all unnatural lusts;[783] all unclean imaginations, thoughts, purposes, and affections;[784] all corrupt or filthy communications, or listening thereunto;[785] wanton looks,[786] impudent or light behaviour, immodest apparel;[787] prohibiting of lawful,[788] and dispensing with unlawful marriages;[789] allowing, tolerating, keeping of stews, and resorting to them;[790] entangling vows of single life,[791] undue delay of marriage,[792] having more wives or husbands than one at the same time;[793] unjust divorce,[794] or desertion;[795] idleness, gluttony, drunkenness,[796] unchaste company;[797] lascivious songs, books, pictures, dancings, stage plays;[798] and all other provocations to, or acts of uncleanness, either in ourselves or others.[799]

---

[766] Exodus 20:14.

[767] Job 31:1; 1 Corinthians 7:34; 1 Thessalonians 4:4.

[768] Colossians 4:6.

[769] 1 Peter 3:2.

[770] 1 Corinthians 7:2,35-36.

[771] Job 31:1.

[772] Acts 24:24-25.

[773] Proverbs 2:16-20.

[774] 1 Timothy 2:9.

[775] 1 Corinthians 7:2,9.

[776] Proverbs 5:19-20.

[777] 1 Peter 3:7.

[778] Proverbs 31:11,27-28.

[779] Genesis 39:8-10; Proverbs 5:8.

[780] Proverbs 5:7.

[781] Galatians 5:19; Hebrews 13:4.

[782] 2 Samuel 13:14; 1 Corinthians 5:1.

[783] Leviticus 20:15-16; Romans 1:24,26-27.

[784] Matthew 5:28, 15:19; Colossians 3:5.

[785] Proverbs 7:5,21-22; Ephesians 5:3-4.

[786] Isaiah 3:16; 2 Peter 2:14.

[787] Proverbs 7:10,13.

[788] 1 Timothy 4:3.

[789] Leviticus 18:1-21; Malachi 2:11-12; Mark 6:18.

[790] Leviticus 19:29; Deuteronomy 23:17-18; 1 Kings 15:12; 2 Kings 23:7; Proverbs 7:24-27; Jeremiah 5:7.

[791] Matthew 19:10-11.

[792] Genesis 38:26; 1 Corinthians 7:7-9.

[793] Malachi 2:14-15; Matthew 19:5.

[794] Malachi 2:16; Matthew 5:32.

[795] 1 Corinthians 7:12-13.

[796] Proverbs 23:30-33; Ezekiel 16:49.

[797] Genesis 39:19; Proverbs 5:8.

[798] Isaiah 23:15-17, 3:16; Ezekiel 23:14-16; Mark 6:22; Romans 13:13; Ephesians 5:4; 1 Peter 4:3.

[799] 2 Kings 9:30; Jeremiah 4:30; Ezekiel 23:40.

Questions 140 – 142

140. Q.   Which is the eighth commandment?

   A.   **The eighth commandment is, Thou shalt not steal.**[800]

141. Q.   What are the duties required in the eighth commandment?

   A.   **The duties required in the eighth commandment are, truth, faithfulness, and justice in contracts and commerce between man and man;[801] rendering to everyone his due; restitution of goods unlawfully detained from the right owners thereof;[802] giving and lending freely, according to our abilities, and the necessities of others;[803] moderation of our judgments, wills, and affections concerning worldly goods;[804] a provident care and study to get,[805] keep, use, and dispose these things which are necessary and convenient for the sustentation of our nature, and suitable to our condition;[806] a lawful calling,[807] and diligence in it;[808] frugality;[809] avoiding unnecessary lawsuits,[810] and suretiship, or other like engagements;[811] and an endeavor, by all just and lawful means, to procure, preserve, and further the wealth and outward estate of others, as well as our own.[812]**

142. Q.   What are the sins forbidden in the eighth commandment?

   A.   **The sins forbidden in the eighth commandment, besides the neglect of the duties required,[813] are, theft,[814] robbery,[815] man-stealing,[816] and receiving any thing that is stolen;[817] fraudulent dealing,[818] false weights and measures,[819] removing landmarks,[820] injustice and unfaithfulness in contracts between man and man,[821] or in matters of trust;[822] oppression,[823] extortion,[824] usury,[825] bribery,[826] vexatious lawsuits,[827] unjust inclosures and depredation;[828] ingrossing commodities to enhance the price;[829] unlawful callings,[830] and all other unjust or sinful ways of taking or withholding from our neighbour what belongs**

---

[800] Exodus 20:15.

[801] Psalm 15:2,4; Zechariah 7:4,10, 8:16-17.

[802] Leviticus 6:2-5; Luke 19:8.

[803] Luke 6:30,38; Galatians 6:10; Ephesians 4:28; 1 John 3:17.

[804] Galatians 6:14; 1 Timothy 6:6-9.

[805] 1 Timothy 5:8.

[806] Proverbs 27:23-27; Ecclesiastes 2:24, 3:12-13; Isaiah 38:1; Matthew 11:8; 1 Timothy 6:17-18.

[807] Genesis 2:15, 3:19; 1 Corinthians 7:20.

[808] Proverbs 10:4; Ephesians 4:28.

[809] Proverbs 21:20; John 6:12.

[810] 1 Corinthians 6:1-9.

[811] Proverbs 6:1-6, 11:15.

[812] Genesis 47:14,20; Exodus 23:4-5; Leviticus 25:35; Deuteronomy 22:1-4; Matthew 22:39; Philippians 2:4.

[813] James 2:15-16; 1 John 3:17.

[814] Ephesians 4:28.

[815] Psalm 62:10.

[816] 1 Timothy 1:10.

[817] Psalm 50:18; Proverbs 29:24.

[818] 1 Thessalonians 4:6.

[819] Proverbs 11:1, 20:10.

[820] Deuteronomy 19:14; Proverbs 23:10.

[821] Psalm 37:21; Amos 8:5.

[822] Luke 16:10-12.

[823] Leviticus 25:17; Ezekiel 22:29.

[824] Ezekiel 22:12; Matthew 23:25.

[825] Psalm 15:5.

[826] Job 15:34.

[827] Proverbs 3:29-30; 1 Corinthians 6:6-8.

[828] Isaiah 5:8; Micah 2:2.

[829] Proverbs 11:26.

[830] Acts 19:19,24-25.

to him, or of enriching ourselves;[831] covetousness;[832] inordinate prizing and affecting worldly goods;[833] distrustful and distracting cares and studies in getting, keeping, and using them;[834] envying at the prosperity of others;[835] as likewise idleness,[836] prodigality, wasteful gaming; and all other ways whereby we do unduly prejudice our own outward estate,[837] and defrauding ourselves of the due use and comfort of that estate which God hath given us.[838]

Questions 142 (cont.) – 144

143. Q. Which is the ninth commandment?
   A. The ninth commandment is, Thou shalt not bear false witness against thy neighbor.[839]

144. Q. What are the duties required in the ninth commandment?
   A. The duties required in the ninth commandment are, the preserving and promoting of truth between man and man,[840] and the good name of our neighbour, as well as our own;[841] appearing and standing for the truth;[842] and from the heart,[843] sincerely,[844] freely,[845] clearly,[846] and fully,[847] speaking the truth, and only the truth, in matters of judgment and justice,[848] and in all other things whatsoever;[849] a charitable esteem of our neighbours;[850] loving, desiring, and rejoicing in their good name;[851] sorrowing for,[852] and covering of their infirmities;[853] freely acknowledging of their gifts and graces,[854] defending their innocency;[855] a ready receiving of a good report,[856] and unwillingness to admit of an evil report,[857] concerning them; discouraging tale-bearers,[858] flatterers,[859] and slanderers;[860] love and care of our own good name, and defending it when need requireth;[861] keeping of lawful promises;[862] studying and practicing of whatsoever things are true, honest, lovely, and of good report.[863]

---

[831] Job 20:19; Proverbs 21:6; James 5:4.
[832] Luke 12:15.
[833] Psalm 62:10; Proverbs 23:5; Colossians 3:2; 1 Timothy 6:5.
[834] Matthew 6:25,31,34.
[835] Psalm 37:1,7, 73:3.
[836] Proverbs 18:9; 2 Thessalonians 3:11.
[837] Proverbs 21:17, 23:20-21, 28:19.
[838] Ecclesiastes 4:8, 6:2; 1 Timothy 5:8.
[839] Exodus 20:16.
[840] Zechariah 8:16.
[841] 3 John 12.
[842] Proverbs 31:8-9.
[843] Psalm 15:2.
[844] 2 Chronicles 19:9.
[845] 1 Samuel 19:4-5.
[846] Joshua 7:19.
[847] 2 Samuel 14:18-20.
[848] Leviticus 19:15.
[849] 2 Corinthians 1:17-18; Ephesians 4:25.
[850] 1 Corinthians 13:7; Hebrews 6:9.
[851] Romans 1:8; 2 John 4; 3 John 3-4.
[852] 2 Corinthians 2:4, 12:21.
[853] Proverbs 17:9; 1 Peter 4:8.
[854] 1 Corinthians 1:4-5,7; 2 Timothy 1:4-5.
[855] 1 Samuel 22:14.
[856] 1 Corinthians 13:6-7.
[857] Psalm 15:3.
[858] Proverbs 25:23.
[859] Proverbs 26:24-25.
[860] Psalm 101:5.
[861] Proverbs 22:1; John 8:49.
[862] Psalm 15:4.
[863] Philippians 4:8.

Question 145

145. Q. What are the sins forbidden in the ninth commandment?

A. The sins forbidden in the ninth commandment are, all prejudicing the truth, and the good name of our neighbours, as well as our own,[864] especially in public judicature;[865] giving false evidence,[866] suborning false witnesses,[867] wittingly appearing and pleading for an evil cause, outfacing and overbearing the truth;[868] passing unjust sentence,[869] calling evil good, and good evil; rewarding the wicked according to the work of the righteous, and the righteous according to the work of the wicked;[870] forgery,[871] concealing the truth, undue silence in a just cause,[872] and holding our peace when iniquity calleth for either a reproof from ourselves,[873] or complaint to others;[874] speaking the truth unseasonably,[875] or maliciously to a wrong end,[876] or perverting it to a wrong meaning,[877] or in doubtful and equivocal expressions, to the prejudice of truth or justice;[878] speaking untruth,[879] lying,[880] slandering,[881] backbiting,[882] detracting, tale bearing,[883] whispering,[884] scoffing,[885] reviling,[886] rash,[887] harsh,[888] and partial censuring;[889] misconstructing intentions, words, and actions;[890] flattering,[891] vain-glorious boasting;[892] thinking or speaking too highly or too meanly of ourselves or others;[893] denying the gifts and graces of God;[894] aggravating smaller faults;[895] hiding, excusing, or extenuating of sins, when called to a free confession;[896] unnecessary discovering of infirmities;[897] raising false rumors,[898] receiving and countenancing evil reports,[899] and stopping our ears against just defense;[900] evil suspicion;[901] envying or grieving at the deserved credit of

---

864 1 Samuel 17:28; 2 Samuel 1:9-10,15-16, 16:3.
865 Leviticus 19:15; Habakkuk 1:4.
866 Proverbs 19:5, 6:16,19.
867 Acts 6:13.
868 Psalm 12:3-4, 52:1-4; Jeremiah 9:3,5; Acts 24:2,5.
869 1 Kings 21:9-14; Proverbs 17:15.
870 Isaiah 5:23.
871 Psalm 119:69; Luke 16:5-7, 19:8.
872 Leviticus 5:1; Deuteronomy 13:8; Acts 5:3,8-9; 2 Timothy 4:6.
873 Leviticus 19:17; 1 Kings 1:6.
874 Isaiah 59:4.
875 Proverbs 29:11.
876 1 Samuel 22:9-10; Psalm 52:1-5.
877 Psalm 56:5; Matthew 26:60-61; John 2:19.
878 Genesis 3:5, 26:7,9.
879 Isaiah 59:13.
880 Leviticus 19:11; Colossians 3:9.
881 Psalm 50:20.
882 Jeremiah 38:4; James 4:11.
883 Leviticus 19:19.
884 Romans 1:29-30.
885 Genesis 21:9; Galatians 4:29.
886 1 Corinthians 6:10.
887 Matthew 7:1.
888 Acts 28:4.
889 Genesis 38:24; Romans 2:1.
890 1 Samuel 1:13-15; 2 Samuel 10:3; Nehemiah 6:6-8; Psalm 69:10; Romans 3:8.
891 Psalm 12:2-3.
892 2 Timothy 3:2.
893 Exodus 4:10-14; Luke 18:9,11; Acts 12:22; Romans 12:16; 1 Corinthians 4:6.
894 Job 27:5-6, 4:6.
895 Matthew 7:3-5.
896 Genesis 3:12-13, 4:9; 2 Kings 5:25; Proverbs 28:13, 30:20; Jeremiah 2:35.
897 Genesis 9:22; Proverbs 25:9-10.
898 Exodus 23:1.
899 Proverbs 29:12.
900 Job 31:13-14; Acts 7:56-57.
901 1 Corinthians 13:5; 1 Timothy 6:4.

any,[902] endeavoring or desiring to impair it,[903] rejoicing in their disgrace and infamy;[904] scornful contempt,[905] fond admiration;[906] breach of lawful promises;[907] neglecting such things as are of good report,[908] and practicing, or not avoiding ourselves, or not hindering what we can in others, such things as procure an ill name.[909]

Questions 145 (cont.) - 151

146. Q. Which is the tenth commandment?
   A. The tenth commandment is, Thou shalt not covet thy neighbour's house, thou shall not covet thy neighbour's wife, nor his man-servant, nor his maid-servant, nor his ox, nor his ass, nor any thing that is thy neighbour's.[910]

147. Q. What are the duties required in the tenth commandment?
   A. The duties required in the tenth commandment are, such a full contentment with our own condition,[911] and such a charitable frame of the whole soul toward our neighbour, as that all our inward motions and affections touching him, tend unto, and further all that good which is his.[912]

148. Q. What are the sins forbidden in the tenth commandment?
   A. The sins forbidden in the tenth commandment are, discontentment with our own estate;[913] envying[914] and grieving at the good of our neighbour,[915] together with all inordinate motions and affections to anything that is his.[916]

149. Q. Is any man able perfectly to keep the commandments of God?
   A. No man is able, either of himself,[917] or by any grace received in this life, perfectly to keep the commandments of God;[918] but doth daily break them in thought,[919] word, and deed.[920]

150. Q. Are all transgressions of the law of God equally heinous in themselves, and in the sight of God?
   A. All transgressions of the law of God are not equally heinous; but some sins in themselves, and by reason of several aggravations, are more heinous in the sight of God than others.[921]

151. Q. What are those aggravations that make some sins more heinous than others?
   A. Sins receive their aggravations,

---

902 Numbers 11:29; Matthew 21:15.
903 Ezra 4:12-13.
904 Jeremiah 48:27.
905 Psalm 35:15-16,21; Matthew 27:28-29.
906 Acts 12:22; Jude 16.
907 Romans 1:31; 2 Timothy 3:3.
908 1 Samuel 2:24.
909 2 Samuel 13:12-13; Proverbs 5:8-9, 6:33.
910 Exodus 20:17.
911 1 Timothy 6:6; Hebrews 13:5.
912 Esther 10:3; Job 31:29; Psalm 122:7-9; Romans 12:15; 1 Corinthians 13:4-7; 1 Timothy 1:5.
913 1 Kings 21:4; Esther 5:13; 1 Corinthians 10:10.
914 Galatians 5:26; James 3:14,16.
915 Nehemiah 2:10; Psalm 112:9-10.
916 Deuteronomy 5:21; Romans 7:7-8, 13:9; Colossians 3:5.
917 John 15:5; Romans 8:3; James 3:2.
918 Ecclesiastes 7:20; Romans 7:18-19; Galatians 5:17; 1 John 1:8,10.
919 Genesis 6:5, 8:21.
920 Romans 3:9-19; James 3:2-13.
921 Psalm 78:17,32,56; Ezekiel 8:6,13,15; John 19:11; 1 John 5:16.

1. From the persons offending[922] if they be of riper age,[923] greater experience or grace,[924] eminent for profession,[925] gifts,[926] place,[927] office,[928] guides to others,[929] and whose example is likely to be followed by others.[930]

2. From the parties offended:[931] if immediately against God,[932] his attributes,[933] and worship;[934] against Christ, and his grace;[935] the Holy Spirit,[936] his witness,[937] and workings[938] against superiors, men of eminency,[939] and such as we stand especially related and engaged unto;[940] against any of the saints,[941] particularly weak brethren,[942] the souls of them, or any other,[943] and the common good of all or many.[944]

3. From the nature and quality of the offense:[945] if it be against the express letter of the law,[946] break many commandments, contain in it many sins:[947] if not only conceived in the heart, but breaks forth in words and actions,[948] scandalize others,[949] and admit of no reparation:[950] if against means,[951] mercies,[952] judgments,[953] light of nature,[954] conviction of conscience,[955] public or private admonition,[956] censures of the church,[957] civil punishments;[958] and our prayers, purposes, promises,[959] vows,[960] covenants,[961] and

---

[922] Jeremiah 2:8.

[923] Job 32:7,9; Ecclesiastes 4:13.

[924] 1 Kings 11:4,9.

[925] 2 Samuel 12:14; 1 Corinthians 5:1.

[926] Luke 12:47-48; James 4:17.

[927] Jeremiah 5:4-5.

[928] 2 Samuel 12:7-9; Ezekiel 8:11-12.

[929] Romans 2:17-24.

[930] Galatians 2:11-14.

[931] Matthew 21:38-39.

[932] 1 Samuel 2:25; Psalm 5:4; Acts 5:4.

[933] Romans 2:4.

[934] Malachi 1:8,14.

[935] Hebrews 2:2-3, 7:25.

[936] Matthew 12:31-32; Hebrews 10:29.

[937] Ephesians 4:30.

[938] Hebrews 6:4-6.

[939] Numbers 12:8-9; Isaiah 3:5; Jude 8.

[940] Psalm 55:12-15; Proverbs 30:17; 2 Corinthians 12:15.

[941] Zephaniah 2:8,10-11; Matthew 18:6; 1 Corinthians 6:8; Revelation 17:6.

[942] Romans 14:13,15,21; 1 Corinthians 8:11-12.

[943] Ezekiel 13:19; Matthew 23:15; 1 Corinthians 8:12; Revelation 18:12-13.

[944] Joshua 22:20; 1 Thessalonians 2:15-16.

[945] Proverbs 6:30-33.

[946] 1 Kings 11:9-10; Ezra 9:10-12.

[947] Joshua 7:21; Proverbs 5:8-12, 6:32-33; Colossians 3:5; 1 Timothy 6:10;.

[948] Micah 2:1; Matthew 5:22; James 1:14-15.

[949] Matthew 18:7; Romans 2:23-24.

[950] Deuteronomy 22:22,28-29; Proverbs 6:32-35.

[951] Matthew 11:21-24; John 15:22.

[952] Deuteronomy 32:6; Isaiah 1:3.

[953] Jeremiah 5:3; Amos 4:8-11.

[954] Romans 1:26-27.

[955] Daniel 5:22; Romans 1:32; Titus 3:10-11.

[956] Proverbs 29:1.

[957] Matthew 18:17; Titus 3:10.

[958] Proverbs 27:22, 23:35.

[959] Psalm 78:34-37; Jeremiah 2:20, 13:5-6,20-21.

[960] Proverbs 20:25; Ecclesiastes 5:4-6.

[961] Leviticus 26:25.

engagements to God or men:[962] if done deliberately,[963] wilfully,[964] presumptuously,[965] impudently,[966] boastingly,[967] maliciously,[968] frequently,[969] obstinately,[970] with delight,[971] continuance,[972] or relapsing after repentance.[973]

4. From circumstances of time[974] and place:[975] if on the Lord's Day,[976] or other times of divine worship;[977] or immediately before[978] or after these,[979] or other helps to prevent or remedy such miscarriages;[980] if in public, or in the presence of others, who are thereby likely to be provoked or defiled.[981]

Questions 151 (cont.) – 154

152. Q. What doth every sin deserve at the hands of God?
     A. Every sin, even the least, being against the sovereignty,[982] goodness,[983] and holiness of God,[984] and against his righteous law,[985] deserveth his wrath and curse,[986] both in this life,[987] and that which is to come;[988] and cannot be expiated but by the blood of Christ.[989]

153. Q. What doth God require of us, that we may escape his wrath and curse due to us by reason of the transgression of the law?
     A. That we may escape the wrath and curse of God due to us by reason of the transgression of the law, he requireth of us repentance toward God, and faith toward our Lord Jesus Christ,[990] and the diligent use of the outward means whereby Christ communicates to us the benefits of his mediation.[991]

154. Q. What are the outward means whereby Christ communicates to us the benefits of his mediation?
     A. The outward and ordinary means whereby Christ communicates to his church the benefits of his mediation, are all his ordinances; especially the Word, sacraments, and prayer; all which are made effectual to the elect for their salvation.[992]

---

[962] Proverbs 2:17; Ezekiel 7:18-19.
[963] Psalm 36:4.
[964] Jeremiah 6:16.
[965] Exodus 21:14; Numbers 15:30.
[966] Proverbs 7:13; Jeremiah 3:3.
[967] Psalm 52:1.
[968] 3 John 10.
[969] Numbers 14:22.
[970] Zechariah 7:11-12.
[971] Proverbs 2:14.
[972] Isaiah 57:17.
[973] Jeremiah 34:8-11; 2 Peter 2:20-22.
[974] 2 Kings 5:26.
[975] Isaiah 26:10; Jeremiah 7:10.
[976] Ezekiel 23:37-39.
[977] Numbers 25:6-7; Isaiah 58:3-5.
[978] 1 Corinthians 11:20-21
[979] Proverbs 7:14-15; Jeremiah 7:8-10; John 13:27,30.
[980] Ezra 9:13-14.
[981] 1 Samuel 2:22-24; 2 Samuel 16:22.
[982] James 2:10-11.
[983] Exodus 20:1-2.
[984] Leviticus 10:3, 11:44-45; Habakkuk 1:13.
[985] Romans 7:12; 1 John 3:4.
[986] Galatians 3:10; Ephesians 5:6.
[987] Deuteronomy 28:15-18; Lamentations 3:39.
[988] Matthew 25:41.
[989] Hebrews 9:22; 1 Peter 1:18-19.
[990] Matthew 3:7-8; Luke 13:3,5; John 3:16,18; Acts 16:30-31, 20:21.
[991] Proverbs 2:1-5, 8:33-36.
[992] Matthew 28:19-20; Acts 2:42,46-47.

Questions 155 – 159

155. Q. How is the word made effectual to salvation?
    A. The Spirit of God maketh the reading, but especially the preaching of the Word, an effectual means of enlightening,[993] convincing, and humbling sinners;[994] of driving them out of themselves, and drawing them unto Christ;[995] of conforming them to his image,[996] and subduing them to his will;[997] of strengthening them against temptations and corruptions;[998] of building them up in grace,[999] and establishing their hearts in holiness and comfort through faith unto salvation.[1000]

156. Q. Is the Word of God to be read by all?
    A. Although all are not to be permitted to read the Word publicly to the congregation,[1001] yet all sorts of people are bound to read it apart by themselves,[1002] and with their families:[1003] to which end, the holy scriptures are to be translated out of the original into vulgar languages.[1004]

157. Q. How is the Word of God to be read?
    A. The holy Scriptures are to be read with an high and reverent esteem of them;[1005] with a firm persuasion that they are the very Word of God,[1006] and that he only can enable us to understand them;[1007] with desire to know, believe, and obey the will of God revealed in them;[1008] with diligence,[1009] and attention to the matter and scope of them;[1010] with meditation,[1011] application,[1012] self-denial,[1013] and prayer.[1014]

158. Q. By whom is the Word of God to be preached?
    A. The Word of God is to be preached only by such as are sufficiently gifted,[1015] and also duly approved and called to that office.[1016]

159. Q. How is the Word of God to be preached by those that are called thereunto?
    A. They that are called to labour in the ministry of the Word, are to preach sound doctrine,[1017] diligently,[1018] in season and out of season;[1019] plainly,[1020] not in the enticing words of man's wisdom, but in

---

[993] Nehemiah 8:8; Acts 26:18; Psalm 19:8.

[994] 2 Chronicles 34:18-19,26-28; 1 Corinthians 14:24-25.

[995] Acts 2:37,41, 8:27-30,35-38.

[996] 2 Corinthians 3:18.

[997] Romans 6:17; 2 Corinthians 10:4-6.

[998] Psalm 19:11; Matthew 4:4,7,10; 1 Corinthians 10:11; Ephesians 6:16-17.

[999] Acts 20:32; 2 Timothy 3:15-17.

[1000] Romans 1:16,10:13-17,15:4, 16:25; 1 Thessalonians 3:2,10-11,13.

[1001] Deuteronomy 31:9,11-13; Nehemiah 8:2-3, 9:3-5.

[1002] Deuteronomy 17:19; Isaiah 34:16; John 5:39; Revelation 1:3.

[1003] Genesis 18:17; Deuteronomy 6:6-9; Psalm 78:5-7.

[1004] 1 Corinthians 14:6,9,11-12,15-16,24,27-28.

[1005] Exodus 24:7; 2 Chronicles 34:27; Nehemiah 8:3-6,10; Psalm 19:10; Isaiah 66:2.

[1006] 2 Peter 1:19-21.

[1007] Luke 24:45; 2 Corinthians 3:13-16.

[1008] Deuteronomy 17:10,20.

[1009] Acts 17:11.

[1010] Luke 10:26-28; Acts 8:30,34.

[1011] Psalm 1:2, 119:97.

[1012] 2 Chronicles 34:21.

[1013] Deuteronomy 33:3; Proverbs 3:5.

[1014] Nehemiah 7:6,8; Psalm 119:18; Proverbs 2:1-6.

[1015] Hosea 4:6; Malachi 2:7; 2 Corinthians 3:6; Ephesians 4:8-11; 1 Timothy 3:2,6;.

[1016] Jeremiah 14:15; Romans 10:15; 1 Corinthians 12:28-29; 1 Timothy 3:10, 4:14, 5:22; Hebrews 5:4.

[1017] Titus 2:1,8.

[1018] Acts 18:25.

[1019] 2 Timothy 4:2.

[1020] 1 Corinthians 14:19.

demonstration of the Spirit, and of power;[1021] faithfully,[1022] making known the whole counsel of God;[1023] wisely,[1024] applying themselves to the necessities and capacities of the hearers;[1025] zealously,[1026] with fervent love to God[1027] and the souls of his people;[1028] sincerely,[1029] aiming at his glory,[1030] and their conversion,[1031] edification,[1032] and salvation.[1033]

Questions 159 (cont.) – 162

160. Q. What is required of those that hear the word preached?

A. It is required of those that hear the Word preached, that they attend upon it with diligence,[1034] preparation,[1035] and prayer;[1036] examine what they hear by the Scriptures;[1037] receive the truth with faith,[1038] love,[1039] meekness,[1040] and readiness of mind,[1041] as the Word of God;[1042] meditate,[1043] and confer of it;[1044] hide it in their hearts,[1045] and bring forth the fruit of it in their lives.[1046]

161. Q. How do the sacraments become effectual means of salvation?

A. The sacraments become effectual means of salvation, not by any power in themselves, or any virtue derived from the piety or intention of him by whom they are administered, but only by the working of the Holy Ghost, and the blessing of Christ, by whom they are instituted.[1047]

162. Q. What is a sacrament?

A. A sacrament is an holy ordinance instituted by Christ in his church,[1048] to signify, seal, and exhibit[1049] unto those that are within the covenant of grace,[1050] the benefits of his mediation;[1051] to strengthen and

---

[1021] 1 Corinthians 2:4.

[1022] Jeremiah 23:28; 1 Corinthians 4:1-2.

[1023] Acts 20:27.

[1024] Colossians 1:28; 2 Timothy 2:15.

[1025] Luke 12:42; 1 Corinthians 3:2; Hebrews 5:12-14.

[1026] Acts 18:25.

[1027] 2 Corinthians 5:13-14; Philippians 1:15-17.

[1028] 2 Corinthians 12:15; Colossians 4:12.

[1029] 2 Corinthians 2:17, 4:2.

[1030] John 7:18; 1 Thessalonians 2:4-6.

[1031] 1 Corinthians 9:19-22.

[1032] 2 Corinthians 12:19; Ephesians 4:12.

[1033] Acts 26:16-18; 1 Timothy 4:16.

[1034] Proverbs 8:34.

[1035] Luke 8:18; 1 Peter 2:1-2.

[1036] Psalm 119:18; Ephesians 6:18-19.

[1037] Acts 17:11.

[1038] Hebrews 4:2.

[1039] 2 Thessalonians 2:10.

[1040] James 1:21.

[1041] Acts 17:11.

[1042] 1 Thessalonians 2:13.

[1043] Luke 9:44; Hebrews 2:1.

[1044] Deuteronomy 6:6-7; Luke 24:14.

[1045] Psalm 119:11; Proverbs 2:1.

[1046] Luke 8:15; James 1:25.

[1047] Acts 8:13,23; 1 Corinthians 3:6-7, 12:13; 1 Peter 3:21.

[1048] Genesis 17:7,10; Exodus 12:1-11; Matthew 26:26-28, 28:19.

[1049] Romans 4:11; 1 Corinthians 11:24-25.

[1050] Exodus 12:48; Romans 15:8.

[1051] Acts 2:38; 1 Corinthians 10:16.

increase their faith, and all other graces;[1052] to oblige them to obedience;[1053] to testify and cherish their love and communion one with another;[1054] and to distinguish them from those that are without.[1055]

Questions 162 (cont.) – 167

163. Q.   What are the parts of a sacrament?
   A.   **The parts of the sacrament are two; the one an outward and sensible sign, used according to Christ's own appointment; the other an inward and spiritual grace thereby signified.[1056]**

164. Q.   How many sacraments hath Christ instituted in his church under the New Testament?
   A.   **Under the New Testament Christ hath instituted in his church only two sacraments, baptism and the Lord's Supper.[1057]**

165. Q.   What is baptism?
   A.   **Baptism is a sacrament of the New Testament, wherein Christ hath ordained the washing with water in the name of the Father, and of the Son, and of the Holy Ghost,[1058] to be a sign and seal of ingrafting into himself,[1059] of remission of sins by his blood,[1060] and regeneration by his Spirit;[1061] of adoption,[1062] and resurrection unto everlasting life;[1063] and whereby the parties baptized are solemnly admitted into the visible church,[1064] and enter into an open and professed engagement to be wholly and only the Lord's.[1065]**

166. Q.   Unto whom is baptism to be administered?
   A.   **Baptism is not to be administered to any that are out of the visible church, and so strangers from the covenant of promise, till they profess their faith in Christ, and obedience to him,[1066] but infants descending from parents, either both, or but one of them, professing faith in Christ, and obedience to him, are in that respect within the covenant, and to be baptized.[1067]**

167. Q.   How is baptism to be improved by us?
   A.   **The needful but much neglected duty of improving our baptism, is to be performed by us all our life long, especially in the time of temptation, and when we are present at the administration of it to others;[1068] by serious and thankful consideration of the nature of it, and of the ends for which Christ instituted it, the privileges and benefits conferred and sealed thereby, and our solemn vow made therein;[1069] by being humbled for our sinful defilement, our falling short of, and walking contrary to, the grace of baptism, and our engagements;[1070] by growing up to assurance of pardon of sin, and of all other blessings sealed to us in that sacrament;[1071] by drawing strength from the death and resurrection of**

[1052] Romans 4:11; Galatians 3:27.

[1053] Romans 6:3-4; 1 Corinthians 10:21.

[1054] 1 Corinthians 12:13; Ephesians 4:2-5.

[1055] Genesis 34:14; Ephesians 2:11-12.

[1056] Matthew 3:11; Romans 2:28-29; 1 Peter 3:21.

[1057] Matthew 26:26-28, 28:19; 1 Corinthians 11:20,23.

[1058] Matthew 28:19.

[1059] Galatians 3:27.

[1060] Mark 1:4; Revelation 1:5.

[1061] Ephesians 5:26; Titus 3:5.

[1062] Galatians 3:26-27.

[1063] Romans 6:5; 1 Corinthians 15:29.

[1064] 1 Corinthians 12:13.

[1065] Romans 6:4.

[1066] Acts 2:38, 8:36-37.

[1067] Genesis 17:7,9; Matthew 28:19; Luke 18:15-16; Acts 2:38-39; Romans 4:11-12, 11:16; 1 Corinthians 7:14; Galatians 3:9,14; Colossians 2:11-12;.

[1068] Romans 6:4,6,11; Colossians 2:11-12.

[1069] Romans 6:3-5.

[1070] Romans 6:2-3; 1 Corinthians 1:11-13.

[1071] Romans 4:11-12; 1 Peter 3:21.

Christ, into whom we are baptized, for the mortifying of sin, and quickening of grace;[1072] and by endeavoring to live by faith,[1073] to have our conversation in holiness and righteousness,[1074] as those that have therein given up their names to Christ;[1075] and to walk in brotherly love, as being baptized by the same Spirit into one body.[1076]

Questions 167 (cont.) – 171

168. Q. What is the Lord's Supper?

A. The Lord's Supper is a sacrament of the New Testament,[1077] wherein, by giving and receiving bread and wine according to the appointment of Jesus Christ, his death is showed forth; and they that worthily communicate feed upon his body and blood, to their spiritual nourishment and growth in grace;[1078] have their union and communion with him confirmed;[1079] testify and renew their thankfulness,[1080] and engagement to God,[1081] and their mutual love and fellowship each with the other, as members of the same mystical body.[1082]

169. Q. How hath Christ appointed bread and wine to be given and received in the sacrament of the Lord's Supper?

A. Christ hath appointed the ministers of his Word, in the administration of this sacrament of the Lord's Supper, to set apart the bread and wine from common use, by the word of institution, thanksgiving, and prayer; to take and break the bread, and to give both the bread and the wine to the communicants: who are, by the same appointment, to take and eat the bread, and to drink the wine, in thankful remembrance that the body of Christ was broken and given, and his blood shed, for them.[1083]

170. Q. How do they that worthily communicate in the Lord's Supper feed upon the body and blood of Christ therein?

A. As the body and blood of Christ are not corporally or carnally present in, with, or under the bread and wine in the Lord's Supper,[1084] and yet are spiritually present to the faith of the receiver, no less truly and really than the elements themselves are to their outward senses;[1085] so they that worthily communicate in the sacrament of the Lord's supper, do therein feed upon the body and blood of Christ, not after a corporal and carnal, but in a spiritual manner; yet truly and really,[1086] while by faith they receive and apply unto themselves Christ crucified, and all the benefits of his death.[1087]

171. Q. How are they that receive the sacrament of the Lord's Supper to prepare themselves before they come unto it?

A. They that receive the sacrament of the Lord's Supper are, before they come, to prepare themselves thereunto, by examining themselves[1088] of their being in Christ,[1089] of their sins and wants;[1090] of the truth

---

1072 Romans 6:3-5.
1073 Galatians 3:26-27.
1074 Romans 6:22.
1075 Acts 2:38.
1076 1 Corinthians 12:13,25.
1077 Luke 22:20.
1078 Matthew 26:26-28; 1 Corinthians 11:23-26.
1079 1 Corinthians 10:16.
1080 1 Corinthians 11:24.
1081 1 Corinthians 10:14-16,21.
1082 1 Corinthians 10:17.
1083 Matthew 26:26-28; Mark 14:22-24; Luke 22:19-20; 1 Corinthians 11:23-24.
1084 Acts 3:21.
1085 Matthew 26:26-28.
1086 1 Corinthians 11:24-29.
1087 1 Corinthians 10:16.
1088 1 Corinthians 11:28.
1089 2 Corinthians 13:5.
1090 Exodus 12:15; 1 Corinthians 5:7.

and measure of their knowledge,[1091] faith,[1092] repentance;[1093] love to God and the brethren,[1094] charity to all men,[1095] forgiving those that have done them wrong;[1096] of their desires after Christ,[1097] and of their new obedience;[1098] and by renewing the exercise of these graces,[1099] by serious meditation,[1100] and fervent prayer.[1101]

Questions 171 (cont.) – 174

172. Q. May one who doubteth of his being in Christ, or of his due preparation, come to the Lord's Supper?
A. One who doubteth of his being in Christ, or of his due preparation to the sacrament of the Lord's Supper, may have true interest in Christ, though he be not yet assured thereof;[1102] and in God's account hath it, if he be duly affected with the apprehension of the want of it,[1103] and unfeignedly desires to be found in Christ,[1104] and to depart from iniquity:[1105] in which case (because promises are made, and this sacrament is appointed, for the relief even of weak and doubting Christians[1106]) he is to bewail his unbelief,[1107] and labor to have his doubts resolved;[1108] and, so doing, he may and ought to come to the Lord's Supper, that he may be further strengthened.[1109]

173. Q. May any who profess the faith, and desire to come to the Lord's Supper, be kept from it?
A. Such as are found to be ignorant or scandalous, notwithstanding their profession of the faith, and desire to come to the Lord's Supper, may and ought to be kept from that sacrament, by the power which Christ hath left in his church,[1110] until they receive instruction, and manifest their reformation.[1111]

174. Q. What is required of them that receive the sacrament of the Lord's Supper in the time of the administration of it?
A. It is required of them that receive the sacrament of the Lord's Supper, that, during the time of the administration of it, with all holy reverence and attention they wait upon God in that ordinance,[1112] diligently observe the sacramental elements and actions,[1113] heedfully discern the Lord's body,[1114] and affectionately meditate on his death and sufferings,[1115] and thereby stir up themselves to a vigorous

---

[1091] 1 Corinthians 11:29.
[1092] Matthew 26:28; 1 Corinthians 13:5.
[1093] Zechariah 12:10; 1 Corinthians 11:31.
[1094] Acts 2:46-47; 1 Corinthians 10:16-17.
[1095] 1 Corinthians 5:8, 11:18,20.
[1096] Matthew 5:23-24.
[1097] Isaiah 55:1; John 7:37.
[1098] 1 Corinthians 5:7-8.
[1099] Psalm 26:6; 1 Corinthians 11:25-26,28; Hebrews 10:21-22,24.
[1100] 1 Corinthians 11:24-25.
[1101] 2 Chronicles 30:18-19; Matthew 26:26.
[1102] Psalm 77:1-4,7-10, 88:1-18; Isaiah 50:10; Jonah 2:4.
[1103] Psalm 31:22, 73:13,22-23; Isaiah 54:7-10; Matthew 5:3-4.
[1104] Psalm 10:17, 42:1-2,5,11; Philippians 3:8-9.
[1105] Psalm 66:18-20; Isaiah 50:10; 2 Timothy 2:19.
[1106] Isaiah 40:11,29,31; Matthew 11:28, 12:20, 26:28.
[1107] Mark 9:24.
[1108] Acts 2:37, 16:30.
[1109] Romans 4:11; 1 Corinthians 11:28.
[1110] Matthew 7:6; 1 Corinthians 5:1-13, 11:27-34; 1 Timothy 5:22; Jude 23.
[1111] 2 Corinthians 2:7.
[1112] Leviticus 10:3; Psalm 5:7; 1 Corinthians 11:17,26-27; Hebrews 12:28.
[1113] Exodus 24:8; Matthew 26:28.
[1114] 1 Corinthians 11:29.
[1115] Luke 22:19.

exercise of their graces;[1116] in judging themselves,[1117] and sorrowing for sin;[1118] in earnest hungering and thirsting after Christ,[1119] feeding on him by faith,[1120] receiving of his fullness,[1121] trusting in his merits,[1122] rejoicing in his love,[1123] giving thanks for his grace;[1124] in renewing of their covenant with God,[1125] and love to all the saints.[1126]

Questions 174 (cont.) – 177

175. Q. What is the duty of Christians, after they have received the sacrament of the Lord's Supper?

A. The duty of Christians, after they have received the sacrament of the Lord's Supper, is seriously to consider how they have behaved themselves therein, and with what success;[1127] if they find quickening and comfort, to bless God for it,[1128] beg the continuance of it,[1129] watch against relapses,[1130] fulfill their vows,[1131] and encourage themselves to a frequent attendance on that ordinance:[1132] but if they find no present benefit, more exactly to review their preparation to, and carriage at, the sacrament;[1133] in both which, if they can approve themselves to God and their own consciences, they are to wait for the fruit of it in due time:[1134] but, if they see they have failed in either, they are to be humbled,[1135] and to attend upon it afterwards with more care and diligence.[1136]

176. Q. Wherein do the sacraments of baptism and the Lord's Supper agree?

A. The sacraments of baptism and the Lord's Supper agree, in that the author of both is God;[1137] the spiritual part of both is Christ and his benefits;[1138] both are seals of the same covenant,[1139] are to be dispensed by ministers of the gospel, and by none other;[1140] and to be continued in the church of Christ until his second coming.[1141]

177. Q. Wherein do the sacraments of baptism and the Lord's Supper differ?

A. The sacraments of baptism and the Lord's Supper differ, in that baptism is to be administered but once, with water, to be a sign and seal of our regeneration and ingrafting into Christ,[1142] and that even to infants;[1143] whereas the Lord's Supper is to be administered often, in the elements of bread and wine, to

---

[1116] 1 Corinthians 10:3-5,11,14, 11:26.

[1117] 1 Corinthians 11:31.

[1118] Zechariah 12:10.

[1119] Revelation 22:17.

[1120] John 6:35.

[1121] John 1:16.

[1122] Philippians 1:16.

[1123] 2 Chronicles 30:21; Psalm 58:4-5.

[1124] Psalm 22:26.

[1125] Psalm 50:5; Jeremiah 50:5.

[1126] Acts 2:42.

[1127] Psalm 28:7, 85:8; 1 Corinthians 11:7,30-31.

[1128] 2 Chronicles 30:21-23,25-26; Acts 2:42,46-47.

[1129] 1 Chronicles 29:18; Psalm 36:10; Song of Solomon 3:4.

[1130] 1 Corinthians 10:3-5,12.

[1131] Psalm 50:14.

[1132] Acts 2:42,46; 1 Corinthians 11:25-26.

[1133] Ecclesiastes 5:1-6; Song of Solomon 5:1-6.

[1134] Psalm 123:1-2, 42:5,8, 43:3-5.

[1135] 2 Chronicles 30:18-19.

[1136] 1 Chronicles 15:12-14; 2 Corinthians 7:11.

[1137] Matthew 28:19; 1 Corinthians 11:23.

[1138] Romans 6:3-4; 1 Corinthians 10:16.

[1139] Matthew 26:27-28; Romans 4:11; Colossians 2:12.

[1140] Matthew 28:19; John 1:33; 1 Corinthians 4:1, 11:23; Hebrews 5:4.

[1141] Matthew 28:19-20; 1 Corinthians 11:26.

[1142] Matthew 3:11; Galatians 3:27; Titus 3:5.

[1143] Genesis 17:7,9; Acts 2:38-39; 1 Corinthians 7:14.

represent and exhibit Christ as spiritual nourishment to the soul,[1144] and to confirm our continuance and growth in him,[1145] and that only to such as are of years and ability to examine themselves.[1146]

Questions 177 (cont.) – 182

178. Q. What is prayer?
A. Prayer is an offering up of our desires unto God,[1147] in the name of Christ,[1148] by the help of his Spirit;[1149] with confession of our sins,[1150] and thankful acknowledgment of his mercies.[1151]

179. Q. Are we to pray unto God only?
A. God only being able to search the hearts,[1152] hear the requests,[1153] pardon the sins,[1154] and fulfill the desires of all;[1155] and only to be believed in,[1156] and worshipped with religious worship;[1157] prayer, which is a special part thereof,[1158] is to be made by all to him alone,[1159] and to none other.[1160]

180. Q. What is it to pray in the name of Christ?
A. To pray in the name of Christ is, in obedience to his command, and in confidence on his promises, to ask mercy for his sake;[1161] not by bare mentioning of his name,[1162] but by drawing our encouragement to pray, and our boldness, strength, and hope of acceptance in prayer, from Christ and his mediation.[1163]

181. Q. Why are we to pray in the name of Christ?
A. The sinfulness of man, and his distance from God by reason thereof, being so great, as that we can have no access into his presence without a mediator;[1164] and there being none in heaven or earth appointed to, or fit for, that glorious work but Christ alone,[1165] we are to pray in no other name but his only.[1166]

182. Q. How doth the Spirit help us to pray?
A. We not knowing what to pray for as we ought, the Spirit helpeth our infirmities, by enabling us to understand both for whom, and what, and how prayer is to be made; and by working and quickening in our hearts (although not in all persons, nor at all times, in the same measure) those apprehensions, affections, and graces which are requisite for the right performance of that duty.[1167]

[1144] 1 Corinthians 11:23-26.
[1145] 1 Corinthians 10:16.
[1146] 1 Corinthians 11:28-29.
[1147] Psalm 62:8.
[1148] John 16:23.
[1149] Romans 8:26.
[1150] Psalm 32:5-6; Daniel 9:4.
[1151] Philippians 4:6.
[1152] 1 Kings 8:39; Acts 1:24; Romans 8:27.
[1153] Psalm 65:2.
[1154] Micah 7:18.
[1155] Psalm 145:18.
[1156] Romans 10:14.
[1157] Matthew 4:10.
[1158] 1 Corinthians 1:2.
[1159] Psalm 50:15.
[1160] Romans 10:14.
[1161] Daniel 9:17; John 14:13-14, 16:24.
[1162] Matthew 7:21.
[1163] Hebrews 4:14-16; 1 John 5:13-15.
[1164] Isaiah 59:2; John 14:6; Ephesians 3:12.
[1165] John 6:27; 1 Timothy 2:5; Hebrews 7:25-27.
[1166] Colossians 3:17; Hebrews 13:15.
[1167] Psalm 10:17; Zechariah 12:10; Romans 8:26-27.

Questions 183 – 186

183. Q. For whom are we to pray?
   A. We are to pray for the whole church of Christ upon earth;[1168] for magistrates,[1169] and ministers;[1170] for ourselves,[1171] our brethren,[1172] yea, our enemies;[1173] and for all sorts of men living,[1174] or that shall live hereafter;[1175] but not for the dead,[1176] nor for those that are known to have sinned the sin unto death.[1177]

184. Q. For what things are we to pray?
   A. We are to pray for all things tending to the glory of God,[1178] the welfare of the church,[1179] our own[1180] or others, good;[1181] but not for anything that is unlawful.[1182]

185. Q. How are we to pray?
   A. We are to pray with an awful apprehension of the majesty of God,[1183] and deep sense of our own unworthiness,[1184] necessities,[1185] and sins;[1186] with penitent,[1187] thankful,[1188] and enlarged hearts;[1189] with understanding,[1190] faith,[1191] sincerity,[1192] fervency,[1193] love,[1194] and perseverance,[1195] waiting upon him,[1196] with humble submission to his will.[1197]

186. Q. What rule hath God given for our direction in the duty of prayer?
   A. The whole Word of God is of use to direct us in the duty of prayer;[1198] but the special rule of direction is that form of prayer which our Savior Christ taught his disciples, commonly called The Lord's Prayer.[1199]

[1168] Psalm 28:9; Ephesians 6:18.
[1169] 1 Timothy 2:1-2.
[1170] Colossians 4:3.
[1171] Genesis 32:11.
[1172] James 5:16.
[1173] Matthew 5:44.
[1174] 1 Timothy 2:1-2.
[1175] 2 Samuel 7:29; John 17:20.
[1176] 2 Samuel 12:21-23.
[1177] 1 John 5:16.
[1178] Matthew 6:9.
[1179] Psalm 51:18, 122:6.
[1180] Matthew 7:11.
[1181] Psalm 125:4.
[1182] 1 John 5:14.
[1183] Ecclesiastes 5:1.
[1184] Genesis 18:27, 32:10.
[1185] Luke 15:17-19.
[1186] Luke 18:13-14.
[1187] Psalm 51:17.
[1188] Philippians 4:6.
[1189] 1 Samuel 1:15, 2:1.
[1190] 1 Corinthians 14:15.
[1191] Mark 11:24; James 1:6.
[1192] Psalm 17:1, 145:18.
[1193] James 5:16.
[1194] 1 Timothy 2:8.
[1195] Ephesians 6:18.
[1196] Micah 7:7.
[1197] Matthew 26:39.
[1198] 1 John 5:14.
[1199] Matthew 6:9-13; Luke 11:2-4.

Questions 187 – 191

187. Q. How is the Lord's Prayer to be used?
  A. The Lord's Prayer is not only for direction, as a pattern, according to which we are to make other prayers; but may also be used as a prayer, so that it be done with understanding, faith, reverence, and other graces necessary to the right performance of the duty of prayer.[1200]

188. Q. Of how many parts doth the Lord's Prayer consist?
  A. The Lord's Prayer consists of three parts; a preface, petitions, and a conclusion.

189. Q. What doth the preface of the Lord's Prayer teach us?
  A. The preface of the Lord's Prayer (contained in these words, Our Father which art in heaven,[1201]) teacheth us, when we pray, to draw near to God with confidence of his fatherly goodness, and our interest therein;[1202] with reverence, and all other childlike dispositions,[1203] heavenly affections,[1204] and due apprehensions of his sovereign power, majesty, and gracious condescension:[1205] as also, to pray with and for others.[1206]

190. Q. What do we pray for in the first petition?
  A. In the first petition, (which is, Hallowed by thy name,[1207]) acknowledging the utter inability and indisposition that is in ourselves and all men to honor God aright,[1208] we pray, that God would by his grace enable and incline us and others to know, to acknowledge, and highly to esteem him,[1209] his titles,[1210] attributes,[1211] ordinances, Word,[1212] works, and whatsoever he is pleased to make himself known by;[1213] and to glorify him in thought, word,[1214] and deed:[1215] that he would prevent and remove atheism,[1216] ignorance,[1217] idolatry,[1218] profaneness,[1219] and whatsoever is dishonorable to him;[1220] and, by his over-ruling providence, direct and dispose of all things to his own glory.[1221]

191. Q. What do we pray for in the second petition?
  A. In the second petition, (which is, Thy kingdom come,[1222]) acknowledging ourselves and all mankind to be by nature under the dominion of sin and Satan,[1223] we pray, that the kingdom of sin and Satan may

---

[1200] Matthew 6:9; Luke 11:2.
[1201] Matthew 6:9.
[1202] Luke 11:13; Romans 8:15.
[1203] Isaiah 64:9.
[1204] Psalm 123:1; Lamentations 3:41.
[1205] Nehemiah 1:4-6; Isaiah 63:15-16.
[1206] Acts 12:5.
[1207] Matthew 6:9.
[1208] Psalm 51:15; 2 Corinthians 3:5.
[1209] Psalm 67:2-3.
[1210] Psalm 83:18.
[1211] Psalm 86:10-13,15.
[1212] Psalm 138:1-3, 147:19-20; 2 Corinthians 2:14-15; 2 Thessalonians 3:1.
[1213] Psalm 145.
[1214] Psalm 19:14, 103:1.
[1215] Philippians 1:9,11.
[1216] Psalm 67:1-4.
[1217] Ephesians 1:17-18.
[1218] Psalm 97:7.
[1219] Psalm 74:18,22-23.
[1220] 2 Kings 19:15-16.
[1221] 2 Chronicles 20:6,10-12; Psalm 83:1-18, 140:4,8.
[1222] Matthew 6:10.
[1223] Ephesians 2:2-3.

be destroyed,[1224] the gospel propagated throughout the world,[1225] the Jews called,[1226] the fullness of the Gentiles brought in;[1227] the church furnished with all gospel-officers and ordinances,[1228] purged from corruption,[1229] countenanced and maintained by the civil magistrate:[1230] that the ordinances of Christ may be purely dispensed, and made effectual to the converting of those that are yet in their sins, and the confirming, comforting, and building up of those that are already converted:[1231] that Christ would rule in our hearts here,[1232] and hasten the time of his second coming, and our reigning with him forever:[1233] and that he would be pleased so to exercise the kingdom of his power in all the world, as may best conduce to these ends.[1234]

Questions 191 (cont.) – 193

192. Q. What do we pray for in the third petition?

A. In the third petition, (which is, Thy will be done in earth as it is in heaven,[1235]) acknowledging, that by nature we and all men are not only utterly unable and unwilling to know and do the will of God,[1236] but prone to rebel against his Word,[1237] to repine and murmur against his providence,[1238] and wholly inclined to do the will of the flesh, and of the devil:[1239] we pray, that God would by his Spirit take away from ourselves and others all blindness,[1240] weakness,[1241] indisposedness,[1242] and perverseness of heart;[1243] and by his grace make us able and willing to know, do, and submit to his will in all things,[1244] with the like humility,[1245] cheerfulness,[1246] faithfulness,[1247] diligence,[1248] zeal,[1249] sincerity,[1250] and constancy,[1251] as the angels do in heaven.[1252]

193. Q. What do we pray for in the fourth petition?

A. In the fourth petition,(which is, Give us this day our daily bread,[1253]) acknowledging, that in Adam, and by our own sin, we have forfeited our right to all the outward blessings of this life, and deserve to be wholly deprived of them by God, and to have them cursed to us in the use of them;[1254] and that neither

---

[1224] Psalm 68:1; Revelation 12:10-11.
[1225] 2 Thessalonians 3:1.
[1226] Romans 10:1.
[1227] Psalm 67:1-7; John 17:9,20; Romans 11:25-26.
[1228] Matthew 9:38; 2 Thessalonians 3:1.
[1229] Zephaniah 3:9; Malachi 1:11.
[1230] 1 Timothy 2:1-2.
[1231] Acts 4:29-30; Romans 15:29-30,32; Ephesians 6:18-20; 2 Thessalonians 1:11, 2:16-17.
[1232] Ephesians 3:14-20.
[1233] Revelation 22:20.
[1234] Isaiah 64:1-2; Revelation 4:8-11.
[1235] Matthew 6:10.
[1236] Job 21:14; Romans 7:18; 1 Corinthians 2:14.
[1237] Romans 8:7.
[1238] Exodus 17:7; Numbers 14:2.
[1239] Ephesians 2:2.
[1240] Ephesians 1:17-18.
[1241] Ephesians 3:16.
[1242] Matthew 26:40-41.
[1243] Jeremiah 31:18-19.
[1244] Psalm 119:1,8,35-36; Acts 21:14.
[1245] Micah 6:8.
[1246] 2 Samuel 15:25-26; Job 1:21; Psalm 100:2.
[1247] Isaiah 38:3.
[1248] Psalm 119:4-5.
[1249] Romans 12:11.
[1250] Psalm 119:80.
[1251] Psalm 119:112.
[1252] Psalm 103:20-21; Isaiah 6:2-3; Matthew 18:10.
[1253] Matthew 6:11.
[1254] Genesis 2:17, 3:17; Deuteronomy 28:15-17; Jeremiah 5:25; Romans 8:20-22.

they of themselves are able to sustain us,[1255] nor we to merit,[1256] or by our own industry to procure them;[1257] but prone to desire,[1258] get,[1259] and use them unlawfully:[1260] we pray for ourselves and others, that both they and we, waiting upon the providence of God from day to day in the use of lawful means, may, of his free gift, and as to his fatherly wisdom shall seem best, enjoy a competent portion of them;[1261] and have the same continued and blessed unto us in our holy and comfortable use of them,[1262] and contentment in them;[1263] and be kept from all things that are contrary to our temporal support and comfort.[1264]

Questions 193 (cont.) – 195

194. Q.   What do we pray for in the fifth petition?
      A.   In the fifth petition, (which is, Forgive us our debts, as we forgive our debtors,[1265]) acknowledging, that we and all others are guilty both of original and actual sin, and thereby become debtors to the justice of God; and that neither we, nor any other creature, can make the least satisfaction for that debt:[1266] we pray for ourselves and others, that God of his free grace would, through the obedience and satisfaction of Christ, apprehended and applied by faith, acquit us both from the guilt and punishment of sin,[1267] accept us in his Beloved;[1268] continue his favour and grace to us,[1269] pardon our daily failings,[1270] and fill us with peace and joy, in giving us daily more and more assurance of forgiveness;[1271] which we are the rather emboldened to ask, and encouraged to expect, when we have this testimony in ourselves, that we from the heart forgive others their offenses.[1272]

195. Q.   What do we pray for in the sixth petition?
      A.   In the sixth petition, (which is, And lead us not into temptation, but deliver us from evil,[1273]) acknowledging, that the most wise, righteous, and gracious God, for divers holy and just ends, may so order things, that we may be assaulted, foiled, and for a time led captive by temptations;[1274] that Satan,[1275] the world,[1276] and the flesh, are ready powerfully to draw us aside, and ensnare us;[1277] and that we, even after the pardon of our sins, by reason of our corruption,[1278] weakness, and want of watchfulness,[1279] are not only subject to be tempted, and forward to expose ourselves unto temptations,[1280] but also of ourselves unable and unwilling to resist them, to recover out of them, and to improve them;[1281] and

---

[1255] Deuteronomy 8:3.
[1256] Genesis 32:10.
[1257] Deuteronomy 8:17-18.
[1258] Jeremiah 6:13; Mark 7:21-22.
[1259] Hosea 12:7.
[1260] James 4:3.
[1261] Genesis 28:20, 43:12-14; Ephesians 4:28; Philippians 4:6; 2 Thessalonians 3:11-12.
[1262] 1 Timothy 4:3-5.
[1263] 1 Timothy 6:6-8.
[1264] Proverbs 30:8-9.
[1265] Matthew 6:12.
[1266] Psalm 130:3-4; Matthew 18:24-25; Romans 3:9-22.
[1267] Romans 3:24-26; Hebrews 9:22.
[1268] Ephesians 1:6-7.
[1269] 2 Peter 1:2.
[1270] Jeremiah 14:7; Hosea 14:2.
[1271] Psalm 51:7-10,12; Romans 15:13.
[1272] Matthew 6:14-15, 18:35; Luke 11:4.
[1273] Matthew 6:13.
[1274] 2 Chronicles 32:31.
[1275] 1 Chronicles 21:1.
[1276] Mark 4:19; Luke 21:34.
[1277] James 1:14.
[1278] Galatians 5:17.
[1279] Matthew 26:41.
[1280] 2 Chronicles 18:3, 19:2; Matthew 26:69-72; Galatians 2:11-14.
[1281] 1 Chronicles 21:1-4; 2 Chronicles 16:7-10; Romans 7:23-24.

worthy to be left under the power of them:[1282] we pray, that God would so overrule the world and all in it,[1283] subdue the flesh,[1284] and restrain Satan,[1285] order all things,[1286] bestow and bless all means of grace,[1287] and quicken us to watchfulness in the use of them, that we and all his people may by his providence be kept from being tempted to sin;[1288] or, if tempted, that by his Spirit we may be powerfully supported and enabled to stand in the hour of temptation;[1289] or when fallen, raised again and recovered out of it,[1290] and have a sanctified use and improvement thereof:[1291] that our sanctification and salvation may be perfected,[1292] Satan trodden under our feet,[1293] and we fully freed from sin, temptation, and all evil, forever.[1294]

Questions 195 (cont.) – 196

196. Q. What doth the conclusion of the Lord's Prayer teach us?

A. The conclusion of the Lord's Prayer, (which is, For thine is the kingdom, and the power, and the glory, for ever. Amen.[1295]) teacheth us to enforce our petitions with arguments,[1296] which are to be taken, not from any worthiness in ourselves, or in any other creature, but from God;[1297] and with our prayers to join praises,[1298] ascribing to God alone eternal sovereignty, omnipotency, and glorious excellency;[1299] in regard whereof, as he is able and willing to help us,[1300] so we by faith are emboldened to plead with him that he would,[1301] and quietly to rely upon him, that he will fulfil our requests.[1302] And, to testify this our desire and assurance, we say, Amen.[1303]

[1282] Psalm 81:11-12.

[1283] John 17:15.

[1284] Psalm 51:10, 119:133.

[1285] 2 Corinthians 12:7-8.

[1286] 1 Corinthians 10:12-13.

[1287] Hebrews 13:20-21.

[1288] Psalm 19:13; Matthew 26:41.

[1289] Ephesians 3:14-17; 1 Thessalonians 3:13; Jude 24.

[1290] Psalm 51:12.

[1291] 1 Peter 5:8-10.

[1292] 2 Corinthians 13:7,9.

[1293] Luke 22:31-32; Romans 16:20.

[1294] John 17:15; 1 Thessalonians 5:23.

[1295] Matthew 6:13.

[1296] Romans 15:30.

[1297] Daniel 9:4,7-9,16-19.

[1298] Philippians 4:6.

[1299] 1 Chronicles 29:10-13.

[1300] Luke 11:13; Ephesians 3:20-21.

[1301] 2 Chronicles 20:6,11.

[1302] 2 Chronicles 14:11.

[1303] 1 Corinthians 14:16; Revelation 22:20-21.

<u>Notes</u>

The Directory for Family Worship

Assembly at Edinburgh, August 24, 1657, Session 10.

The language has been modernized for better understanding.

Act for observing the Directions of the General Assembly for secret and private Worship, and mutual Edification; and censuring such as neglect family worship.

THE General Assembly, after mature deliberation, doth approve the following Rules and Directions for cherishing piety, and preventing division and schism; and doth appoint ministers and ruling elders in each congregation to take special care that these Directions be observed and followed; as likewise, that presbyteries and provincial synods enquire and make trial whether the said Directions be duly observed in their bounds; and to reprove or censure (according to the quality of the offence), such as shall be found to be reprovable or censurable therein. And, to the end that these directions may not be rendered ineffectual and unprofitable among some, through the usual neglect of the very substance of the duty of Family-worship, the Assembly doth further require and appoint ministers and ruling elders to make diligent search and enquiry, in the congregations committed to their charge respectively, whether there be among them any family or families which use to neglect this necessary duty; and if any such family be found, the head of the family is to be first admonished privately to amend his fault; and, in case of his continuing therein, he is to be gravely and sadly reproved by the session; after which reproof, if he be found still to neglect Family-worship, let him be, for his obstinacy in such an offence, suspended and debarred from the Lord's Supper, as being justly esteemed unworthy to communicate therein, till he amend.

Directions of the General Assembly, concerning secret and private worship, and mutual edification; for cherishing piety, for maintaining unity, and avoiding schism and division.

BESIDES public worship in congregations, founded in several places in the world by the mercy of God, it is fitting and proper that individual devotions, and private worship of families, be encouraged and established; that, with continuing reformation in the Church, the practice of godliness, both personally and in the family home, be advanced.

I.   And first, for private worship, it is most necessary that everyone in the family practices prayer and meditation individually. For in this practice is the untold benefit of God's grace to those who do it diligently. Private worship or devotion is the daily means by which each family member communes with God, and it makes him or her prepared for all other Christian duties. Therefore, it is fitting for pastors and elders to encourage their families to practice regular family worship, at times suitable to the family but preferably each morning and evening. Yet, it is most incumbent upon the head of the household to ensure the daily and diligent practice of individual and family worship.

II. The ordinary practical piety of families ought to include: 1) Prayer and praise for both the needs of the church, and the kingdom of God, and the individual needs of family and friends; 2) the reading of Scripture, along with teaching the appropriate catechism, so that each family member may be assisted in their understanding of Scripture when it is read in public worship; 3) godly discussion of the Scripture in order to build up the faith of each family member, and; 4) warning and correction to all the members of the family by the head of the house, especially if the particular passage read contained any duty or commandment.

III. Though the duty and authority of interpreting Scripture is only given to those duly called and appointed by God in the Church, the scriptures may be read by any who have the ability. However, it is preferred that the head of the house should read to the family, but may appoint whoever is to read. Upon the reading and hearing, the family should discuss the passage in order to get good use from it. It is especially beneficial to recognize if any sin is associated with the selected passage so that each family member is warned to be watchful against that sin in their own lives, so that they do not likewise fall into judgment. Moreover, if there is a duty or promise spoken of in the passage, it will be good to discuss how

IV. The head of the family should take care that no one member of the family withdraw themselves from family worship. Ministers and elders should also encourage and train each head of household so that they do not become lax, but become fit and able to lead family worship. If the ministers and elders of the church do not find the head of the family to be fit to lead, they may appoint another member of the family to lead. From time to time, ministers and elders are encouraged to visit the family and lead them in family worship. However, he should only do so with the whole family included, except in cases where he needs to impart a private word of admonition or correction to particular members of the family.

V. At no time should an outside person lead family worship who: 1) has no calling (i.e., is not ordained by God and the church); 2) has a dubious calling (i.e., his credentials cannot be confirmed); 3) is known to be teaching errors, or; 4) is divisive or schismatic.

VI. Normally, each family should worship as an individual family unless other families or individuals are staying in their home, or sharing a meal with them, or on an appropriate special occasion.

VII. Although times of blended family worship may have been beneficial in different times and places, families should not regularly blend in private worship except at those times already mentioned. The practice of regular blending should be discouraged because it may depreciate the public worship of God, may hinder each family from the good effects of private worship, and may cause unnecessary offenses, which could cause grief, hardening of hearts, and divisions within the church.

VIII. Especially on the Lord's Day, the head of the family should prepare all the members of the family for public worship. He or she should carefully explain all the elements in which the family will participate, and remind them about each element's benefits and proper uses. After the time of public worship, the head of the family should pray about and discuss all they heard, and spend the rest of the day in catechizing, discussing, and meditating upon the Word. The family may do this jointly or separately as appropriate. In all, each member should be encouraged by the means of grace, and reminded of all the graces of Christ, both in this life, and eternal life to come.

IX. As it is important for each member of the family to pray, they ought to be encouraged to pray. For some family members, a form of prayer may be warranted. For others, they ought to be encouraged to pray in their own words. To this end, the head of the family ought to teach each member the proper attitude and spirit of prayer; that they should pray often; that they should pray in earnest, truly seeking God for His help, not only for themselves, but for the family. The following suggestions should be considered as "parts" of each member's prayer and meditation:

A. They ought to confess their unworthiness to come before God's majesty; to ask God for the proper attitude they should have to come before Him in prayer.

B. They ought to confess their sins in true humility; they not only should confess their own sins, but also confess the sins of the family. By doing this, they judge and condemn themselves before God, and humbly ask for forgiveness.

C. They ought to pour out their souls to God, in the name of Christ, by the help of the Holy Spirit, so that He may forgive them their sins. They ought to ask for His grace and mercy; that He allow them the grace to repent, believe, and obey His commands; that He would help them to be godly, and serve Him with joy.

D. They ought to give thanks to God for His mercy, not only to themselves, but to their families, and their church. They ought to thank Him for His love in Christ, and for His grace in giving the light of the Gospel.

E. They ought to pray for whatever spiritual or physical needs they have at the time.

F. They ought to pray for the Christ's Church in general, especially for those who suffer for the name of Christ. They ought to pray for their government and its leaders. They ought to pray for their other family members, friends, and neighbors.

G. They ought to end their prayers, thanking God for hearing their prayers, asking for God to glorify Himself in all the world, and for His will to be done in all things.

X. These family prayers ought to be offered with great sincerity, and with an appropriate amount of time set aside, and in the proper environment with as many hindrances removed. Ministers and elders ought to encourage the families of the church to pray diligently, and inquire regularly of the effect it has been having on the family.

XI. Families should be encouraged to do all of the regular duties above, but should also participate in special times of fasting and prayer, either public or private, as is called for by the church.

XII. Because our society is in such moral decline, it is that much more important to consider one another and stir up one another to love and good works. As such, every member of the church ought to stir up themselves, and one another; to build each other up by instruction, warning, correction, encouragement in order to: 1) show forth the grace of God in putting off ungodliness and worldly desires; 2) live godly, soberly, and righteously in this present world; 3) comfort the weak, and; 4) pray with and for one another. All of these things ought to be done at all times, but especially, when in times of hardships or great difficulties, members seek counsel or comfort. Or, when a member must confront another member regarding a sin or offense, or when that sin or offense must be told to the church.

XIII. When a sin or offence is between two parties, and after all other private means have been exhausted, it may be necessary to involve another person like a pastor, elder, or some experienced Christian to share in the matter. Moreover, if a member's conscience is troubled, and they require a godly, grave, discreet person to be with them when meeting for prayer and discussion, it ought to be permitted.

XIV. If a family member is traveling or away from home, they should be careful not to neglect these duties, but should seek out others with whom they might participate in these private times of worship. However, they should also take care that they edify and minister to one another, and not be engaged in unwholesome speech or behavior.

The purpose of these directions is twofold. First, this directory serves to encourage all ministers, elders, and members of the Church, according to their various callings and places, to take care to practice and advance their own godliness, and likewise, to suppress their own ungodliness and minimize unfruitful times of worship. And secondly, this directory hopes to minimize worship practices that may breed error, scandal, schism, contempt, and disregard for public worship, ordinances, or church leaders; and to encourage all not to neglect their duties, but perform them in the Spirit, and not in the flesh, which is contrary to truth and peace.

Valley of Vision – Selected Prayers

The prayers included below are devotional prayers each family may pray together over the course of a week, both morning and evening. Use these prayers to begin with, then form your own prayers over time.

Lord's Day Morning

O Lord, we live before Your face every day, but week days are not like the Lord's Day, and our week day concerns make our Lord's Day remembrances fade. Therefore, we bless You for this day, which is sacred to our souls, when we may come before You and be refreshed. We thank You for establishing this day so that we may come near to You, and You to us. We rejoice in another Lord's Day, when we may stop thinking about all our cares in this world, and turn our attention towards You. Please let our resting today be devoted to You, let our conversations build up ourselves and others, let our reading of Your Word be reverent, and let our hearing of Your Word be profitable to us, so that our souls may be alive and soar to Your heavenly places. We are going to Your house to pray; please pour out Your Spirit of grace so that we see our need of Your help. We are going to Your house to praise You; please help us to be thankful and cheerful as we praise You. We are going to Your house to learn about You; please help us to learn more and more about You when Your Word is preached, and glorify Yourself in all our hearts as we hear it. Would You help us to see the light of Your Word? Would you help us to understand how we are to live? Would You help us to stay close to You, so that You may strengthen and comfort us? Would You make us to be Your people, ready to do what You have called us to do? Lord, be with those who cannot come today, and comfort them. Please gather Your people to come, who have not yet come. And, Lord, bless us with good will towards our family, with forgiveness in our hearts for all who have wronged us, with peace in our hearts towards everyone, and with acceptance towards all Your people. In Jesus' name, Amen.

Lord's Day Evening

O God, we bless You, our Creator, the one Who preserves us, the one Who provides for us, the one Who teaches us. We bless You for helping us understand our world when we see all You have created, the work of Your hands. But today, we have seen even more than what nature confesses about You. You have taught us what You would have us to do, and what You have done for us. Even more than this, You have taught us what You have promised to give us, and that gift is Jesus. We ask You for even more understanding about the way He has saved us from our sins, and how He wants us to be like Him; enjoying Him and being helped to live because of His Spirit, freely given to us. Help us not to be uncertain about being Your servants, and what You have called us to do. Help us to know by Your Spirit, that we are Your children, and that You have saved us. Bless us even more with a sense of Your wonderful salvation. Since we have been shown the light of salvation in Christ, help us to see even more amazing things. Since we have been made alive with Christ, help us to live our lives to the full every day. Since we have been made strong by Jesus, help us to get even stronger day by day. Help us to stay close to Jesus, so that our lives are made fruitful by Him, so that we may want to obey Him more and more, so that we may be totally His and experience the fullness of His joy, and so that we may serve Him as best as we can. Please Lord, work in us so that our faith is strengthened in Jesus, so that we may love Him and all Your people. In the name of Christ, we pray, Amen.

Monday Morning

O God All-Sufficient, You have made all things, and You make them all work to Your glory, by the Word of Your power. The Bible tells us that Your dwelling place is in a place unseen; that You walk on the wings of the wind; that all the nations of the world are as nothing before You; and that centuries of men have been born and have died, yet still You are God. Everything You have created, the earth and the heavens, will one day be as nothing, as a dream. But You never change, and You will never fade away, because You are, forever and ever, God over all, the blessed eternal One. Your greatness and glory can never be measured, yet You have called us Your children and have cared for us. Your hands made us and you have watched over us with love that goes beyond any human love. You have held onto our souls so that we will never be parted from You. In Your power, You have given us everything we need for our lives, and have taught us how we should live before You. Please help us to bless You at all times, and help us not to forget how you forgive our sins, heal us when we are sick, keep us from being destroyed, give us the crown of Your love and mercy, give us good food to eat, and refresh our strength like the eagle. Let your Holy Word today give us instruction, so that we may know Your holy will, and so that we might show everyone we meet, we love Your Word and what You have taught us in it. Through Jesus Who strengthens us, Amen.

Monday Evening

Great God and only King, You have made summer and winter, day and night. And each one of these shows us that You care about our well-being, and that You are full of kindness towards us. You have already given us great gifts in the teachers You provide for our learning, in the laws You have given for our well-being, in our homes that give us shelter, in our food that makes us grow and become strong, in our clothes that protect us from the heat and the cold, and in keeping us healthy and growing in our understanding and love for You and for others, reminding us that our wills must be aligned with Yours. But like the stars we cannot see because the sun rises, we also do not fully see all You have given us in the grace and wisdom of Your Son, Jesus, and of His great love in saving us from our sins. We bless You, Jesus, for being the One who is mighty and willing, and who was even able to go to the cross in order to save us. Lord, please make us fully aware of our need of His saving grace, of His blood that cleanses us from our sins, and of the great eternal rest we have been promised in Him. Even more than this, be pleased, O Lord, to give us His righteousness by our faith in Him, the only righteousness that will justify us in our guilt, give us the guarantee of eternal life, and full possession of the Holy Spirit in this life. Help us to love the salvation that comes through Jesus, and be joyful of His making us holy. Give us faith to understand Your promises and the hope that they bring, and provide us with the strength to go through every trial and temptation, so that we might not sin against You. Keep our hearts from straying from You, and help our desires to be bound to Your will. Please let us live, not like the world does, yet still in the world to be of use in Your kingdom. Help us to be willing to do all You have asked us to do, in the place You have called us to serve. Through Christ, our Lord, we pray, Amen.

Tuesday Morning

Most High God, all Your creation, the universe and the millions of creatures You have made, are Yours. They were all made by Your speaking them into existence. You keep them by Your power, and You rule over them by Your will. But You are also our merciful Father, the God of all grace; the One who comforts us, and has protected us from our own destructive natures. You have remembered us, You have come near to us, You have preserved us; You have given us a wonderful inheritance in Your Holy Word, in the gospel of our salvation, and in Jesus, our saviour. We come to You in His name, and not with any righteousness of our own, but only in His righteousness. We do not come in our own obedience, but His. We plead with You to remember His sufferings on our behalf. Jesus obeyed all of the law for us, He paid the penalty for our sins, and He showed the great honour of God's justice. We ask that You justify us by the blood He shed for us, for we are saved by His life, and we are joined with His Spirit. Help us to take up His cross and follow Him. Please let Your grace prepare us for what You have in store for our lives. Help us to be willing to serve You, no matter what we gain or lose, suffer or enjoy. If You bless us with wealth, help us to use it wisely, and not fall into the trap of relying on it instead of You. Help us to bear any trial with patience and cheerfulness. We know these things are necessary for You to make us who You want us to be. Help us also when we are tempted. Please protect our way, help us hate sin, and help us not to desire the evil things of this world. And Lord, help us to hope in the great blessings that await us, when we are forever with You; where no one will ever be sick again, and where the sun will always be shining. In the name of Christ, we pray, Amen.

Tuesday Evening

Our great God who is in control of everything, the fullness of Your greatness can never be discovered. Your name is the most excellent. Your glory reaches above the heavens. Ten thousand serve before Your throne, and ten thousand times ten thousand stand before Your throne room. In Your awesome presence, we are less than nothing. We are not coming before You now because we think we deserve it. We know we are sinners. But we come before You because we need a saviour, and You give us comfort because of Your promises. Our broken hearts cause us to cry out to You because we see Jesus drawing others to Himself, and we believe He is drawing us as well. Please look upon us and be merciful to us, O Lord. Convince us of our sins and the punishment we deserve because of them. Give us faith to believe in Jesus so that we might have life through Him. Help us to bear His sufferings along with our own so that we might see Your Almighty hand at work in Your perfect providence. Please do not let our cries for help hinder our telling forth Your praise. Please do not let us feel sorry for ourselves so that we do not do as You have commanded. Although we live in an ever-changing world, help us not to forget that we have a city that never changes and will endure for all time. Please be with us until we reach that city, so that we may glorify You, both in this life and that which is to come. We bless You, Father, for Your constant care, supplying us daily with mercy, and we commit all we are and have to Your keeping. Please allow no evil or sickness or fear to come near us. Help our guilty consciences to be silent, our hearts to be pure, and our sleep to be sweet and restful. We pray all these things, knowing that ten thousand times ten thousand are blessing Your name forever, and we join with them even now, as we praise the Lamb, who is to receive blessing, honor, glory, and power, forever and ever, in the name of the Lamb, Amen.

Wednesday Morning

Lord of Heaven, Your goodness cannot be put into words and goes beyond our understanding. In Your work of creation, You are almighty. In the pouring out of Your great grace, You are all-wise. In Your gospel of grace, You are all love. In Your only Son, You have provided our deliverance from sin, our justification through faith in Him, our sanctification by which You continue to make us holy, and the preservation of our souls in this life. Though Your law thunders against us so that we are terrified, You have also allowed us to hear the soft whisper of the hope of the gospel. Though we know we are stained with sin, You show us the fountain by which we may be made clean. Though we are empty vessels, You show us how we may have the fullness of life, never to be emptied. Please grant to us the knowledge, that to walk with Jesus, is better than any other thing we might do, or think, or imagine. Keep us from turning our thoughts away from eternal things. Save us from the lies people in this world believe about themselves. Help us to stay constant in our service to You, to be truly converted, to have new hearts, and to show forth the light of Christ, and our confidence in Him. Help us to judge ourselves, rightly. Help us to be dependent upon the Lord Jesus, to love Him, to bend our wills to His, and to grow in the knowledge of Him. Give us a great desire to truly worship, and to progress in our faith, so that our faith may stay the course and grow stronger; so that we may live and work by the Spirit; so that we may be benefitted by godly discipline; and so that we do not give in to our fleshly desires. In the name of Christ, we pray, Amen.

Wednesday Evening

King of glory, Divine Majesty, all of the perfection of Your nature makes Your throne beautiful and enduring. The heavens and the earth are Yours. The world is Yours and all its fullness. In Your great power, You created everything from nothing. In Your great wisdom, You have ruled over all nations, families, and individuals. Your goodness is without limit. All Your creatures wait before You, and are to be provided for by You, and are to be satisfied with nothing less than You. With all of this, how even more precious are the thoughts of Your great mercy and grace. How excellent is Your covenant love and mercy which draws all Your people unto You. Teach us, O Lord, to find our happiness in no other place but in Your blessedness, which is everything compared to the dead things of this earth. Help us never to ask for those things which satisfy blind fools. Rather, help us to continue to ask for the light of Your face, to plead for the joy of salvation in Jesus, to find heaven in no one else but You, Father. You have cared for our joy more than we have, and though we do not know what we need, You have never neglected us. In Your love and pity, You have provided us a saviour, justified us and applied His redemption to our hearts. And You continue Your work in us so that we may be holy before You. We confess we have sinned, and we plead Your forgiveness and mercy. We grow tired, please give us rest. We are foolish and stupid, please make us wise to salvation. We are weak and helpless, please let Your strength perfect us. We are poor and needy, please enrich us with Christ's unsearchable riches in glory. We are confused and tempted, please help us to remember that You have promised never to leave us or forsake us. For all these things we bless Your holy and strong name, Jehovah, Lord of hosts, and we pray in those strong names. Amen.

Thursday Morning

Creator God, the One who sustains all things, and Who is the author of all things, we understand that there is no place we can go where You are not there. There is no place outside Your control. We have no desire to even imagine such a place. It is our privilege, O Lord, to be ruled by Your almighty power, to be governed by Your righteousness, to be taught by Your wisdom, to be perfected by Your careful and patient work in us, and to be filled with Your mercy and grace; for You love us with a love that is more than we can understand. We praise You for Your goodness, we are amazed by Your power, and we tremble at the thought of Your holiness and our wickedness. But when we think of Your goodness, it causes us not to tremble, instead it gives us the desire to come into Your presence, and to confess our sins and turn from them. We confess our past sins before You, and of our worthlessness before You now. And we bless You for Your steadfast love and mercy, which are the grounds for our hope and future happiness. You have told us of Your great grace and mercy by showing us the glory of nature, and the way You made all things come to pass. But we are even more greatly shown your grace and mercy in Your Word, and in the gift of Your Son, and in the gospel of our salvation. Lord, please make us willing to be saved Your way and not our own, because we know that our way will lead to death, but Your way leads to life in Jesus. Help us not only want to receive Him, but also to walk in Him, depend on Him, be in communion with Him, and to follow wherever He leads us. Help us, because we are not perfect, to continue to press forward, not complaining about the work You have called us to, or murmuring about where You have brought us, but being thankful for this place and thankful for our rest. In all these things help us, so that in our service to You, we may speak loudly the gospel to silence the foolish and stupid. In Christ's name, Amen.

Thursday Evening

O Lord God, You preserve us, rule over us, save us, and will one day judge us. Quiet our souls so that we may call upon Your name. Help us to be separated from our evil, fleshly desires. Show us the great power of faith. Grow us up so that we may know the power of the Spirit in order that we may serve You. Give us delight and show us how beneficial it is to be a servant of the Great King. Let our service before You to be pleasing so that we might receive the assurance of Your love. Show us the danger we may fall into if we do not flee to You for salvation. Make us aware of the sickness in our souls that we may come to You, the Great Physician, for healing. Bind us to the cross of Christ so that the rebellion in our hearts may be killed. Help us to be watchful so that we may be servants who are able to behave like we should, and keep our hearts from sinning. When we lose strength, revive us. When we are lazy, help us to work as we ought. When we go away from You, bring us back. Put in us more faith so that we may see how important it is to be godly. Make us to be rich in faith, to be strong in faith, to live by faith, to walk by faith, to experience the joy of faith, to work in faith, and to hope through faith. Let us see nothing in ourselves but the wisdom, righteousness, holiness, and salvation of the Lord Jesus Christ, in Whose name we pray, Amen.

Friday Morning

O God Most High, Creator of the ends of the earth, Ruler over all the universe, Judge of all creation, Head of the Church, and Saviour of Sinners; the ends of Your greatness cannot be discovered, Your goodness is without end, Your lovingkindness never fails, Your faithfulness in bringing to pass all things is without limit, and Your mercy is new every morning. We bless You for speaking to us the words of our salvation. We praise You for all the things You have taught us, all the promises You have made us, and Your gracious invitation to be members of Your family through the gospel of Jesus Christ. Though we were born in our sinful state and completely lost without You, You have shown us the good news of everlasting life in Jesus. Though we are weak, You have taught us that You are mighty to save. Though we are poor, You have taught us that You will help us seek riches in Christ that would not otherwise ever be found. Though we are blind, You have given us eyes to see the treasures of wisdom and knowledge which are to be found in Christ Jesus. We thank You for Your gift that could not be expressed in words alone. This gift, the Lord Jesus, is our only salvation, and is the ground of our hope and confidence. We depend solely upon His death for our sins, we rest in His righteousness alone, and we greatly desire for His image to be stamped upon our souls. Let His glory fill our minds, His love control our desires, and His cross make our hearts enflamed with love for God. As Christians, let us do what You have called us to do, escaping the traps this world places in our path, so that we may serve You in whatever circumstances You have placed us. Help us also to find joy in our lot in life, and improve our lives with the gifts You give us. Let us be helpful to everyone, and build up our neighbour. Through Jesus Christ, our Lord, Amen.

Friday Evening

O God of Abraham, Isaac and Jacob, we put our hope in Your Word. In Your Word, we see You, not on a fearful throne of judgment, but on a throne of grace, always willing and able to be gracious and to show mercy. On this throne of grace, we do not hear you say to us, "Depart from Me, you transgressors of the law," but, "Look to Me and be saved, for I am God and there is none other." We do not hear Your fearful judgment because You have taught us Your holy name, and to put our trust in You alone. We know You are rich in mercy and grace because of all the saints now in glory who have been Your witnesses, who have been saved from their sins by Your Son. All of Your witnesses confess that they were saved by You, and these eternally cry out, "Not to us, but unto Your name give glory, for the sake of Your mercy and truth." You provided to them and to us the same Mediator, in Whom all the fullness of the godhead dwells, and Who has been named a Prince and a Saviour. To this One we look and on Him we depend. Through Him we are justified. Help us to endure the fellowship we have in His sufferings. And help us to do so without ceasing to hate our sins, or to cease from desiring holiness before You. Let His blood cleanse our hearts and minds so that we no longer feel the pain of guilt. Let us not only delight in His sacrifice for our sins, but also let us delight in our service to Him. Help us to be ruled by His love. Help us to live to Him instead of living to ourselves. Help us to have thankful hearts and be cheerful in our trials, not complaining and grumbling. And Help us, O Lord, to remember the greatness and numerous blessings we have in You. May we praise You at all times, Jehovah, God of all Love. In Your name we pray, Amen.

Saturday Morning

Sovereign Lord, Your will is supreme in heaven and earth, and every being You made by Your power is Yours. You are the Father of our souls. When You breathed out Your Word, You gave us understanding by which we know that You are in control of all things. But, O God, we are sinners in Your sight. You have said so, and if we deny it, we make You a liar. Yet in Christ Jesus, You have reconciled us so that we are no longer Your enemies. Please give us ears to hear Him by faith. Please give us eyes to see Him by faith. Please give us hands to receive Him by faith. Please give us appetites to feed on Him by faith. Lord, without Your giving us these things, we cannot know what light, riches, honour, and everlasting life we might have by faith in Him. But You have invited us, help us to hear You when You call. You are the almighty teacher, help us to learn of You so that we may live for You. You dwell in light that may not be approached, either by men or angels. You have hidden Yourself and You may only be found if You allow Your people to seek Your face through Christ. Fill our minds with the greatness of Your perfection, for we know that Your love to us in Christ Jesus never changes. More than that, Your love is such that nothing can separate us from it, and the enjoyment of which we will never be disappointed. Help us not to insincere and merely outward in our worship and service of You. Help us to remember what You are, and what we are; You are holy, and we are unworthy. Help us to approach You humbly, for our nature clings to pride, presumption, ignorance, wickedness, disobedience, all of which flow from the deceitfulness of our hearts. Let us not forget how much You have been patient with us, how You have dealt with us wisely, how powerful You are, how faithful You have been, how much care You have taken with us. And let us never stop responding to Your call of the gospel, of salvation, and of service.

Saturday Evening

O Lord God, there is nothing for which we could ask that you would be unable to give. There is no promise You have failed to fulfil. We know You have already given great blessings to the saints without number, who were all as guilty and unworthy as we are. But we plead with You, Lord, make us willing to receive what we need from the abundant supply of Your grace. In order to make us willing, help us to see how sinful we are, and soften our hard hearts. Help us to see how foolish, how unthankful, how prideful, how full of unbelief, how rebellious, and how corrupt we have been. Lord, teach us, by the thunder of Your law, how blessed we are that we may look into the glory of Your name, in the Substitute You have provided, so that we may submit ourselves to You and be saved from our sins. Give us the hope of salvation so that we need not be ashamed. Give us a love that drives us to holiness. Give us a joy in You because You have been our strength. Give us a faith in Christ, who loved us and died for us. Help us never to grow tired of doing what You have called us to do, especially when we become distracted by the world. Help us to wait upon You and keep Your commandments. Help us to be humble and sincere when we call upon Your name. Help us to live continually with eternity in view. Let us serve You freely no matter what is going on in our lives. Help us submit ourselves to You so that we may follow Your guidance and not the world's. Help us to put away the things we enjoy if You require it, because You know what is best for us. When we sin against You, turn our hearts so that we will be thankful for Your means of grace, and to Lord's Day worship. Teach us to treasure these more than we have done in the past. Help us to be in the Spirit on the Lord's Day. Help us approach Your day with humility, solemnity, mindful of our service before You, and of the great privilege it is to worship You. Help us to set all things aside that are not involved in Your worship. Help us to be encouraged and strengthened by worshipping with the saints tomorrow. In the name of Christ Jesus, we pray, Amen.

Catechism Memorization Tracking

Date	Name	Catechism (i.e. Children's, WSC)	Question Numbers

Date	Name	Catechism (i.e. Children's, WSC)	Question Numbers

Date	Name	Catechism (i.e. Children's, WSC)	Question Numbers

Date	Name	Catechism (i.e. Children's, WSC)	Question Numbers

Date	Name	Catechism (i.e. Children's, WSC)	Question Numbers

Date	Name	Catechism (i.e. Children's, WSC)	Question Numbers

Date	Name	Catechism (i.e. Children's, WSC)	Question Numbers

Date	Name	Catechism (i.e. Children's, WSC)	Question Numbers

Date	Name	Catechism (i.e. Children's, WSC)	Question Numbers

Date	Name	Catechism (i.e. Children's, WSC)	Question Numbers

Dictionary of Theological Terms

These definitions are taken from *Westminster Dictionary of Theological Terms*, © 1996 Donald K. McKim (Westminster John Knox Press, Louisville, KY)

a

absolution (From Lat. *Absolvere, 'to set free'*) – The formal act of pronouncing forgiveness of sins.

active obedience (of Christ) – Theological description of the fulfillment of the will of God by Jesus Christ, in that He fully obeyed the law of God on behalf of the elect.

agnosticism – The view that it is not possible to have any certain knowledge beyond ordinary experience, so that one cannot know whether or not God exists.

already…not yet – The view of some New Testament Scholars, according to which Jesus taught that the kingdom of God was "already" here in His own life and ministry, but is "not yet" fully here and will not be until His second coming.

amillennial – A view first suggested by Augustine that the "thousand years" of Christ's reign (Re 20:4ff.) should be interpreted symbolically rather than literally.

amyraldianism – The theological system of Moïse Amyrald (1596-1664), which modified orthodox Calvinism's teachings on God's eternal decrees in favor of a decree of universal redemption with no decree for reprobation.

Anabaptists (From Gr. *ana*, 'again,' and *baptein*, 'to dip in water') – Those who advocated rebaptism in certain instances. Most prominently, the 16th century reformers who renounced infant baptism, stressed the literal reading of Scripture, and supported the separation of church and state.

analogy of faith (Lat. *analogia fidei*) – The Protestant principle that individual doctrines are to be understood in light of the whole understanding of Christian faith, that obscure passages of Scripture are to be understood in light of clearer portions, and the Old Testament in light of the New Testament (Romans 12:6).

analogy of Scripture – Protestant belief that since Scripture has an ultimate unity because it is inspired by God, a Scripture passage may be understood more fully as it is studied in conjunction with other passages.

annihilationism – The belief that those not believing in Jesus Christ will be directly obliterated by God because of their sin; that there is no eternal punishment.

antediluvium (From Lat. *ante*, 'before,' and *diluvium*, 'flood') – A term for the materials in the book of Genesis that are recorded prior to the flood that covered the earth in the story of Noah (Genesis 6-8).

anthropomorphism (From Gr. *anthrōpos*, 'human,' and *morphē*, 'form') – The attribution of a human quality to God, such as "eyes," "hands," or "arms." It uses analogous and metaphorical language (see Genesis 3:8; Psalm 18:15).

antinomian (From Gr. *anti*, 'against,' and *nomos*, 'law') – The view that there is no need for the law of God in the Christian life (Romans 3:8; 6:15). It has appeared periodically throughout church history.

apocalypse (From Gr. *apokalypsis*, 'revelation,' 'unveiling') – The final "revealing" of divine mysteries. It is a type of revelatory literature. The book of Revelation is also called the Apocalypse.

apologetics – The endeavor to provide a reasoned account of the grounds for believing in the Christian faith.

apostasy – (Gr. *apostasis*, 'rebellion') Falling away from or renouncing the Christian faith.

Arianism – The teaching of the 4th century theologian Arius (c. 250-336) that Jesus is the highest created being but does not share the same substance as God the father. It was declared heretical by the Council of Nicaea (325).

Arminianism – The teaching of Jacobus Arminius (1560-1609), which conflicted with Calvinism, particularly on issues of human sinfulness, predestination, and whether or not salvation can be lost. It stressed human response to the gospel, conditional election, unlimited atonement, and resistible grace.

aseity (of God) – Literally, "of itself." The view that God is entirely self-sufficient and not dependent upon anything else.

assurance of pardon – In corporate worship, the declaration that the sin of the congregation is forgiven on the basis of God's promises to forgive sin in Jesus Christ (1 Jo 1:9).

Athanasianism – Views based on the writings of Athanasius (c. 293-373), bishop of Alexandria, who vigorously defended the teachings of the Council of Nicaea (325) that Jesus Christ was eternally divine and fully God (of the same substance). He contended against Arianism.

atonement (From English 'at one') – The death of Jesus Christ on the cross, which effects salvation as the reestablishment of the relationship between God and sinners.

b

benediction (Lat. *benediction*, 'blessing') – A blessing that is spoken at the close of a worship service (Numbers 6:24-26).

biblical theology – The attempt to arrange biblical teachings or themes in a more systematic way while maintaining biblical images, frameworks, and worldviews.

c

Calvinism – The developed and systematized teachings of John Calvin (1509-1564), which spread throughout Europe and internationally from the 16th century to the present day. It is also called the Reformed tradition. Calvinism embraces both theological beliefs and a way of life.

catechism (Gr. *katechein*, 'to instruct by word of mouth') – A means of instruction, often in question-and-answer form, that conveys a summary of Christian theological beliefs.

chiliasm (Gr. *chilioi*, 'thousand') – Another name for millenarianism and the belief that Christ will return to earth for a thousand-year reign prior to the final consummation (Revelation 20:1-5).

Christological – Referring to the doctrines of Jesus Christ.

communicant – One who participates in the Lord's Supper. More generally, communicants are those who are church members and are entitled to participate. The term may be used synonymously for "church members."

confessionalism – The view that a church must have a confession of faith to be constituted as a church or denomination.

congregational (form of Church government) – A Church government in which authority is with the local congregation, which is autonomous and independent.

covenant of grace – The relationship into which God entered to provide, by grace, the promise of salvation to sinful humanity. It extends throughout the Old Testament by means of various covenants to its final fulfillment in Jesus Christ.

covenant of redemption (Lat. *Pactum Salutis*) – Theological description of the agreement between God the Father and God the Son to provide for the salvation of sinful humanity by Christ's death on the cross.

covenant of works – Theological term, found in some streams of Reformed theology, used to describe God's initial covenant with humanity (in Adam) before the fall into sin. A perfect relationship with God could be enjoyed as long as Adam maintained perfect obedience to God's law.

covenant theology – A theological perspective most developed by 17th century Reformed theologians. It focuses on the ways in which the divine-human relationship has been established by "covenants."

creatio ex nihilo – The Christian view that God created all things out of "nothing" and is thus the ultimate cause and source of meaning for the whole created order.

credobaptism – The belief that baptism may be administered only to those who have made a conscious and credible profession of faith in Christ.

d

diaconate – The church office originating from those who "served" at meals (Ac 6:1-6) and emerging in the early church with social duties, particularly the care of the poor.

Decalogue (Gr. *dekalogos*, 'ten words') – The Ten Commandments (Exodus 20:1-17) which express the will and law of God and deal with the relation between man and God as well as man and man.

Deism – A view contrasting to atheism and polytheism. It emerged in 17th and 18th century England. It holds that the knowledge of God comes through reason rather than revelation, and that after God created the world, God has had no further involvement in it.

Dispensationalism – A view of God's activities in history expounded in *The Scofield Reference Bible* and traced to John Nelson Darby (1800-1882). Each dispensation is a different time period in which man is tested in responding to God's will. Seven dispensations cover creation to judgment.

divine economy – God's plan for salvation and ongoing providence, which is cosmic in scope. It embraces all aspects of human existence and the universe itself.

Docetism (Gr. *dokein*, 'to seem') – The belief that Jesus only "seemed" or appeared to have a human body and to be a human person. The view was found during the period of the early church among Gnostics, who saw materiality as evil. It was condemned by Ignatius of Antioch (c. 35 – c. 107).

doctrine (Lat. *doctrina*, from *docere*, 'to teach') – That which is taught and believed to be true by the church as it pertains to the Holy Scriptures.

double predestination – The view that God has freely chosen both to save some people (the elect) and to damn others (the reprobate). It is "double" in that it recognizes both election and reprobation as divine decrees.

e

easy believism – Popular slogan for the view that one simply has to "believe" in order to be saved and that there is no corresponding need for a committed life of Christian discipleship.

ecclesiology – The study of the church as a biblical and theological topic. The New Testament presents various images of the church that the early church struggled with as it sought its self-understanding in light of the gospel and controversies.

eisegesis – Reading meaning "into" a biblical text as opposed to "out of" a biblical text. (See exegesis.)

elder (Gr. presbyteros, 'presbyter,' or 'elder') – In early Christian churches, a leader with governmental oversight. The Reformed tradition distinguishes between "teaching" and "ruling" elders.

Election (Gr. eklogē, 'a choice') – God's choosing of a people to enjoy the benefits of salvation and to carry out God's purposes in the world (1 Thessalonians 1:4; 2 Peter 1:10). This doctrine has been of particular importance in Reformed theology.

episcopal (form of Church government) – A Church government in which bishops oversee a diocese, as in Roman Catholicism and Anglicanism. These also espouse a single office (papacy or patriarchy) over the Church who resides as final earthly authority.

epistemology – Study of how human knowledge is obtained, its bases, forms, and criteria.

eschatology (From Gr. eschatos, 'last,' and logos, 'study') – Study of the "last things" or the end of the world. Theological dimensions include the second coming of Jesus Christ and the last judgment.

Eucharist (Gr. eucharistein, 'to give thanks') – A term for the Lord's Supper deriving especially from Jesus' prayer of thanks for the bread and wine, which he related to his body and blood given for those he loved.

Evangelicalism – An interdenominational movement in American Protestantism that emphasizes the spreading of the gospel through evangelism and the need for a personal relationship with God in Jesus Christ through faith. It has been marked by a more pronounced social concern than is common in fundamentalism.

exegesis (Gr. exēgēsis, 'interpretation,' from exēgeisthai, 'to draw out or to explain') – the act of interpreting or explaining the meanings of verses or passages of Scripture.

expiation (Lat. expiatus, from ex, 'out,' and piare, 'to seek, appease, or purify through sacred rite') – Release from sin as well as the means by which this release is accomplished in relation to the work of Christ.

expository sermon – A sermon that seeks to interpret and explain a passage of Scripture.

f

Faith (Gr. pistis, Lat. fides, 'trust,' 'belief') – In Christianity, belief, trust, and obedience to God as revealed in Jesus Christ. It is the means of salvation (Ephesians 2:8-9) or eternal life (John 6:40). Faith affects all dimensions of one's existence: intellect, emotions, and will.

federal headship – The view that Adam acted as a representative of the whole human race and that through the fall into sin (Genesis 3), the whole human race now experiences the consequences of this sinful act (Romans 5:12,17-19).

forensic act – A legal act or declaration, used in relation to "righteousness" and "justification" in Protestant theology. It indicates that God "declares" a sinner righteous or justified (not "makes" one righteous) through Jesus Christ.

Forgiveness (Gr. aphesis, 'letting go') – Pardoning or remitting an offense. It restores a good relationship with God, others, or the self after a sin is committed.

Fundamentalism - A late 19th and early 20th century Protestant movement that opposed the accommodation of Christian doctrine to modern scientific theory and philosophy, specifically Darwinian evolution. Identified as anti-intellectual, Fundamentalism prompted the rise of neo-Evangelicalism.

g

general assembly – In Presbyterian churches, the annual meeting of elected pastors and elders from each presbytery that forms the church's highest governing body.

Gnosticism (From Gr. gnōsis, 'knowledge') – An amorphous movement during the early church period which featured complex views that focused on the quest for secret knowledge transmitted only to the "enlightened" and marked by the view that matter is evil. Gnostics denied the humanity of Christ.

gospel (Gr. euangelion, 'good news') – The central message of the Christian church to the world, entered on God's provision of salvation for the world in Jesus Christ. Also delineates the first four books of the New Testament.

grace – Unmerited favor. God's grace is extended to sinful humanity in providing salvation and forgiveness through Jesus Christ that is not deserved, and withholding, the judgment that is deserved (Romans 3:24; Ephesians 1:7; Titus 2:11).

grace (common) – God's universal, nonsaving grace in which blessings are given to humanity for physical sustenance, pleasure, learning, beauty, etc., as expressions of God's goodness. It is particularly contrasted in Reformed theology with God's special or saving grace.

grace (saving) – God's gracious favor for salvation on the basis of the work of Jesus Christ.

grammatico-historical exegesis – The interpretation of biblical texts by focusing on their syntactical construction, cultural and historical contexts.

h

hamartiology (From Gr. *hamartia*, 'sin,' 'missing the mark') – A theological term for the study of the doctrine of sin.

hermeneutics (Gr. *hermēneutikē*, 'interpretation') – The rules one uses for searching out the meaning of writings, particularly biblical texts.

homiletics (From Gr. *homilētikos*, from *homilein*, 'to be in company,' 'to converse') – The theological discipline that deals with the preparation, construction, and delivery of sermons. Also, the study of preaching.

i

illumination (Lat. *illuminatio*) – The work of the Holy Spirit in conveying to sinners the knowledge and grace of the gospel through the ministry of the Word of God. The biblical image is of being "enlightened" (Ephesians 1:18; Hebrews 6:4, 10:32).

imputation (Lat. *imputatio*, from *imputare*, "to reckon in") – To attribute or ascribe in the sense of reckoning. The concept relates to sin, guilt, or righteousness, as when Paul indicates that through Adam's sin, death, and guilt are imputed to all (Ro 5:12-14), while through Christ's work, righteousness is "reckoned" or "imputed" to those who believe (Romans 4:22-24, 5:15-21).

incarnation (From Lat. in, 'in,' and carnis, 'flesh') – The doctrine that the eternal second Person of the Trinity became a human being and "assumed flesh" in Jesus of Nazareth. Jesus Christ was the "Word made flesh" (John 1:14). The doctrine holds that Jesus was one divine person with both a divine and a human nature.

inerrancy (biblical) – A way of expressing a commitment to the belief that the Bible contains no "errors" of any sort and is completely truthful on all matters on which it teaches such as history, science, and biology.

infallibility (biblical) – Commitment to a belief that the Bible is completely trustworthy as a guide to salvation and the life of faith and will not fail to accomplish its purpose.

inspiration (biblical) (Gr. *theopneustos*, 'God breathed') – Belief that God is the source behind biblical writings and acted through the Holy Spirit with the biblical writers to communicate what God wills to reveal of Himself (2 Timothy 3:16).

invisible church – A term used particularly in Reformed theology with roots in the thought of Augustine (354-430) to indicate the company of those who truly believe in Jesus Christ and are the recipients of salvation (the elect), both those who are currently alive and those who have died. (See visible church.)

j

judicatory – An ecclesiastical body beyond a local church that conducts church business and/or church discipline such as, in a Presbyterian system, a presbytery, or general assembly.

Justification (Gr. *dikaioō*; Lat. *iustificatio*, 'a reckoning or counting as righteous') – God's declaring a sinful person to be "just" on the basis of the righteousness of Jesus Christ (Romans 3:24-26, 4:25, 5:16-21). The result is God's peace (Romans 5:21), God's Spirit (8:4), and thus "salvation."

l

legalism - The wrong use of the Law as the basis for righteousness or sanctification.

licentiate (From Lat. *licentia*, "permission") – One who is licensed and accorded certain ministerial privileges and responsibilities.

liturgy (From Gr. *leitourgia*, 'work of the people') – The service of God offered by the people of God in divine worship.

LXX – A designation for the Septuagint version of the Old Testament, prepared during the 3rd century B.C. It derives from the legend that the translation from Hebrew into Greek was made in seventy days by seventy scholars.

m

Marcionism – The teachings of Marcion (d. c. 160), which featured a sharp disjunction between the "God of wrath" of the Old Testament and the "God of love" of the New Testament and the view that Christ never became flesh. In Marcionism, Christianity replaces Judaism. Its canon was Luke's Gospel and ten Pauline letters.

marks of the church – The "notes" of the church as found in the Nicene Creed are the church as "one, holy, catholic, and apostolic" (or unity, holiness, catholicity, and apostolicity). Protestant Reformers emphasized the marks as preaching the Word and the right administration of church discipline, and the right administration of the sacraments.

mediator (Lat. *medius*, 'middle') – One who stands between parties in order to effect a reconciliation. The term is applied to Jesus Christ as the "one mediator between God and man" (1 Timothy 2:5), who has effected reconciliation by overcoming sin (cf. Hebrews 8:6, 9:15, 12:24).

missiology – The study of the mission of the Christian church.

modalism – A view of the Trinity considered by the early church as heretical. It was believed that the one God was revealed at different times in different ways and thus has three manners (modes) of appearance rather than being one God in three persons.

monergism – The view that the Holy Spirit is the only agent who effects regeneration in Christians. It is in contrast with synergism, the view that there is a cooperation between the divine and the human in the regeneration process.

moral law – A term for the Ten Commandments, or Decalogue, or for the law of Moses. Its purpose is to regulate conduct and ethical choices and it is distinct from Israel's ceremonial and civil law.

mortification (Lat. *mortificare*, 'to mortify,' from *mors*, 'death,' and *facere*, 'to make') – A theological term for the subduing or putting to death of the life of sin through repentance. In some traditions particular stress is on subduing sensual appetites and using ascetic practices.

O

ordo salutis (lit. order of salvation) – A term found particularly in Calvinistic theology to indicate the temporal order of the process of the salvation of the sinner according to the work of God. Elements include: election, predestination, gospel call, inward call, regeneration, conversion (faith & repentance), justification, sanctification, and glorification. (Romans 8:29-30).

overture – A term used in a Presbyterian form of church government for a formal communication from a presbytery to the General Assembly.

P

passive obedience (of Christ) – Jesus Christ's sufferings on the cross in that He obeyed to the point of death with the payment of the penalty due sin in view. It was not His own sin that put Him on the cross, but the sins of the elect.

Pelagianism – The theological views associated with the British monk Pelagius (c. 354-c.420), who in theological debate with Augustine argued for a totally free human will to do good and held that divine grace was bestowed in relation to human merit. These views were condemned at the Council of Ephesus (431).

Pentateuch (From Gr. *pentē*, 'five,' and *teuchos*, 'book') – A term for the first five books of the Old Testament: Genesis, Exodus, Leviticus, Numbers, and Deuteronomy. They are known in Judaism as the Torah or books of the law.

piety (Lat. *pietas*, 'duty to God') – Devotion and commitment to God expressed in the Christian life through a variety of actions. Different expressions and emphases for piety are found throughout Christian history. The term is sometimes used synonymously with "spirituality."

pneumatology (From Gr. *pneuma*, 'spirit,' and *logos*, 'study') – Theological doctrine of the Holy Spirit. In the early church, the doctrine of the Spirit began in the 4th century with controversies about the Spirit's divinity.

Post-millennialism – Eschatological view that teaches Jesus Christ will return following the millennium or thousand-year reign mentioned in Revelation 20:1-7.

posttribulationism – The eschatological belief that the church will endure a time of suffering during the tribulation period, until the return of Jesus Christ at the end of that period.

Pre-millennialism – The belief that Jesus Christ will return to earth prior to a period of one thousand years during which He will reign.

presbyter (Gr. *presbyteros*, 'elder') – A term used in Presbyterian forms of church government for elders who govern local congregations. It is derived from the functions of the New Testament leaders (Acts 14:23; 15:4; 1 Timothy 4:14; James 5:14). Also used for "bishops" (Titus 1:5-9), priests, and ministers.

presbytery – The grouping of Presbyterian churches in a particular area that assumes governmental oversight over the individual churches through representative elders and clergy. Also, the jurisdiction of a presbytery.

preterist (From Lat. *preteritus*, 'past') – An interpretive view of the book of Revelation that maintains all its prophecies have already been fulfilled and are past or were being fulfilled when the book was being written.

pretribulationism – A view of the future which teaches that the Christian church will escape the coming period of great tribulation by virtue of being removed from the earth (raptured) at the return of Jesus Christ.

propitiation (Lat. *propitius*, 'favorable') – A theological term for making atonement for sin by making an acceptable sacrifice. The term is used in Romans 3:25; Hebrews 2:17; 1 John 2:2, 4:10, to describe the death of Christ.

Protestant (From Lat. *protestari*, 'to bear witness,' 'to testify') – One who adheres to the theological views that emerged from the 16th century Reformation in Europe.

protoevangelium – The "first gospel," a reference to the statement in Ge 3:15, which has been taken by biblical interpreters as predicting the defeat of satan by the victory of Jesus Christ and thus as the first promise or "gospel" of a coming Redeemer.

Puritanism – Sixteenth and seventeenth century Protestant religious movement that sought to "purify" the Church of England in more Reformed Protestant directions. It designates differing groups. The movement was Calvinistic in theology and Presbyterian or Congregational in church government.

q

Qumran – Site at the northwest end of the Dead Sea where the Dead Sea Scrolls were found (1947). A Jewish group called the Essenes lived at Qumran during biblical times (c. 150 B.C. – A.D. 70).

r

Redemption (literal: "to buy back.") Jesus redeemed us, "not with gold or silver, but with his holy precious blood and his innocent suffering and death (Luther)" (see "Atonement," "Propitiation," "Reconciliation.").

Rapture - A 19th century end-time notion based upon a faulty interpretation of 1 Thessalonians 4:15-17. Rapturists believe that they will be "snatched" out of this world prior to the great tribulation (see "Tribulation"). Those who believe in a rapture are pre-millennialists (see "Pre-millennialism") and are a thorn in the side of the post-millennialists. (see "Post-millennialism") Amillennialists (see "Amillennialism") simply smile and say, "You're both wrong!"

Reconciliation (literal: "overcoming an estrangement") - Theologically, because of the sacrificial (see "Sacrifice," "Atonement") death of Jesus Christ, God has reconciled sinners unto himself. God has made us his friends because of Christ (see "Propitiation").

Reconstructionism - The Post-millennial (see "Post-millennialism") teaching that the Church, by the preaching of the Gospel, will be enabled to reconstruct the culture around biblical laws (see "Theonomy").

Reformation Theology - A theology based upon the five solas (literal: "alone") of the 16th century Reformation. We are saved by Grace Alone, through Faith Alone, in Christ Alone, to the Glory of God Alone. These truths are drawn from Scripture Alone. Today there is a significant revival of Reformation theology to counter the experience-based theology of modern Evangelicalism (see "Evangelicalism") and the Pelagianism (see "Pelagianism") of Revivalism (see "Arminianism," "Revivalism").

Regeneration (literal: "to be born-again" John 3: 3-5) - We need to be born-again because we were born wrong (in Adam) the first time. The new birth is totally the work of God (see "Monergism"). Much controversy exists over when that new birth takes place. Lutherans believe in "baptismal regeneration" (see "Baptism").

Repentance (literal: "to change your mind") - Reformation theology (see "Reformation Theology") teaches that repentance is the combination of contrition (sorrow over sin) and faith in the forgiveness of sins promised in Jesus Christ. Such repentance is the result of hearing the Law and the Gospel. Many Evangelicals (see "Evangelicalism") erroneously teach that repentance is a human decision to forsake sin and live a moral life prior to coming to faith.

Revivalism - A 19th century movement spearheaded by Charles Finney. Finney, a classic Pelagian, (see "Pelagianism") taught that man is not dead in his trespasses and sin (see "Decision Theology," "Total Depravity") but is capable of deciding to be a Christian. The new birth (see "Regeneration"), according to Finney, was nothing more than an individual deciding to repent (see "Repentance") and live a moral life. Finney was a perfectionist (see "Perfectionism") who rejected the cardinal truth of justification (see "Justification"). His influence is widely felt today in much of Evangelicalism (see "Evangelicalism").

s

Sacrament (literal: from the Latin sacramentum, "mystery") - According to the Reformation perspective: A sacrament is a sacred act, instituted by the Lord Jesus, containing visible elements in which God promises and offers the forgiveness of sins. According to this definition, there are two sacraments: Baptism (see "Baptism") and the Lord's Supper (see "Lord's Supper"). The Roman Catholic definition of a sacrament allows for five additional sacraments: Confession, confirmation, marriage, ordination, and last rites.

Sacrifice - God appointed sacrifices as a means whereby the guilty could offer acceptable worship. The idea of sacrifice pervades the whole Bible.

Salvation (literal: "to be delivered, taken out of a snare, or set free.") - Salvation involves the totality of what God has done for us in the death and resurrection of Jesus Christ. We have been delivered from sin, death, and the power of the devil. It is God who has saved us in Christ.

Sanctification (literal: "to be set apart or separated") - As a theological category, sanctification defines the Christian life lived as a result of justification (see "Justification"). While justification and sanctification must be distinguished and not confused, they can never be divided. While justification is a completed work in Christ, sanctification is progressive.

Sin - The transgression of God's Law. Original sin defines human nature (see "Total Depravity"). Actual sins are thoughts, words, and deeds contrary to God's Law or the failure to do the good that God commands. We sin, because we are sinners from birth.

t

Theonomy (literal: "God's Law.") - The post-millennial (see "Post-millennialism") view that God's Law will be established in the earth prior to the coming of the Lord Jesus (*see* "Reconstructionism").

Trinity - The biblical doctrine specifically formulated at the Council of Nicea (325 A.D.) defining the person of God. There is one God in Three Persons: the Father, the Son, and the Holy Spirit. All Christian denominations embrace the Doctrine of the Trinity.

Total Depravity - Also know as the doctrine of Original Sin. Man from birth is spiritually dead and alienated from God and totally unable to contribute anything toward his salvation (*see* "Monergism")

Tribulation - The view taught by pre-millennialists. (*see* "Pre-millennialism") The tribulation is a seven year period of time in which the anti-Christ will be revealed prior to the coming of Jesus to establish his earthly reign. Most teach that Christian will not experience the tribulation but will be raptured (*see* "Rapture").

W

Word/Faith Movement - A distorted and in some cases heretical view held by many Charismatics (*see* "Charismatic"). Word/Faith teachers claim that faith is a power which, when joined to a positive confession and, for some, visualization, will produce results. Our words have the same power and effect as God's Word. It is claimed that we are "little gods." Also known as "name it and claim it," or prosperity teaching.

Worship - A response to what God has done for us, especially in Christ Jesus. We are enabled to worship God because God himself has made us holy and acceptable to him in Christ Jesus (*see* "Justification," "Sacrifice"). Historic Christian worship is a structured response to God in which context his grace is also received in the Word and the Sacraments.

Reformation Solas Song

We know from So - la Scrip - tur - a,

We are saved by So - la Gra - ti - a, Through So - la

Fi - de, In So - li Chris - to, To So - li

De - o Glo - ri - a.

Kevin C. Easterday   2014© Psalm One Publishing

Irregular
Kevin C. Easterday

Scripture Index

II. New Testament

95293341R00112

Made in the USA
Lexington, KY
07 August 2018